Disaster in the Pacific

Books by Denis and Peggy Warner

The Tide at Sunrise: A History of the Russo-Japanese War, 1904-1905

The Great Road: Japan's Highway to the Twentieth Century

The Sacred Warriors (with Commander Sadao Seno)

Books by Peggy Warner

Don't Type in Bed

Asia Is People

The Coffin Boats (with Commander Sadao Seno)

Books by Denis Warner

Out of the Gun

Hurricane from China

The Last Confucian

Certain Victory: How Hanoi Won the War

Denis and Peggy Warner
with Sadao Seno

DISASTER IN THE PACIFIC

NEW LIGHT ON THE BATTLE OF SAVO ISLAND

NAVAL INSTITUTE PRESS
Annapolis, Maryland

Library of Congress Cataloging-in-Publication Data
Warner, Denis Ashton, 1917–
Disaster in the Pacific: new light on the Battle of Savo Island/ Denis and Peggy Warner, with Sadao Seno.
p. cm.
Includes bibliographical references and index.
ISBN 0-87021-256-7
1. Savo Island, Battle of, 1942. I. Warner, Peggy. II. Seno. Sadao, 1925– . III. Title.
D774.S318W37 1992
940.54′26--dc20 92-2602
CIP

Printed in the United States of America on acid-free paper ∞

9 8 7 6 5 4 3 2

First printing

For Nancy Milne

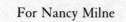

A mob of men, without indoctrination, and without training in concerted action, does not constitute an army. It can safely be said that a collection of ships, which has never operated together before, and under a strange commander, does not constitute a fleet.

Admiral W. J. Pye, USN

The vitally interesting part of the [Hepburn] report is what I did not put in it.

Rear Admiral Donald J. Ramsey, USN

Contents

Maps

Introduction

The guns had fallen silent, but beyond Mariveles, across the narrow ribbon of water separating Corregidor from Bataan in the Philippines, exploding American ammunition dumps rumbled on. If 9 April 1942 was not a day to remember, neither was it a day to be easily forgotten. Bataan had surrendered. Along the sides of the Malinta tunnel on Corregidor, in air reeking with sweat and creosote, and dank from dripping rocks, soldiers bearing all the telltale signs of defeat huddled in exhausted sleep. Corregidor, the garrison knew, was doomed.

For a small group of cryptanalysts making their way out of the tunnel and down the hill to what remained of the much-bombed pier, fate and the U.S. Navy offered another choice. They sailed by submarine that night for Australia, where they were soon to provide intelligence that contributed substantially to victory in the Pacific—and to some of the background of this book.

In January 1942 the Imperial Japanese Navy, having decided to invade Australia, presented its plans to Imperial General Headquarters.[1] For the next fifty days the plans were keenly debated. The navy argued that the main force of the U.S. Pacific Fleet had been destroyed at Pearl Harbor. Britain had lost the *Repulse* and the *Prince of Wales,* the core of its Eastern Fleet, near Kuantan off the Malayan coast. The combined American-British-Australian-Dutch force had been defeated in the Java Sea. There were no obstacles blocking a direct invasion of Australia. The country was weak militarily, and Japan's prospects in the war would be enhanced by its capture. Admiral Osami Nagano, chief of the Naval General Staff and supreme naval adviser to the emperor, strongly supported the plans. The army opposed them.[2] It would need at least twelve divisions to invade and maintain its hold on Australia, and more than a million tons of shipping to transport the invading force.

On 15 March, three weeks before the fall of Bataan, Imperial General Headquarters compromised. It decided to cut the American-Australian line of communications by seizing Port Moresby on New Guinea's southern shore, Fiji, Samoa, and New Caledonia.[3] Australia would be isolated and helpless. Under the code name Operation F. S. (Fiji and Samoa Islands Area Operation), planning began.

The army envisaged no problems. It believed that three brigades would be sufficient to seize the smaller Pacific island groups, and began to prepare accordingly. The navy for its part assigned the Eighth Fleet, under the command of Vice Admiral Gunichi Mikawa, to the task. The fleet consisted of the heavy cruisers *Chokai, Kako, Furutaka, Aoba,* and *Kinugasa,* the light cruisers *Yubari, Tenryu,* and *Tatsuta,* the auxiliary ship *Soya,* and four destroyers. Plans included the exploitation of the nickel mines on New Caledonia, and the use of Noumea as a submarine base to attack ships running the blockade from the United States to Australia.

The Coral Sea battle having upset plans for the seaborne seizure of Port Moresby, Japan was forced to try and take it from the rear.[4] The Japanese set out on an extraordinary march through the world's highest jungle and over the almost impassable Owen Stanley Range, meanwhile extending their pincer movement through the Solomons to the South Pacific.

Paymaster Commander Eric Nave had worked on the Japanese naval code, JN 25, and the British had passed the key to the U.S. cryptanalysts on Corregidor before they went by submarine to Australia.[5] In Melbourne, with the help of Nave and a handful of Australian and British cryptanalysts and traffic analysts, they and their fellow navy code breakers in Pearl Harbor and Washington provided the U.S. Joint Chiefs of Staff with detailed and accurate forecasts of Japanese naval movements and plans. These were used to guide the Allied counteroffensive through New Guinea and the Solomons.

This rich lode of intelligence brought victory at Midway. Not everyone was easily persuaded, however, that the information was reliable.[6] General Douglas MacArthur, who had arrived in Australia from the Philippines to become Supreme Commander, Southwest Pacific Area, only two days after Imperial Japanese Headquarters decided its strategy, refused to believe that the Japanese could cross the Owen Stanleys in sufficient strength to threaten Port Moresby. General Sir Thomas Blamey, Commander Allied Land Forces, was no less skeptical. Working on the vital intelligence of naval code breakers and traffic analysts, however, the Joint Chiefs of Staff set in motion plans for the First U.S. Marine Division to preempt Japanese moves southward through the Solomons. The Joint Chiefs also instructed MacArthur to initiate offensive operations against Japanese positions at Lae and Salamaua, on the northeast coast of New Guinea, as a prelude to the ultimate seizure of the major Japanese base at Rabaul in New Britain.

Operation Watchtower, the hastily planned operation in the Solomons, began well, but like the campaign in New Guinea, it quickly ran into trouble. This was largely because of a serious underestimation of the Japanese capacity for surprise as well as the neglect of intelligence originating with traffic analysts and air and sea reconnaissance. Central to the grave problems now facing the Allies was the disastrous Battle of Savo Island, "the blackest day," as Admiral Ernest J. King, chief of naval operations and Commander in Chief, U.S. Fleet, called it.[7] Just after 0143 on 9 August 1942, Japanese shells shattered the bridge of the Australian heavy cruiser *Canberra.* A little more than a minute later she had stopped dead in the water, listing 10 degrees to starboard and blazing amidships, her captain fatally wounded and many others dead. The Japanese cruiser force, under Vice Admiral Mikawa, raced on to scatter and destroy the U.S. cruisers protecting the transports that two days earlier had begun to land the First Marine Division at Guadalcanal and Tulagi.

The heavy cruiser USS *Quincy* went down at 0235. The heavy cruiser USS *Vincennes* sank fifteen minutes later, followed some hours later by the heavy cruiser USS *Astoria.* A last desperate shot at short range destroyed Mikawa's chart room in the heavy cruiser *Chokai.* Other ships scored minor hits on the Japanese, but the force escaped virtually unscathed. Long before daylight Admiral Mikawa was far from the waters off Savo Island in which this battle—if that is the proper word for such a brief and one-sided action—had been fought. Behind him he left chaos. In thirty-seven minutes, more than a thousand American and Australian sailors had been killed, fatally injured, or forced into the sea, where they would drown. Another seven hundred were wounded. Four invaluable cruisers had been lost, and the U.S. Navy had suffered the worst open-sea defeat in its history. The U.S. carrier force, which might have intercepted Mikawa's squadron as it approached on 8 August, and battered it during the retreat on 9 August, had already departed. The carriers played no part in the action. As they headed south away from the Solomons, they were followed by the transports and their escorts, leaving the marines perilously exposed on the beachheads without essential air cover, supporting naval gunfire, vital weapons, munitions, or supplies. The sea lines of communication between Australia and the United States were now jeopardized, a danger aggravated by the Japanese drive across the mountains in New Guinea toward Port Moresby. The two developments caused alarm in Canberra. Prime Minister John Curtin began to bombard his allies in London and Washington with requests for help in protecting Australia from what was perceived to be the renewed threat of Japanese invasion, and the immediate danger of isolation from the United States.

Ever since the ignominious defeat suffered by the Allied force off Savo Island, the crew of a Royal Australian Air Force Hudson reconnaissance bomber, which had sighted the Japanese force east of Bougainville Island on the morning of 8 August, has been blamed. Rear Admiral Samuel Eliot Morison, the U.S. historian, wrote of one RAAF pilot: "Instead of breaking radio silence, as he had orders to do in an urgent case, or returning to base, which he could have done in two hours, [he] spent most of the afternoon completing his search mission, came down at Milne Bay, had his tea, and then reported the contact. . . . Thus, the faulty and long-delayed report of one pilot completely misled both American commands as to Japanese intentions." This is wrong in most of the details. The report was faulty, but the pilot did break radio silence and warn the American commands, did return quickly to base, pausing only long enough to drop bombs near a Japanese submarine, most certainly did not have tea, and was debriefed immediately after landing. But the story has persisted, repeated with embellishments ever since. According to one history, "The pilot was an inexperienced and not very intelligent Australian who winged his way blithely on to complete his reconnaissance leg without breaking radio silence and sending the crucial information from his plane. He then landed and nonchalantly drank his tea before reporting. This prevented tracking the Japanese force. . . ."[8]

Another history enlarged on the Morison story, blaming not just one but two pilots involved for failing to break radio silence.[9] Tourists visiting the Solomon islands read the story in an official government brochure describing the Battle of Guadalcanal.

The facts are altogether different. Thanks to the warning by a Hudson, which came in ample time for counteraction, the news had reached the task forces that a Japanese force was close by and could launch a surface attack that night on the assembled warships and transports off Savo Island. The Hudson's signal was intercepted by the Japanese flagship *Chokai.*[10] Major ships in the Allied force, which had been briefed in advance about the search area to be covered and the radio frequency to be used by planes in an emergency, received one and possibly two signals during daylight on 8 August.

Admiral Mikawa, fearful that he had lost the vital element of surprise and conscious of the enormous risk that he was now taking, elected to proceed with his mission. During what seemed a dangerously long afternoon on 8 August, with the expectation every mile of air attack, he sped on to Savo Island.

Admiral King did not exaggerate when he described the defeat at Savo Island as the U.S. Navy's blackest day. Aside from the losses, much was now in doubt. What had appeared likely to be a quick and not too painful surgical operation on Guadalcanal became a desperate struggle to survive. For months it was touch and go, for the marines and also for the Australians in New Guinea. Japan's plan to isolate Australia teetered on the brink of success.

Any critique based on the assumption that the task force got the news about the Japanese too late to do anything about it was likely to differ substantially from one that would demonstrate that the Allies had an early warning. The declassification in the United States of the work of cryptanalysts and traffic analysts shed much new light on the battle. The office files of Admiral Morison and the papers of Admirals Turner and Hepburn were no less revealing. All previously published accounts, including Morison's, the Hepburn report, and the Naval War College's otherwise admirable and detailed *The Battle of Savo Island: Strategical and Tactical Analysis* (in this book referred to as *War Analysis*), have been seriously flawed. We acknowledge our debt to Nancy Milne, wife of the leader of the Hudson group.

It would be easy, and inexcusable, to overlook the human stresses involved in the disaster off Savo Island. Two days of combat—for most their first ever—had exhausted officers and men alike. They had not developed the wells of knowledge from which they drew so successfully in later campaigns in the Pacific. The crews had been inadequately trained, especially in night fighting. Ships that had not exercised together found it difficult to fight together. It would nevertheless be a disservice to those who gave their lives and to others whose reputations were unfairly damaged not to record the facts as we have found them.

Part One

WARNING SIGNALS

1

"So They've Arrived, Have They?"

The sea was as blue as the Mediterranean on an early summer day, the cumulonimbus cloud that would gather so densely and soar so high toward evening no more than a wisp in the sky. For the crew of the Royal Australian Air Force (RAAF) Hudson, a reconnaissance bomber now approaching the halfway mark in a long patrol, there had been nothing to report. Then, ahead, they saw eight ships. The biggest with its raked stack led four others, all well and evenly spaced in line astern. Some distance away, visible through the slight haze, were three smaller vessels heading southeast at a leisurely pace. Their wakes were small white ribbons on the calm surface of the sea. For the crew of the RAAF Hudson, not knowing they were about to experience their first contact with the enemy, it seemed a tranquil scene.

The time was 1027 on 8 August 1942, the place some 40 miles north of the coastal village of Kieta on the island of Bougainville, about 340 air miles from Guadalcanal. The Hudson's signal lamp blinked the letter of the day to the cruisers and destroyer below. The answer should have been the corresponding letter. Instead, it came in sudden, brilliant flashes from the larger ships. "My God, they're Japs!" shouted Sergeant Bill Stutt, twenty-four-year-old pilot of the plane, A-16-218.[1]

Days before, five Hudsons of the Thirty-second and Sixth Squadrons, RAAF, had moved from their base camp at Horn Island off the northern tip of Cape York on the Australian mainland. They were to carry out armed reconnaissance flights from the Fall River base at Milne Bay, which opens like the jaws of a crocodile at the eastern end of New Guinea. Stutt and his crew, just finished with advanced training, were on their fourth operational flight. Two other Hudsons had not seen action; a fourth had had only limited combat experience. Twenty-six-year-old Flight Lieutenant Lloyd Milne, who had completed his tour of duty with the Thirty-second Squadron and volunteered to lead the Hudsons on their missions from Milne Bay, was in charge of the fifth.

Formed on 21 February at the Seven Mile Aerodrome, Port Moresby, from the remains of the Twenty-fourth Squadron, which had lost all but two of its aircraft at Rabaul during the previous two months, the Thirty-second had been in continuous action ever since. In April, as Japanese air raids grew more intense, the squadron moved to Horn Island, where there were better facilities for dispersing aircraft among shrubs and trees, and fewer enemy air attacks. But Horn Island was too distant for the conduct of the urgent reconnaissance that the situation now demanded in the Solomons. Hence the move to Fall River Air Field at Milne Bay. Carved out of a coconut plantation, it had become operational only twelve days before. Its facilities were primitive, its amenities nonexistent. The low-lying, swampy terrain, deluged by rainfall that ran to a hundred inches a year, was mosquito infested. One-fifth of the Australians and Americans unfortunate enough to be stationed there suffered from malaria. Although thwarted in their plans to take Port Moresby by direct invasion from the sea because of losses in the Battle of the Coral Sea, the Japanese planned to use Milne Bay as a staging post to support their overland drive from Buna, on the north coast of New Guinea.

By the standards of the day, Lloyd Milne's Hudsons were ideal for the task of reconnaissance. With a maximum speed of 261 miles per hour (mph) and a cruising speed of 224 mph, they could search for better than eight hours, and they carried two small bombs for use against targets of opportunity. Their search area covered the approaches to the Solomon islands from Rabaul. Southwest Pacific Area Command had established the search area on 5 August and notified Commander in Chief, Pacific, Pearl Harbor (CinCPac), as well as all task force commanders then converging on the Solomons for the landings at Tulagi and Guadalcanal. The signal designated standard Southwest Pacific Air Search (B), bounded by Tagula Island, east of Milne Bay, and central New Georgia.[2] Planes were to sight Buka, Kieta, the Bougainville straits, and Gizo Island.

The Hudsons' orders were to radio immediately upon spotting a target, and to remain in the vicinity until recalled or forced to retire.[3] The air force ground station to which a contact report was transmitted was to repeat the entire message in acknowledgment. Arrangements had also been made between the Southwest Pacific and South Pacific commands that any signals originating from the Hudsons would be immediately rebroadcast, so that if direct communication was not established between the plane and the task forces, the signals would still get through.

The frequency allocated to the Hudsons was 6,700 kilocycles.[4] Parent stations for coastwatchers in the Gilbert, Ellice, Phoenix, and Tonga islands reported to Suva in Fiji on this frequency. The commanding officers in Samoa and Efate, in the New Hebrides, and the port director at Suva were required in the operational plan for the offensive in the Solomons to summarize, encipher, and address these reports to all ships and bases in the South Pacific Area.

Only three of the Hudsons sent to Milne Bay were serviceable on the morning of 8 August. Lloyd Milne allocated their search pattern, which was advised by radio to all task forces in the Solomons, together with the number of aircraft participating and their call signs. Much of the vital stretch of sea in the central Solomons, covering the approaches to what was soon to be known as the Slot because it formed a channel between the Santa Isabel and New Georgia islands, was the Hudsons' responsibility. Any Japanese force approaching from the northwest toward Guadalcanal, where the marines had landed on 7 August, was likely to come through the Slot from Rabaul. Although General Douglas MacArthur's boundary had been fixed at 159° East longitude, the arrangement limited the Hudsons' area of responsibility to 158° 10′ East, centered in the channel between Choiseul and Santa Isabel islands; for increased effectiveness, aircraft from the South Pacific Command would overlap by 2 degrees, or 120 nautical miles.

Milne's briefing was just that, brief.[5] In the absence of any senior RAAF officers at Milne Bay, a junior intelligence officer said there was a slight chance the three Hudsons scheduled to make the flight on 8 August might see American ships in the waters east of the Solomons. Beyond that, the briefing officer had nothing to offer. No word of the landing by U.S. Marines on Tulagi and Guadalcanal the previous day, or of the air battle that had taken place over the landings. No word that American Flying Fortresses had seen Japanese cruisers near Rabaul, or that a submarine had sighted a naval force off Cape St. George, at the southern tip of New Ireland, traveling southeast at high speed. Twenty-four hours had passed since the marines had landed. If the Australian planes had been shot down and their crews captured, they would not

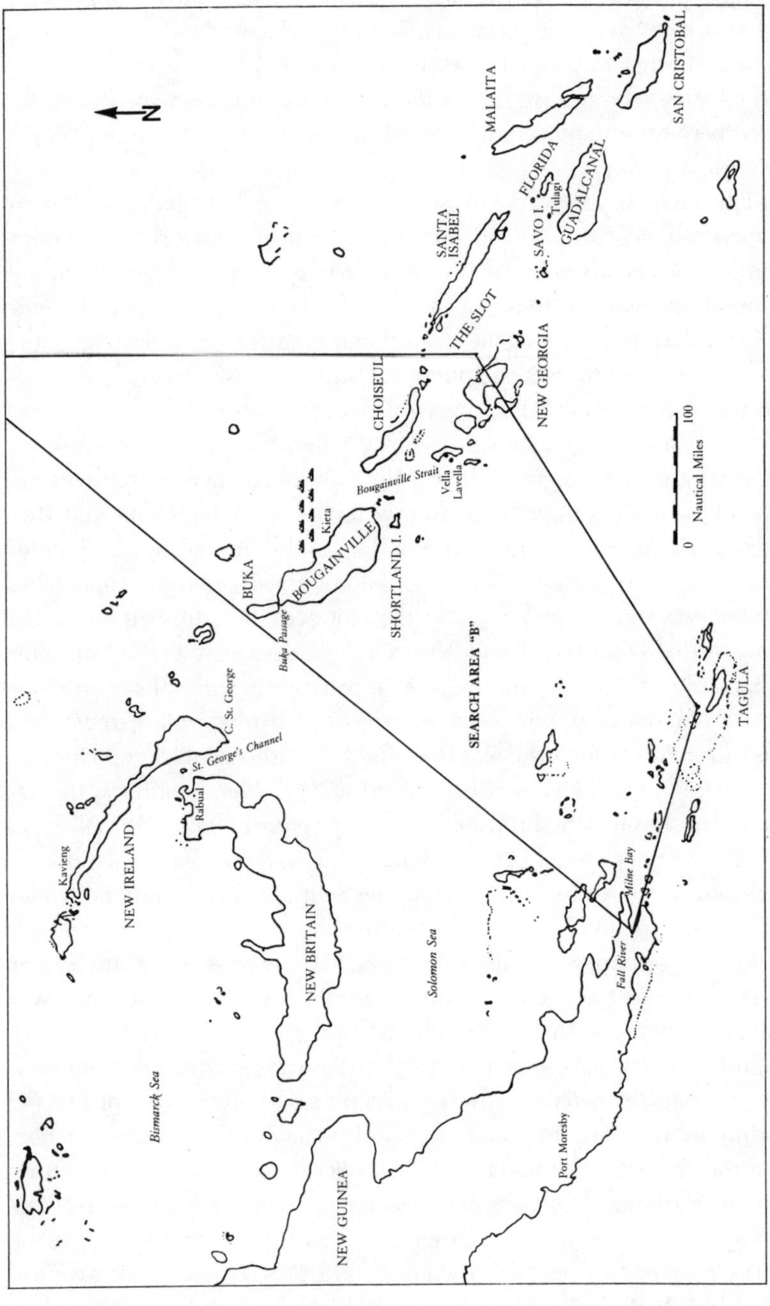

The RAAF Hudsons' Search Area, 8 August 1942

have been able to tell the enemy any more about the landings than he himself knew.

The landing at Guadalcanal had gone much more successfully than anyone dared hope. Tulagi proved much tougher, a dress rehearsal for the bloody amphibious operations that the marines would have to make later against the heavily defended Central Pacific islands. For the first time, but not the last, the marines met troops who preferred to die by their own hands rather than surrender, who fought without food or water or hope, or, it seemed, even reason, until their last round of ammunition had been spent.

Still, despite heavy casualties on Tulagi, there was no danger that the landings would be thrown back on the beaches. An air raid on 7 August had not seriously disturbed the operation. The major problem facing the marines when Stutt saw the Japanese force was that the landing of equipment and supplies was running far behind schedule.

Stutt came from a pioneer aviation family. During World War I his father had been chief test pilot for the War Office in London and a senior instructor for Britain's Royal Flying Corps. Later, his father became the first man to fly nonstop from Melbourne to Sydney. Flying was very much in Bill Stutt's blood.

His shout, "My God, they're Japs!" did not resolve the crew's dilemma. Everyone thought the ships were Japanese, but if they were American and word was sent by radio, Stutt and his men— navigator Sergeant Wilbur Courtis, radio operator Sergeant Eric Geddes, and gunner Sergeant John Bell—would be in real trouble. Wilbur Courtis had no doubts.[6] This was not a case of mistaken identity.

While Stutt and his crew were considering the implications, they saw two floatplanes that appeared just to have taken off from the ships. In fact, the planes were Jakes, the Japanese navy's low-winged, single-engine reconnaissance aircraft, either returning from search missions ordered before dawn that morning or employed on an inner air patrol to guard against submarine attack. Each of the planes, with the exception of one detailed for the much longer flight to Tulagi, was to search for a radius of 250 miles, then fly a crossleg for 30 miles. Stutt believed the planes to be the naval seaplane version of the Zeke, with a maximum speed of 270 mph, much faster than the Hudson and thus apparently ominous.

Stutt identified the ships as three cruisers, three destroyers, and either two gunboats or two seaplane tenders. What he was looking at, in fact, were the heavy cruisers *Chokai, Aoba, Kako, Kinugasa,* and

Sergeant Bill Stutt

Furutaka, the light cruisers *Tenryu* and *Yubari,* and the destroyer *Yunagi.* The error, caused no doubt by the fact that the cruisers carried the Jakes that Stutt and his crew thought had been launched to attack their plane, proved unfortunate but understandable: two Japanese seaplane tenders, the *Chitose* and the *Chiyoda,* were similar in length and beam to the cruisers, flush-decked and armed with 5-inch guns. The *Furutaka* and the *Kako* displaced only 8,100 tons, the *Chitose* and the *Chiyoda* 11,023 tons. Both seaplane tenders had been designed for conversion to high-speed oilers, submarine tenders, or even aircraft carriers. That the cruisers could have been mistaken for gunboats is more difficult to explain, although two of the gunboats in Japanese service were converted destroyers.

Radio operator Geddes hastily abandoned the signal lamp and turned to the radio.[7] Geddes, who had topped his class at the RAAF's radio school, tried to raise Milne Bay without success. Home base could not hear. Others could, including the Japanese. A detailed action report from the *Chokai* read: "At 0826 sighted an enemy plane Lockheed

[Hudson] which shadowed us at some 30,000 meters in the bearing 240°, and missed it in the bearing of 310° after about ten minutes. At 0903 recognized the plane, which had kept shadowing us, and drove it off by main battery firings.[8] The plane found our fleet. Intercepted its report as follows: '0927 three cruisers, three destroyers, two seaplane tenders or gunboats 05° 49′ South, 156° 07′ East, course 120° at 15 knots.'"

The times are important, if confusing. The Japanese operated on Japanese standard time, zone 9, the Hudsons on zone 10, and the allied forces in the Solomons on zone 11. That 0826 in the *Chokai*'s action report was 0926 aboard the Hudson and 1026 at Guadalcanal. And 0903, the time at which the *Chokai* saw a second Hudson, was 1103 Guadalcanal time and 1003 aboard the Hudson. Finally, 0927, the sighting time indicated on the Hudson's intercepted message, was 1027 Guadalcanal time.

Since the action report was not specific about the time at which the *Chokai* intercepted Stutt's signal, and it did not indicate that two Hudsons were involved, it seems likely that the intercept took place some time between the *Chokai*'s two sightings, that is, between 1026 and 1103.

When he failed to contact Fall River, Geddes sent the signal repeatedly in the clear, and getting no response concluded that his set was out of order, not unusual in those days. He recalls trying for about half an hour before giving up.

Had the *Chokai* intercepted the Hudson's message when it was transmitted from the aircraft? Any doubt that it had not, but rather that it had picked the message up later when it was sent from Fall River in cypher, is resolved by comparing the two messages. The message in cypher, which the Japanese could not read, went out in 183 groups at 1450 zone 10 time. It read: "FR/W1 8/8 FORM WHITE F R62 A16(-)? 218 FR 623 AT 2325Z7 IN POSITION 05 49S 156 07 E SIGHTED EIGHT WARSHIPS COURSE 180 DEGREES T SPEED 15 KNOT FORCE CONSISTED OF THREE CRUISERS THREE DESTROYERS TWO SEAPLANE TENDERS OR GUNBOATS(.) AIRCRAFT ENDEAVORED TO DO RECOGNIZED APPROACH 1,000 FEET BUT ON SEEING AIRCRAFT CATAPULTED FROM ONE CRUISER TOOK AVOIDING ACTION(.) ONE CRUISER (1) THREE SHORT RAKED FUNNELS LARGE SUPERSTRUCTURE RAKED RESPONSE(.)."[9]

The Japanese were confused by the two sightings. The 0826 sighting was of Stutt's plane, the one at 0903, according to the documents, of Flying Officer Merv Willman's. Records show that the *Chokai* identified the number of Stutt's tail plane but not the number of the second.

If there was alarm aboard the Hudson when the Jakes appeared, there was consternation among staff officers in the *Chokai.* Captain Shigenori Kami, flag captain for the Eighth Fleet, confident that its cruisers could launch an effective night attack against the American and Australian ships provided the circumstances were favorable, had sold a daring plan to Vice Admiral Gunichi Mikawa, commander in chief of the Eighth Fleet. Tokyo had at first wanted to veto the raid. Then, reluctantly, it gave its approval. After launching their aircraft in the early morning, the Eighth Fleet's heavy cruisers had dispersed and were some distance from the two light cruisers and the destroyer. With the return of the search planes, they had been ordered once again to concentrate. Stutt, then, saw all eight ships as he approached. Now, while deciding what action to take, the heavy cruisers again changed course, and the Hudson, still unaware that its radio message had not gotten through to the task forces, headed for Milne Bay with its urgent report.

The sky at this time was generally clear, if hazy, the only cloud near Kieta on the course back to Milne Bay. The Hudson headed for it. The plane emerged from the cloud over the west coast of Bougainville. Immediately, it saw two vessels. "We hadn't gone very far when we saw these two big ships on the surface," said Courtis. "They were both submarines. Even today I am still amazed how big they were."

The RO-33, which had sunk the 300-ton freighter *Mamutu* in the Gulf of Papua on 7 August and later machine-gunned the survivors in the water, had been ordered to Guadalcanal, but she could not have covered the distance so quickly. The I-121 was en route from Rabaul to Tulagi; in June 1990, however, her captain had no recollection of any incident at this time. Then there was the I-122, which had passed through St. George's Channel the previous day. She may have been involved.

Equipped with maps lacking in accuracy and detail, Stutt had crossed Bougainville at a safe 7,000 feet to avoid the island's two active volcanoes. He was making a slight descent to work up speed when he saw submarines. At first he intended to ignore them. Then, spotting a red sun on the conning tower of one, he decided to attack. The submarines were proceeding in line ahead. The Hudson dropped two bombs on one. "From my position in the nose of the aircraft," Courtis said, "I clearly saw the submarine, which had two wide yellow bands across the deck, and the bombs entering the water." Neither of the bombs hit.

The Hudson landed at Milne Bay at 1255 local time, three hours and twenty-eight minutes after first sighting Vice Admiral Mikawa's force. Stutt had two reasons for not continuing to track it: the perceived threat of attack by what he thought were Zeke-type fighters and, more importantly, the need to get his message through as quickly as possible. He had not received acknowledgment of his radio signals and had no idea that they had been intercepted.

Patrols being scheduled for approximately eight hours, the Hudson returned to Milne Bay earlier than expected. "We parked the aircraft by the side of the landing strip, unloaded our gear, and told the armorers that the aircraft needed to have the bombs replaced," said Geddes. "The ground crews were quite excited. We were whisked away from them. . . . Bill Stutt was taken to the operations room—as I remember it, a large, native-style thatched hut—and the rest of us were left standing in the clearing outside." According to Stutt, "We landed, jumped out of the plane in wild excitement, got into the jeep and went straight to the debriefing hut."[10] Within minutes of the landing, he had reported the encounters with Mikawa's force and the submarines.

He denies accusations that he wasted time. He did not pause for a cup of tea; he hates the stuff. And lunch followed the debriefing, it did not precede it.

At 1100, about twenty minutes after Stutt had headed for home, Willman's Hudson, A-16-185, sighted part of Mikawa's force.[11] Dismayed that he had been discovered, Mikawa had turned northwest to conceal his intentions while his staff officers deliberated the significance of Stutt's warning that the Japanese ships were heading in the direction of Guadalcanal.

The Japanese opened fire as Willman dropped two bombs and passed overhead. At his debriefing, he reported what he believed to be two heavy cruisers, two light cruisers, and one small, unidentified vessel. One of the ships, he added, seemed to be similar to a British *Southampton*-class cruiser.

Sergeant John Davies, Willman's navigator, recorded the sighting in notes he made at the time. "1000. Saw ships 05 24 South 156 05 East. Ships ten miles South. 1010 Fired on Bolted. 1020. On course again behind cloud."

The third Hudson, A-16-157, piloted by Milne, saw a single Japanese cruiser southwest of Buka Island at 0945. The ship, not part of Mikawa's force, opened fire. Sergeant "Dutch" Holland, Milne's radio operator, after great difficulty, succeeded in raising Port Moresby to report the cruiser's position. Milne later saw two corvettes, one of which opened

Lloyd and Nancy Milne

fire and was, in turn, bombed by Milne. Later Milne reported shadowing Mikawa's force for half an hour.

Rear Admiral Richmond Kelly Turner, the amphibious force commander, subsequently interpreted Willman's report as meaning that Mikawa's squadron had shed the "seaplane tenders" reported earlier by Stutt, while the main force headed back to Rabaul.[12]

Another interpretation could have been that the Hudsons' sightings were no more than confirmation that a substantial Japanese naval force was heading for Guadalcanal. For days, naval communications intelligence at Pearl Harbor had been warning task force commanders of the buildup of Japanese naval strength in the area.[13] Little enemy naval activity passed unnoticed by American traffic analysts. Aircraft, submarines, cruisers, and destroyers were all arriving to reinforce the already formidable Japanese force. All were noted in the traffic of 7 August. Moreover, it was obvious that they were receiving urgent operational orders. On 8 August, communications intelligence sent another warning that enemy cruisers were near Rabaul. Air and sea surveillance also signaled what should have been regarded as urgent warnings.

On 7 August, seventeen B-17s from MacArthur's command had taken off from Horn Island and Port Moresby to attack Vunakanau Air Field at Rabaul. Twenty-seven miles to the north they sighted what they believed to be one heavy cruiser, three light cruisers, and one destroyer traveling west at a speed of thirty knots. In St. George's Channel, B-17s saw six warships, described as large to medium, heading southeasterly. South Pacific Command received these signals at midnight. More information came from USS S-38, an eighteen-year-old submarine that had been in action since December. At best, she could muster fourteen knots on the surface and about eleven knots submerged. Under the command of Lieutenant Commander H. G. Munson, she was on patrol in St. George's Channel. Just after sunset on 7 August, Munson saw two ships that he believed to be destroyers. Five minutes later the ships passed close by. Three minutes later at least three larger ships passed directly overhead, one so close the submarine had to roll several degrees. Munson was unable to position himself to attack. The ships headed southeast at high speed. Failing to track—the submarine was soon outdistanced—he broke radio silence and reported. The signal reached the task forces off Guadalcanal at 0738 on 8 August.

Munson continued his vigil in St. George's Channel and next morning torpedoed the troop transport *Meiyo Maru,* which was to have been the spearhead of a Japanese landing force following Mikawa's attack. She went down with 342 men, rare luck for the Allies. Mikawa ordered other transports bound for Guadalcanal to return to Rabaul, a godsend for the U.S. Marines, who were far from ready to cope even with a small amphibious landing by fresh Japanese troops. As mentioned, the *Meiyo Maru* carried most of the force. If any of the other ships had been sunk, the operation would have continued as planned.

Like the Hudsons, both the B-17s and the S-38 underestimated the size of the ships they had seen or heard. The "destroyers" noted by Lieutenant Commander Munson were the light cruisers *Tenryu* and *Yubari,* screening the *Chokai,* while the force seen twenty-seven miles north of Rabaul consisted of the *Chokai* and the four ships of Cruiser Division 6, the *Aoba, Kako, Kinugasa,* and *Furutaka.* Warnings by naval communications intelligence at Pearl Harbor were now reinforced by impressive visible sightings. Since the silhouettes of the *Tenryu* and the *Chokai* were unmistakable, these were bad errors, and no doubt bore some responsibility for the almost complacent attitude that prevailed on most Allied ships the evening of 8 August.

Before 1800, the sun had disappeared behind Guadalcanal's dark mountains. From shore came occasional flashes of gunfire. In the roadstead a stricken transport, victim of the air raid earlier in the day, turned from a pillar of smoke into a ball of fire. Lieutenant Commander E. J. B. Wight, the *Canberra*'s intelligence officer, made his way to the compass platform after sunset.[14] "We've had high-level torpedo attacks and dive-bombing attacks," he said. "The only thing left is surface craft, and judging from the reports, we'll probably get that tomorrow morning."

"I don't think so," replied Captain Frank E. Getting, the commanding officer, who had discussed the reports with other members of his staff earlier that day. "I think you'll find that those ships in the reports were operating between Rabaul and somewhere in the vicinity of Buka Passage."

Lieutenant Commander J. S. Mesley, the navigation officer, asked Getting if he wanted to see the position of the ships on the chart.[15] "No," he replied. He believed all the messages referred to normal island traffic, pointing out that at Navy Office, Melbourne, there were constant reports of similar traffic.

Altogether the *Canberra* had received no less than three reports about Mikawa's force. As Wight remembered them, they had all given roughly the same number of ships but varying courses, up to fifty miles apart. Mesley realized that any of the ships mentioned in the reports could arrive in the transport area before dawn if they increased speed sufficiently. He reckoned that for them to reach the transport area, their speed would have to be 23.8 knots. He also noted a disconcerting lack of information about what air reconnaissance was being carried out. Vice Admiral Frank Jack Fletcher's Task Force 61, with three aircraft carriers, was in the vicinity, but the *Canberra* had no knowledge of its activities.

Lieutenant Commander John Plunkett-Cole, torpedo officer in the *Canberra,* also remembered three warnings during daylight hours of possible enemy surface attacks.[16] Because the fatigue of the crew would not allow continuous maximum readiness, it was decided, he said, that the time to relax was by night. "In other words," he added, "the greatest danger apprehended was from air attack."

Light cruiser HMAS *Hobart* regarded the Hudsons' signals as so secret that only her captain, signal officer, and operations officer were aware of their contents. When he heard the gunfire in midwatch, Lieutenant Commander Richard Peek called Captain H. A. Showers from the bridge, where Peek was principal control officer. "So they've arrived, have they?" said Showers, who, like others who had received the signal during the day, believed that it came from a coastwatcher.[17]

The cruiser USS *Vincennes* apparently received two signals. Since the ships in the second sighting were close to where they had been during the first, the conclusion was that they were the same force.[18] Willman's observation that one of the cruisers resembled the *Southampton* class was noted. Captain F. L. Riefkohl, commanding officer of the *Vincennes,* had no doubt that the signals from the Hudsons portended trouble. He assumed that the force was escorting the seaplane tenders reported by Stutt to some base where the planes would be unloaded and ready to attack at dawn. The cruisers and destroyers could then proceed at high speed and attack the Allied force sometime during the midwatch, a prescient observation. He made note of this in his night orders, stressing the importance of vigilance.

In the aircraft carrier USS *Enterprise,* Lieutenant Elias B. Mott, assistant gunnery and antiaircraft officer, remembers a signal being put on the carrier's status board.[19] From the position given, the ship's officers estimated that if the force continued on its way to Guadalcanal it could be expected around 0100 on 9 August.

In the USS *Wasp,* Stutt's signal caused an immediate debate about whether surface ships or aircraft should be sent to attack Mikawa's force. Clark Lee, a war correspondent aboard the carrier, described the reaction to the signals in his book, *They Call It Pacific:* "That afternoon aboard the carrier I heard that a small Japanese warship force was coming down toward Guadalcanal. . . . One of the torpedo plane pilots came to me. 'Get your life jacket and helmet,' he said. 'Maybe we'll be taking off to hit the babies. They seem to be well within range. . . . It hasn't been decided yet whether we'll send in surface ships or planes. . . . Better to be ready to take off with us if you want to see the fun.' "

The long-delayed message from Pearl Harbor confirming Stutt's signal sent on the morning of 8 August was still being deciphered in the USS *Astoria* when Japanese ships opened fire. The communications officer had no recollection of receiving any other signal during the day. Yet Captain William G. Greenman, the commanding officer, remembered receiving the Stutt report either in the morning of 8 August or sometime before the attack by Japanese aircraft in the afternoon.[20] Like others, he was confused about its origin. He was told the report originated with a coastwatcher near Bougainville.

Commander Elijah W. Irish, navigator of the USS *Chicago,* apparently recalled two reports.[21] "Sometime during daylight of the eighth we received a contact report of two small enemy detachments approaching our position from different routes from the north. The captain had me figure out their position and time of arrival. From my calculations, it could have been anytime after midnight, depending upon the speed." He did not recall exactly the source of the reports.

Though their recollections are hazy, the fact that these officers recall the messages coming in daylight hours eliminates the doubt that any signal reached the task forces before the confirmation of sightings arrived in cypher after dark. Sunset in the Solomons on 8 August was at 1816. Nine months after the battle, Captain Riefkohl believed that he might have received the first message as early as 1015—some fifteen minutes before it could have been dispatched! Since the amphibious command ship had an arrangement for guarding the scouting plane circuit, it seems likely that, like the *Chokai,* she picked up Stutt's signal in the morning, although Rear Admiral Turner, the amphibious commander, remembered that he had received it in the afternoon.[22] The fact that the signal was sent on a coastwatcher frequency means that it may have been transmitted several times, perhaps in slightly different form. Several officers thought the sightings were made by a coastwatcher, although no coastwatcher sighted Mikawa's force off Bougainville or anywhere else.

When he learned of the presence of the Japanese force north of Choiseul Island in the afternoon of the eighth, Admiral Turner got out the disposition order prepared by Rear Admiral Victor Crutchley, RN, the screening force commander, read it again thoroughly, and decided to make no changes.[23] "It seemed then to me to be an excellent order," he remarked. "All vessels had this dispatch concerning the contact. I considered that everything was as nearly ready as could be expected. I hoped the enemy would attack. I believed they would get a warm reception."

After he received the report, during the day, Admiral Crutchley discussed it with his senior staff, who were sceptical about the RAAF and its intelligence-gathering capabilities. Later, Crutchley asked Admiral Turner what he believed Japanese intentions to be. Turner replied that in his opinion the force was headed for Rekata Bay on the northern tip of the island of Santa Isabel, about 120 miles away; from there, it would possibly operate torpedo-carrying planes against Allied forces. Thus they would expect two torpedo attacks a day instead of one. He had requested a full-scale bombing the following day on the ships expected in Rekata Bay.

Admiral Turner considered two other courses of action.[24] The first, to send surface forces out that night to attempt interception, he dismissed, as it would have left the transports naked to attack. The second, to send surface forces out to find and engage Mikawa's force after the expected withdrawal of the transports on the morning of the ninth, he held in abeyance pending further information. Neither air nor surface forces went out to intercept Mikawa's force. Instead, Admiral Fletcher withdrew with the aircraft carriers that had been providing cover and general support. In the midwatch, Mikawa struck.

Part Two

POINT, COUNTERPOINT

2

Coming Events

Long before the bombs rained on Pearl Harbor Japanese reconnaissance aircraft had appeared over the Solomon islands, which stretch for 600 miles southeast from New Guinea in a long volcanic and coral chain. The British established a protectorate over the southern islands in 1893, with their administrative headquarters on the island of Tulagi. The Australians seized the German-controlled northern islands of Buka and Bougainville in 1914, administering them from Rabaul after World War I as part of the Trust Territory of New Guinea. By 1942, when World War II encroached upon the South Pacific, neither Britain nor Australia could claim to have made much effort to develop their colonial dependencies. The settlement on the two-mile-long island of Tulagi provided British colonial administrators with comfort and convenience, including a cricket field and a golf course, while a mountain of bottles offshore attested to the spirit with which the expatriates devoted themselves to overcoming the hydra-headed evils of malaria, heat, and humidity. The mails came once every six weeks by way of Fiji, where the British high commissioner had his headquarters. Roads were virtually nonexistent. On Tulagi there were no cars. People walked and went by launch to the smaller islands of Gavutu and Makambo, where Lever Brothers and Burns, Philp, the island traders, kept their headquarters. Beyond, on the bigger islands, district officers went about their duties on foot, along muddy tracks and accompanied by native policemen, men bearing rations and bedding, and defaulters loaded down with padlocked boxes containing official documents and silver coins collected as tax.

The first bombs fell on Tulagi on 27 January 1942. Eleven days later, when the steamship *Morinda,* her morale and rivets shaken by near misses during a Japanese bombing attack, tied up at Gavutu, residents clamored aboard for berths. The ship could accommodate only a small number, and when the list of fortunate ones was read out, many people had to return to shore. Some tried to force their way back on board. Unseemly fights broke out. The police had been discharged, and with no one to preserve order, looters wrecked the shops in Chinatown while shopkeepers and their families fled in small boats.

Among the *Morinda*'s incoming passengers was twenty-six-year-old district officer Martin Clemens, returning from an abruptly terminated leave in Sydney. He walked about Tulagi, once a manicured park bright with bougainvillea and hibiscus, and scattered with white, red-roofed houses, and found nothing but a bleak stretch of smashed crockery and furniture. He tried to stop looters from loading up canoes but abandoned the task as hopeless. Ahead of him were much more difficult and dangerous tasks on the island of Guadalcanal.

Seven-and-a-half miles northeast of Guadalcanal, and eighteen miles almost due west of Tulagi, was Savo Island, standing sentinel over the northern approaches to what would soon become known as Ironbottom Sound. Swimmers from Tulagi gave it wide berth. In accordance with their religious beliefs, Savo islanders disposed of their dead by throwing the bodies into the sea. Sharks infested offshore waters, accustomed to a diet of human flesh. Here a lonely Scandinavian, Lafe Shroeder, one of the only surviving European settlers, ran a trading post and for a time used a radio transmitter to warn a small RAAF detachment with seaplanes at Tulagi of approaching Japanese raids. Savo Island was volcanic, about four miles in diameter, rising from a circular base to a height of 1,675 feet. Deep water ran close to its shore.

As for Guadalcanal, some ninety miles long and twenty-five miles wide, it had mountains in the center that rose sharply to more than 8,000 feet. Dense tropical rain forest, interlaced with short but fast-flowing rivers, covered most of the land. About fifty European planters, traders, prospectors, and missionaries from several Christian denominations lived among the fifteen thousand islanders. Coconut plantations were concentrated around Kukum on the northern coast, where there were also large patches of kunai grass growing to a height of five feet. On Guadalcanal, British colonialism had barely scratched the surface. As for the rest of the world, until the bombs fell on Tulagi and the Japanese moved in, it managed quite well without giving its neighbors in the southern Solomons a thought.

With the uncontested fall of the islands, no great prize passed into Japanese hands. Strategic position, not material wealth, was what now sounded warning signals in Washington and Canberra.

The initial Japanese timetable had envisaged the occupation of Port Moresby in early May, and of Fiji, Samoa, and New Caledonia in July—plans that Coral Sea and Midway ruined. But if the timetable had changed, goals and intentions had not—of this the Joint Chiefs in Washington, thanks to cryptanalysts and radio traffic analysts, were well aware. General Douglas MacArthur, who had arrived in Australia from the Philippines on 17 March, wanted the British fleet moved from the Indian Ocean to the Pacific. "Lack of sea power in the Pacific is, and has been, the fatal weakness in our position since the beginning of the war," he wrote in a dispatch on 23 May. "Much more than the fate of Australia will be jeopardized if this is not done. The United States will face a series of disasters."

After all these years, it is still not possible to determine whether MacArthur believed everything he wrote or said. He was passionately committed to his "defeat Japan first" policy, and his pronouncements, with the exception of those made at times of clear crisis, have to be considered in light of this fact. However, on this occasion, Admiral Ernest J. King, chief of naval operations and commander in chief of the U.S. Fleet, agreed with him about the gravity of the situation. The first bombs had only just fallen on Tulagi when he proposed an offensive in the Solomons. Against the opposition of General George C. Marshall, chief of staff of the army, the plan made no headway at this stage. After the battle of Midway in early June, King again proposed an attack on Tulagi, while MacArthur countered with a much more reckless stratagem. He wanted to seize Rabaul, using the U.S. First Marine Division under his command. This proposal did not commend itself to the navy.

Early in May, Admiral Chester W. Nimitz had been appointed commander in chief, Pacific Ocean Areas (CinCPOA) as well as CincPac. Under this decision, MacArthur's eastern boundary extended only to 160° East longitude, embracing the most northerly and westerly part of Guadalcanal, where the Japanese were about to construct an airfield, but excluding Tulagi, where they had established a seaplane base. The arrangement did not please MacArthur. "The whole scheme in regard to the setup in the Pacific was to give the U.S. Navy the maximum degree of control," he complained.

A compromise agreement gave the navy, under Admiral Nimitz,

responsibility for a limited operation to take Tulagi and the Santa Cruz islands to the east. MacArthur would take over the final two phases of the campaign, which was to end with the seizure of Rabaul. MacArthur recommended that the three phases be undertaken successively. The Joint Chiefs declined to commit themselves initially. At this stage, they envisaged only landings by the First Marine Division on Tulagi and neighboring areas, and the occupation of the Santa Cruz islands, 300 miles to the east, to protect the right flank of MacArthur. He was then to assume strategic control with a pincer movement through Lae and Salamaua in New Guinea, converging ultimately on Rabaul.

To execute the first phase of the plan, Vice Admiral Robert L. Ghormley, USN, was appointed Commander, South Pacific Area, a subdivision of Nimitz's command.

MacArthur remained strongly opposed to a naval officer commanding land operations. With the passage of time and the strengthening of Japanese defenses at Rabaul, however, his enthusiasm for bold action had diminished. He considered that the Joint Chief's plan would be risky, since the Solomons would become a salient. If covering U.S. naval and air forces were redeployed and the Japanese forces reinforced, the Solomons, he believed, would be highly vulnerable. So when the Joint Chiefs ordered the operation, MacArthur argued that it could not be effectively organized within the time allowed.

Like MacArthur, Ghormley believed that he was in no position to launch a major amphibious operation in such a hurry. After talks in Melbourne, he and MacArthur advised delaying the operation until there had been a more adequate buildup of Allied forces. "It is our joint opinion," they reported in a prescient submission to the Joint Chiefs, "that the initiation of the operation at this time, without reasonable assurance of adequate air cover during each phase, would be attended with the gravest risk." They recommended no more than an infiltration operation until the three phases of the operation could be mounted as one continuous effort.

To facilitate the operation by the marines under Ghormley's command, the eastern boundary of the Southwest Pacific Area Command was altered from 160° to 159° East longitude. This kept part of the Solomons within the Southwest Pacific Area Command but, more importantly, brought the pending operations on Guadalcanal and Tulagi under Ghormley's direction. MacArthur's forces were to be responsible only for the interdiction of air and naval operations west of the operational area.

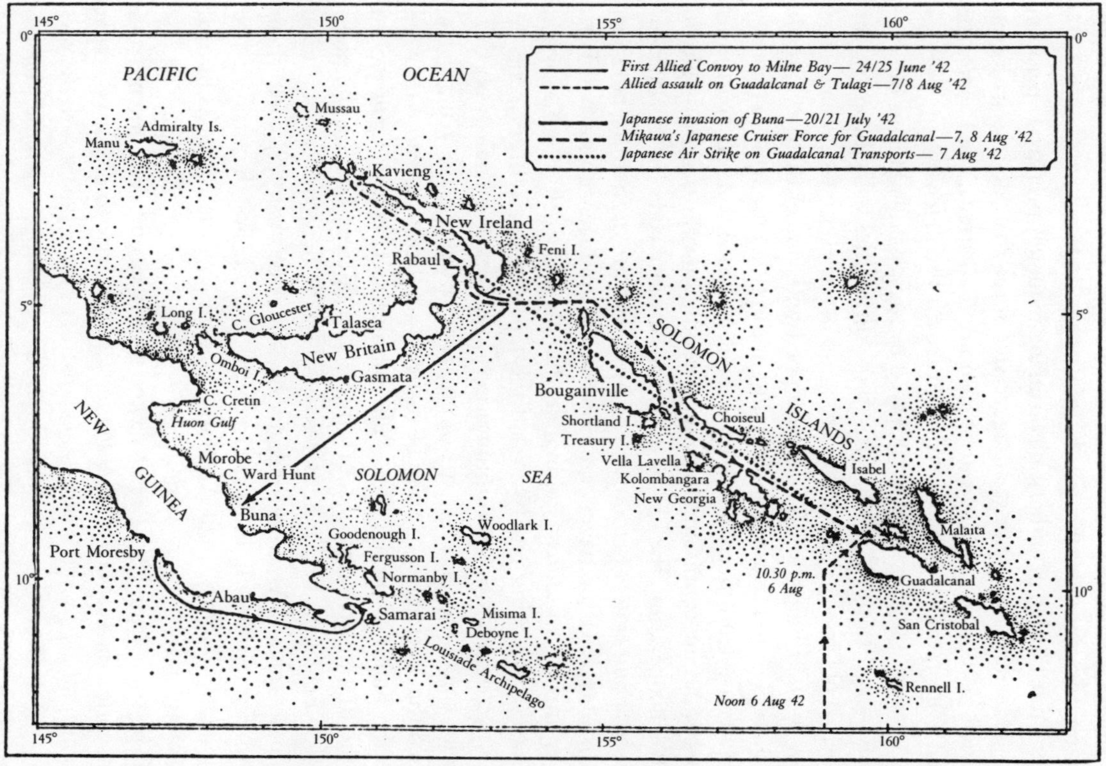

Moves in the Solomons–New Guinea Area, June–August 1942. (Courtesy Australian War Memorial)

Before his appointment, Admiral Ghormley had been leader of the U.S. naval mission in Britain. Recalled to Washington, he arrived on 17 April 1942, the eve of MacArthur's assumption of power as Supreme Commander, Southwest Pacific Area, and the Doolittle raid on Tokyo. Taking command of the South Pacific on 19 June, he assumed the unenviable burden of embarking on an inadequately prepared operation into terra incognita against an aggressive force that, despite its losses, showed no sign of running out of steam. On all fronts, the Pacific, the Middle East, and Russia, the Allies were on the defensive.

Admiral King was now well served by highly skilled teams of cryptanalysts and traffic analysts. After some difficulties with the army, the navy had obtained approval for setting up its intercept station on Corregidor in the Philippines. There, equipped with one of the few "purple machines"—none was available at this time to either the army or the navy in Hawaii—ten officers and fifty-one enlisted men worked in a tunnel that had an air-conditioned receiving room and offices and, thanks to British cooperation, the key to the Japanese naval code JN 25. This enabled the unit closely to monitor enemy moves into the South China Sea.

In May 1941 the naval communications intelligence unit had been set up in Hawaii under Commander Joseph J. Rochefort and assigned the task of working on JN 25 and the Japanese flag officers' code.

Since the sixty-one communications intelligence specialists on Corregidor constituted a large part of the navy's trained team, King determined that every effort had to be made to get them out before they fell into the hands of the Japanese. The submarine USS *Seadragon* picked up the first detachment of four officers and thirteen men on the night of 4–5 February 1942 and set sail for Java, then under increasing Japanese threat. A second submarine, the USS *Snapper,* took them on to Exmouth Gulf in Western Australia, whence they traveled to Melbourne to join a small Australian unit in Victoria Barracks headed by Commander Jack Newman.

The submarine USS *Permit* picked up the second detachment from Corregidor on 16 March. The *Permit* gave priority to offensive action over cryptanalysts, and when it met a patrol of three Japanese destroyers about midnight it fired two torpedoes, both of which missed their target. The Japanese replied with depth charges that could easily have ended the rescue effort then and there. The detonations blew bunks from the bulkheads and light bulbs from their sockets, but miraculously, the boat sprang not a leak. Further adventures awaited the submarine off the coast of Western Australia, where it was attacked, unsuccessfully, by an

Allied patrol bomber. By this time the team could have been forgiven if they thought that Corregidor might be better than this most hazardous of escapes.

Bataan fell on 9 April, the day after the second group finally landed in Fremantle. That night, the third and final group embarked from Corregidor in the *Seadragon.* Although they encountered a Japanese destroyer off the mouth of Manila Bay, they reached Fremantle safely on 26 April and took a train to Melbourne, where they arrived on 6 May. Here they joined the unit hitherto led by Commander Newman, who had become chief of staff of the combined unit Frumel (Fleet Radio Unit, Melbourne, code-named Cast), and now led by Commander Rudolph J. Fabian, USN.

Paymaster Commander Eric Nave, RN, an Australian, was a key figure in the effort to break Japanese codes. Sent to Japan at the end of World War I to study Japanese, he passed a British embassy language test with the highest marks ever recorded and then went on in 1925 to organize wireless interception for Britain's China station. Nave's wireless operators found interception virtually impossible because the Japanese used forty-five Kana signs and not the English alphabet of twenty-six. So he bought some blank phonograph records to study the material in slow time. In this way he worked out the Japanese signal alphabet and was soon able to read their language messages and then their codes.

When the Japanese moved from simple to more sophisticated codes, Nave moved with them. "I grew up with their codes," he said. "I came to understand the Japanese methods and where they were going." As early as 1926 he had broken his first Japanese naval code, and though the Imperial Japanese Navy switched codes frequently, Nave had little difficulty adjusting to the changes.

In 1940 ill health brought him back to Australia from Singapore, where he had been working with the British. He established the Special Intelligence Bureau in Melbourne to concentrate on Japanese consular messages and naval traffic in the mandated territories of the Central Pacific. Just before the outbreak of the Pacific war, he advised that a Japanese naval force was probably heading for Pearl Harbor. Nave predicted that an attack would take place there the weekend of 7–8 December. His accuracy matched that of the Japanese carrier planes when they unleashed their deadly attack.

Signals intelligence, or sigint, was then and still is one of the most secret branches of intelligence work. Nancy Milne, who later worked for RAAF intelligence at MacArthur's headquarters in Brisbane, had the task of keeping the Japanese order of battle up to date from material provided by cryptanalysts, traffic analysts, and other Ultra sources. The work was rigidly compartmentalized. Milne worked in a room with an Australian who was half Japanese and five American officers. No one discussed his or her work. Nor did Squadron Leader Percy Feltham, a Melbourne lawyer in charge of the Australians, elaborate on more than the essential details of each job. Raw material fed into the office continuously during the day came mostly in the form of signals from Central Bureau. These always bore the word Ultra in heavy red letters. The typescript was also in red. Although only authorized personnel entered the room, orders were that signals should always be kept face down to help to maintain secrecy.

Neither Nancy Milne nor her fellow workers were told how the Japanese signals were received or decoded, or translated at such speed. It was not hard, however, to conclude that code-breaking machines had been involved in the process. The speed of decoding was such that, for example, a signal relaying the transcript of the preliminary interrogation of two Allied airmen was on Milne's desk within hours of their being shot down and captured.

From the constant stream of Japanese signals covering the movement of aircraft, the ordering and distribution of spare parts and machinery, construction work, and the posting of personnel, it was possible to build up a card system for quick reference showing where Japanese squadrons were posted, where they might be shifted, the type of aircraft they were flying, and what facilities were being installed at various centers for their use.

In the early days of the Pacific war, however, Washington lost track of its wandering cryptanalysts. Conditions for cryptanalysis, moreover, appear to have been less than adequate. There were shortages of paper and typewriters, and the facilities in Melbourne's Victoria Barracks left much to be desired. A list of complaints included the following: "No fire hoses (fun in case of fire); no window blinds in WRAN [Women's Royal Australian Navy] sleeping hut (fun for the sentries); no bath or washbasin plugs (no fun for anybody); no refrigerating machine in the meat room (oversight)." Two years after it had been established, the unit was still sending out impassioned pleas for six standard correspondence typewriters to be shipped by rapid means, "disguising the contents." Its Townsville intercept office was still awaiting teleprinters to begin operations. There was also an urgent need for teleprinters in Melbourne. Four had arrived but without keyboard units.

Cast was to have moved to a building in downtown Melbourne, but this was vetoed because of its central location. Instead, a room in a block of flats, the Monterey building on St. Kilda Road, was chosen. Cast took over the middle floor, Nave's Special Intelligence Bureau the top floor, the Directorate of Naval Communications the ground floor. For a time Washington remained confused. Cast used a radio station in Canberra to transmit its messages. On the international call list, the station was designated Radio Belconnen Australia. Belconnen was in Canberra, as was the transmitter, although it was controlled by the receiving station at Moorabbin, a Melbourne suburb, where it was operated by Jack Newman's unit.

Cast was directly responsible to Admiral King in Washington. It passed on to MacArthur only what it saw fit on the grounds that its primary concern was the Japanese navy. MacArthur soon appreciated the need for his own special intelligence and established the Central Bureau, commanded and staffed principally by Americans, with radio interception done by the Australian Special Wireless Group.

The various Allied naval cryptanalysis and radio traffic analysis organizations now began to pay big dividends for the Allies in predicting Japanese offensive operations. The most immediate and important results came from Melbourne and Commander Rochefort's naval communications intelligence unit in Hawaii. As early as April, Rochefort had warned that Port Moresby was in Japanese sights. A month later he confidently predicted that Midway was the next Japanese objective.

Although the Japanese changed their main cryptographic system on 28 May, only days before Midway, and the new code took weeks to break, traffic analysis now served as an excellent substitute, accurately predicting Japanese intentions and providing the Joint Chiefs of Staff in Washington with highly accurate forecasts of enemy intentions.

Lieutenant Commander Edwin T. Layton, the fleet intelligence officer at Pearl Harbor, prepared a weekly bulletin for CinCPac. In his report Layton gave, *inter alia,* the location and organization of all Japanese naval units down to destroyers and submarines.

3

Operation Shoestring

The British garrison at Tobruk surrendered on 20 June 1942 while Prime Minister Winston Churchill was staying at the White House in Washington. "I am ashamed," he told Lord Moran, his doctor. "I cannot understand why Tobruk gave in. More than 30,000 of our men put up their hands. If they won't fight . . . " The news could scarcely have been less timely. Churchill's military advisers wanted ever more emphasis put on men and materiel for Europe and the Middle East. The Pacific would have to wait.

However, on 25 June, the last day of Churchill's visit, Admiral King had his way. King had been made commander in chief of the U.S. Navy after Pearl Harbor and in March had taken on additional duties as chief of naval operations. He wanted the Japanese blocked in the Solomons, and on that day his operation was approved by the Joint Chiefs of Staff. Rear Admiral Richmond Kelly Turner had fathered the plan in the belief that to leave the Solomons occupied by the enemy, athwart the line of communications from the United States to Australia and New Zealand, would have been fatal.[1] Turner regarded the operation as a holding offensive, or as a defensive offensive, to prevent the Japanese from cutting the supply line to Australia. There was also a need to keep the enemy from opening a second front against the hard-pressed Russians, and to start a war of attrition, wearing him down while U.S. factories were moving into gear for war production.

A week after the operation was approved, the three key admirals met in San Francisco[2]—King, at sixty-three, the toughest and perhaps the most brilliant of them all; Chester Nimitz, unassuming, quiet spoken, and little known outside the navy; and Turner, explosive, opinionated, domineering (but not, needless to say, in King's presence). Meanwhile the crisis deepened on the Russian front. Hand-to-hand fighting was taking place in Sebastapol, a mammoth tank battle continued near Kursk, and a new German offensive against Moscow seemed to be in the making. There were serious doubts whether the Soviet Union could continue to hold out.

Adding to the concern of the admirals in San Francisco, serious leaks in Washington threatened to compromise the operation. An article in the *Dominion,* a newspaper out of Wellington, New Zealand, virtually tipped off the Japanese.[3] "Bombing is not enough," said the author. "What is needed is to drive the Japanese out of their positions and convert them to their [our] own use. The only way to take positions such as Rabaul, Wake Island and Tulagi is to take physical possession of them." The same article quoted the *New York Times* to similar, and potentially more damaging, effect: "It may also be significant that the censor passed the news of the arrival of the completely equipped expeditionary force of American Marines at a South Pacific port recently, as marines are not usually sent to bases where action is not expected. It may well be that we are preparing to reap the fruits of the Coral Sea and Midway victories. Sooner or later the present stalemate in the South Seas will be broken on a battlefield of our own choosing." When marines in Wellington began to reload the transports, even an uneducated guess might have tipped the enemy on Tulagi as to their destination. The risk had to be taken. There could be no turning back now.

Admiral King now advised MacArthur that the situation in the Solomons was too critical to permit any delay, an opinion based on cryptanalysis reports and confirmed by the latest intelligence. Cryptanalysts and radio traffic analysts operating from Melbourne, Pearl Harbor, and Washington knew from the first day of July that the Japanese were preparing for major new operations in the South and Southwest Pacific.[4] Pinpointing this, naval communications intelligence at Pearl Harbor reported that there was noticeable Japanese activity in the Solomons. Then, on 5 July, came the firm and alarming intelligence that the Japanese were building an airfield on Guadalcanal. Documents captured in New Guinea confirmed the increased activity in New Britain. Orders had been issued to the Eleventh and Thirteenth Pioneer Detachments to go to Guadalcanal, while the Fourteenth Pioneer Detachment and the Fifth Sasebo Special Landing Force had orders to land on the east coast of New Guinea.

The Japanese had occupied Tulagi on 2 May, established a seaplane

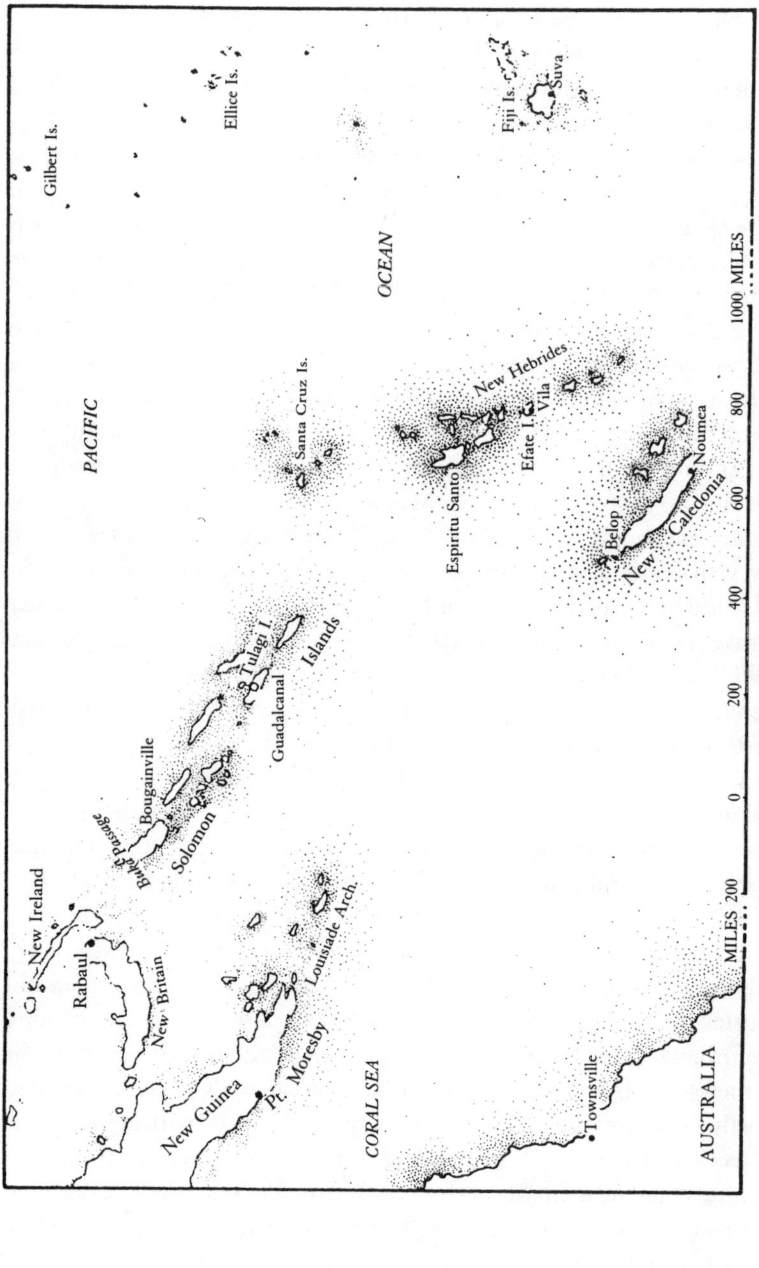

Noumea to Rabaul. (Courtesy Australian War Memorial)

base there, and sent reconnaissance parties across to Guadalcanal. On 8 June a section of the Tulagi garrison occupied the coconut plantations at Lunga, on the north coast of Guadalcanal, and in the following weeks burnt the kunai grass about two miles south of Lunga Point in preparation for the construction of the airfield. Much of this was known to the Allies. *The Role of Radio Intelligence in the American-Japanese Naval War* observed the following:

> As early as 1 July 1942 it was noticed by U.S. Naval Communications Intelligence that the hitherto obscure Solomon Islands had become a center of much Japanese activity. The full significance of the enemy's movements was not lost on the allied naval and military commands, for they well appreciated the strategic importance of the islands. If the Japanese were to gain control of them, it was almost inevitable that the supply lines from America to Australia would be badly disrupted by land-based enemy planes. In addition, it was believed that the Solomons would be used as a stepping stone for the invasion of the Australian mainland.

Vice Admiral Frank Jack Fletcher was less than enthusiastic about the Solomons operation, believing it to be too hazardous. In conferences with Nimitz and Turner at Pearl Harbor, he pointed out that the carriers would have to limit their stay in the Guadalcanal area. Nimitz, he later said, gave him the impression that the landing force could be ashore in two days and would be able to dig in and accept enemy air attacks.[5]

Turner flew to Auckland on 16 July, to Wellington the next day, and assumed tactical command of the amphibious force on 18 July, only four days before he was due to sail for a rendezvous with the rest of his force in the vicinity of Fiji.

Intense and highly secret efforts had been made to put the necessary forces together. The Americans' First Marine Division, en route to New Zealand to complete its training, was the only ground force available. Three of the four aircraft carriers now in the Pacific were to provide direct air support, a decision that caused concern for Fletcher, who did not relish the idea of operating in the close waters of the Solomons. Somehow air bases had to be finished in New Caledonia and the New Hebrides to provide land-based air support. This was to be reinforced by long-range air support from the Southwest Pacific Area Command.

Three Australian cruisers, HMAS *Australia, Canberra,* and *Hobart,* which had come under overall American command on 22 April, were detached from the Southwest Pacific Area Command and placed under Admiral Ghormley's command for what was now called Operation Watchtower (the first phase of Operation Pestilence), the code name under which Allied air, surface, and land forces were, for the first time in the Pacific war, to take combined initiative. It was also to be the first time in the war that an Allied force undertook an opposed landing.

Of necessity, Operation Watchtower, perhaps more appropriately known to its participants as Operation Shoestring, was conceived in haste and delivered without the careful planning that was to distinguish so many other operations in the Pacific. All the major participants lacked experience both in the planning and the implementation of complex amphibious operations. Moreover, as Ghormley and MacArthur had argued, time was needed, and there was none to spare.

Under his command, Admiral Ghormley established three task forces to carry out the operation. Fifty-seven-year-old Vice Admiral Fletcher commanded both Task Force 61, the carrier group, and the expeditionary force. At the Battle of the Coral Sea he had lost the carrier USS *Lexington,* and at Midway the USS *Yorktown.* He did not want to lose any more.

Long before these losses, Fletcher had proved himself to be a cautious, some said far too cautious, commander. The week following the Japanese attack on Pearl Harbor, he arrived there to command a task force built around the *Saratoga,* which was to support the marine garrison on tiny, isolated Wake Island. Wake was under direct threat of Japanese invasion. One landing had been thwarted by gunfire unleashed by the small garrison against the light cruiser *Yubari* and destroyer transports carrying the troops. A much bigger Japanese effort was in the making.

Fletcher's task was to thwart it. He not only failed, he failed to try. He ordered his ships to refuel when they might have been speeding to the attack, and in any case, Vice Admiral William Pye, interim CinCPac, ordered him to turn back. As Wake was falling, some members of Fletcher's staff begged him to ignore Pye's order. Fletcher chose to obey, a decision that caused furious dissension and lasting bitterness in the U.S. Navy.

For Operation Watchtower, Fletcher had his flag in the *Saratoga* and had with him two other aircraft carriers, the *Wasp* and the *Enterprise,* the new battleship *North Carolina,* five cruisers, one light cruiser, and fifteen destroyers. Although designated as expeditionary force commander, he limited himself to the command of the three carrier groups.

Vice Admiral Frank Jack Fletcher, USN. This photograph was taken on 17 September 1942. (80-G-14193, National Archives)

The strain of war had begun to show, his contemporaries noted. Fletcher was tired.

Rear Admiral Turner, also fifty-seven years old, commanded Task Force 62, the amphibious force, from the transport *McCawley*. Her hasty conversion into a command ship had been less than successful. Her quarters were cramped and inconvenient, especially as she had to carry a complement of troops. Worse, her communication facilities were far from adequate for the operation. She had a total of two radio transmitters and five receivers suitable for operations. In addition, there was one inefficient commercial set that could not be depended on and a TBS voice radio. Because of a short, not discovered for another three months, it was capable of operating over about eight miles instead of the usual twenty. This meant that during operations, exchanges between the *McCawley* and ships off Tulagi, fifteen miles away, had to be relayed through a destroyer on the outer screen of the X-ray transport group in Lunga Roads. To supplement these facilities, an additional sixteen field sets were set up in various parts of the ship. "It is doubtful," Admiral Turner later noted, "if an operation has ever been conducted in the United States Navy which required so complicated a communication organization; certainly, none has been conducted with such inadequate radio facilities."

Turner, an initially reluctant but ultimately highly successful amphibious commander, was responsible for planning Operation Watchtower. He had come from the operations section of war plans at the U.S. Navy Department, where he had clashed with other naval officers and army planners, who accused him of distrusting his sister services. A highly intelligent, dominating, often arrogant officer with a furious Irish temper, a biting tongue, and a habit of calling a spade a spade, he was described by one of his peers as a relentless taskmaster, the Patton of the navy, and by his juniors as Terrible Turner. A prodigious worker, and while not at sea, a heavy drinker, he commanded little affection but much respect. Listening to a complaint once about Turner's drinking habits, Admiral Nimitz said that if he knew his brand of whiskey he would recommend it to some of his other admirals.

In the spring of 1939, as captain of the *Astoria,* Turner had transported the ashes of Hiroshi Saito, the former Japanese ambassador to the United States, to Japan. In Honolulu, on the way to Yokohama, newspapers reported that the *Astoria*'s mission would cement Japanese-American relations. One described Saito as one of the most beloved ambassadors in Washington, "a man of charm with a gift for making and understanding friends. He understood [the United States] and our people and was always for U.S.-Japanese friendly relations."

Japan welcomed Turner with fanfare and fun. Turner lunched with the foreign minister and Ambassador Joseph G. Grew. A garden party followed, with beer, sake, and a Japanese girl for each American sailor. The Japanese lavished gifts on their guests and presented them with a specially commissioned ode:

Today God commands the sea to subside.
The angels walk dry-shod from wave to wave.

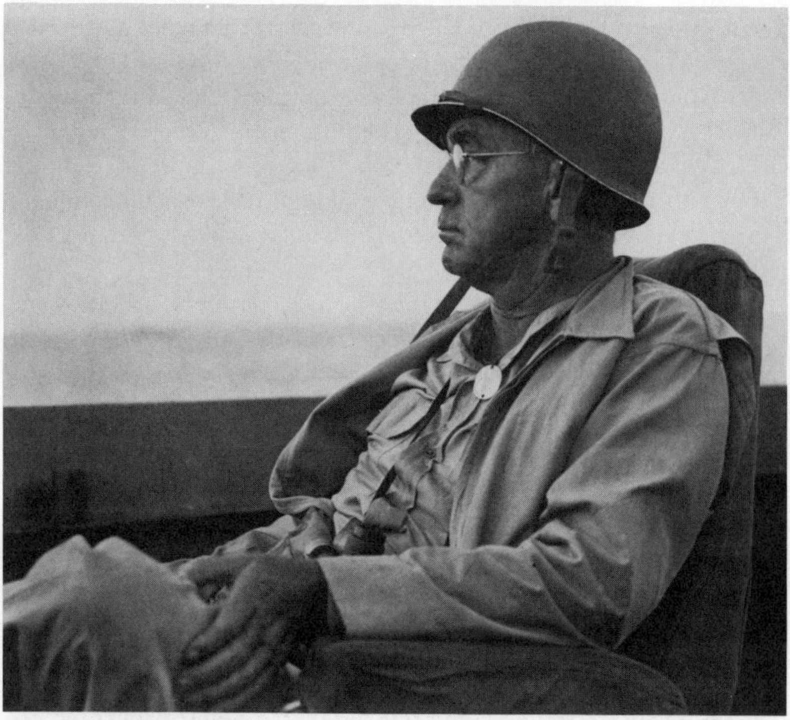

Rear Admiral Richmond Kelly Turner, USN. This photograph was taken aboard the USS Rocky Mount *on 17 June 1944 after he had been promoted to vice admiral. (80-G-231988, National Archives)*

The sea flows calmly for the noble dead that returns home.
The sea flows calmly for the seamen that bring peace with death.
Ah! be glad the world is one song.
The upward look and vision, and never night again.

A man with strong prejudices, and even more strongly expressed views, Turner had refused a proposal by naval communications intelligence at Pearl to have one of its mobile intelligence units aboard the *McCawley,* a decision that was to prove costly.[6] Turner, well aware of the difficulties of working with a combined force, also had reservations about commanding Australian and U.S. ships in Task Force 62 and had asked to be assigned only American ships. Admiral Fletcher disapproved his recommendation. Curiously, considering his views, Turner then elected to name the English rear admiral commanding the Australian Squadron as his deputy.

As second in command to Turner, and commander of the Australian Squadron (Task Force 44), fifty-one-year-old Rear Admiral Victor Alexander Charles Crutchley, RN, took tactical command of the two fire-support groups for Guadalcanal and of the screening group (Task Group 62.6). Crutchley had not wanted the job. It was more appropriate, he told Turner, that an American flag officer should have tactical command. Turner, who would retain his confidence in Crutchley through all that followed, rejected the protest.

At Crutchley's disposal were the 8-inch-gun cruisers, USS *Vincennes,* USS *Quincy,* USS *Astoria,* USS *Chicago,* and HMAS *Australia* (his flagship); HMAS *Canberra;* the light cruisers USS *San Juan* and HMAS *Hobart;* fifteen destroyers; and five mine-sweeping destroyers.

A tall, striking figure with a bright red beard and a mustache to hide the scar from a wound, known to Australian sailors as Old Goat's Whiskers, Crutchley was the personification of a senior Royal Navy officer. As a lieutenant at the Battle of Jutland in World War I, he took part in two attempts to block the harbors of Zeebrugge and Ostend and thereby to bottle up the German submarine fleet. For his part in the first attempt, in April 1918, he won the Distinguished Service Cross. When this attempt failed, he volunteered for a raid in May and won both the Victoria Cross and the Croix de Guerre. Before being promoted to rear admiral in June 1942, he commanded the British battleship *Warspite* and the Royal Navy barracks at Devonport. Although he had commanded HMNZS *Diomede* in 1935–36, he was new to the Pacific, and to his role as rear admiral commanding the Australian Squadron. The last Briton to be appointed to this position, Crutchley had taken up his post only two months before. The *Australia,* for reasons of security that were nonsensical, had no voice radio for talking between ships, and her radar was so inadequate that Turner considered asking him to move his flag to the *Chicago.*

Crutchley's staff officer for operations and intelligence was thirty-five-year-old Commander Galfrey Gatacre, RAN, who like Crutchley himself had recently arrived from service with the Royal Navy in the Atlantic. He had won the Distinguished Service Cross in 1941 for his part in the sinking of the German battleship *Bismarck.* Gatacre's conviction was that reports from RAAF aircraft could not be trusted. His doubts about the RAAF's capacity to identify naval ships was based curiously on his observation that a RAF Whitely bomber had once failed to see the British battleship *Rodney* in which he served, even though the ship had had the aircraft in view for some time. Concerning Bill Stutt's

Rear Admiral Crutchley, RN, (right) *on board HMAS* Australia *with Rear Admiral R. S. Berkey, USN. (106691, Australian War Memorial)*

report of the Japanese force he was to comment, "At least the air crew could add up to eight!"

Another influential figure was Captain H. B. Farncomb, RAN, commanding officer of HMAS *Australia* and Crutchley's flag captain, later to become the first Australian to achieve flag rank. Not quite an Australian Turner, he shared the American's fondness for off-duty drink and was often offensively rude. He was also capable. In the forthcoming operation, Farncomb would leave most of the staff work to Gatacre, but he would participate in a key discussion with Crutchley when they considered the Hudsons' reports.

He shared Gatacre's views on the RAAF. In a letter to Commander R. B. M. Long, chief of Australian naval intelligence, six weeks after the Savo Island battle, he wrote:

> Compared with [the efforts of] the army and the RAAF, who respectively magnify every puerile skirmish in New Guinea into a battle and a glorious victory, or never fail to describe in the utmost and inexact detail every abortive air raid they carry out, our own press efforts are childish. We, who know how inefficient our South-West Area Air Force is, feel extremely angry when we read the highly colored accounts in the press of their imaginary exploits.[7]

Carrier Air Support Task Group 61.1 was the responsibility of Rear Admiral Leigh Noyes in the *Wasp.* Until a few weeks before the Solomons operation, Noyes had been Fletcher's senior. This changed on 15 July with the announcement that Fletcher had been promoted to vice admiral. This added some sensitivity to the relationship, but nothing like that which existed between Noyes, formerly director of naval communications, and Admiral Turner.

Late in 1940, the U.S. Army and Navy and the British Chiefs of Staff had agreed on a full exchange of cryptographic information. The Americans had agreed to give the British at Bletchley Park a purple machine to decipher Japanese diplomatic messages. The British were in turn expected to hand over the Enigma cryptograph used to break the German code. In fulfillment of the agreement, a U.S. team arrived in London with two purple machines. One had been intended originally for Commander Rochefort's naval communications intelligence team at Pearl Harbor when it was set up in May 1941. Now Rochefort had to wait. Worse, the Foreign Office refused to hand over the Enigma cryptograph on the grounds that the British Chiefs of Staff had no

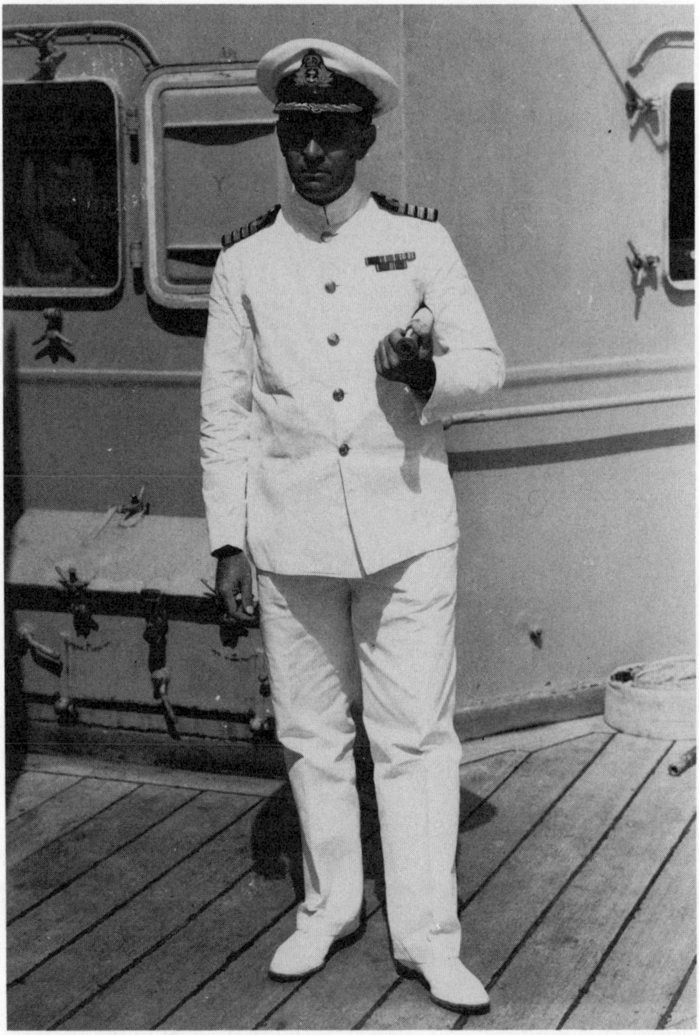

Captain H. B. Farncomb, RAN. (1220, Australian War Memorial)

authority to enter into such a contract. Noyes, usually an equable officer, fell out furiously with the explosive Turner, blaming him for the one-sided deal. The quarrel, which reached its peak in the critical days before Pearl Harbor, was never patched up.

Captain Forrest Sherman, later to become the brilliant head of Admiral Nimitz's planning staff, commanded the *Wasp*. His entreaties to Admiral Noyes in the early hours of 9 August to proceed north at high speed and attack the withdrawing Japanese fleet would go unheeded. The action he recommended would not have saved the American and Australian cruisers from destruction, but it might have inflicted painful wounds on the victorious Mikawa. Unkind critics were to suggest that Noyes's nose was out of joint because Fletcher had been promoted above him. Others would say that the quarrel with Turner was to blame for Noyes's attitude. No proof exists to substantiate either allegation, but one cannot dismiss these personal tensions as wholly irrelevant to the events that unfolded in the early hours of 9 August.

Two officers were to have flag responsibilities thrust upon them unexpectedly. They were Captain Frederick L. Riefkohl, captain of the *Vincennes,* the first American from Puerto Rico to have graduated from Annapolis, and Captain Howard D. Bode, in command of the *Chicago.* Both Riefkohl and Bode had served in World War I and seemed destined for more senior commands. For Bode, however, the Pacific war had begun badly. Like Noyes, he had fallen out with the formidable Turner on the eve of war. As head of foreign intelligence at the Office of Naval Intelligence in Washington, D.C., Bode wanted to send a critical Japanese intercept to Admiral Kimmel at Pearl Harbor. Turner not only refused, he was responsible for removing Bode as head of foreign intelligence. Following this, Bode was appointed to command the battleship *Oklahoma.* Ashore at Pearl Harbor when the Japanese struck, he saw his ship go down. After taking command of the *Chicago* he was again ashore, dining with Rear Admiral C. Muirhead-Gould, RN, flag officer in charge of the Sydney station, when Japanese midget submarines attacked in Sydney Harbor on the night of 31 May 1942, narrowly missing the *Chicago.*

Under the general direction of Admiral Turner, an imposition that was to cause him considerable concern, fifty-five-year-old Major General Alexander A. Vandegrift, USMC, commanded the land phase of Operation Watchtower. When Ghormley told him in July that his First Marine Division would land on Tulagi and Guadalcanal, Vandegrift, like so many others, did not even know where they were. He had been planning optimistically to spend six months in New Zealand training his still far from adequately prepared division. To add to his difficulties, because of the haste with which the operation had been put together, he had no more than five weeks after landing in New Zealand to send the marines across the beaches, and this without proper maps and no intelligence to indicate whether they were likely to be defended. A tall, quiet, unassuming man, known to the marines as Sunny Jim, Vandegrift was to prove unflappable in action, even when he had no more than one day's supply of ammunition.

His serious problems began in Wellington. Ships of the first echelon, having been unloaded, were released for Operation Torch, the campaign to clear the northern coast of Africa and to open the Mediterranean and secure Allied traffic. New Zealand waterside workers, as Vandegrift soon discovered, liked to take their time. When rain fell, work ceased. With the arrival of more ships, the marines, still not recovered from their long voyage in crowded transports, and working three shifts on a twenty-four-hour day in Wellington's bitter winter weather, took over the job.

In the midst of these problems, Vandegrift traveled from Wellington to Auckland in July to meet Admiral Ghormley. "I've got some disconcerting news," said Ghormley, who proceeded to brief him on the Joint Chiefs' directive. Vandegrift was amazed. One regiment of the First Marines was with him in New Zealand, a second was in Samoa to protect it against Japanese invasion, and a third was on the high seas.

"I just don't see how we can land anywhere on the first of August," he said.

"I don't see how we can land at all," Ghormley replied.

Despite the combined protest by Ghormley and MacArthur, the attempt nevertheless had to be made, and Vandegrift, who had now heard of Guadalcanal for the first time, went to work. He assigned eleven thousand marines for the landing on Guadalcanal's beach, east of the mouth of the Tenaru River, five miles west of Lunga Point, and close to the airfield the Japanese were building. Another four thousand marines were earmarked for the landings on Florida, Tulagi, and Gavutu. The division's reserve was to move to Ndeni, in the Santa Cruz islands, where coastwatcher Ruby Boye was at work.

Rear Admiral John S. McCain, commander of Task Force 63, was responsible for ground- and tender-based air support as well as long-distance reconnaissance. His bombers from Noumea, and from hastily built strips at Efate and Espíritu Santo in the New Hebrides, were to soften up Japanese defenses on Tulagi and Guadalcanal. His air search was to cover the approach to, and the operation within, the Tulagi-Guadalcanal area. In addition to B-17s in the New Hebrides and New Caledonia, PBY flying boats supported by tenders were deployed at Ndeni, and following the seizure of Tulagi, at Malaita, eighty-three miles from Lunga Point. The latter began operations only on 8 August. Since the B-17s were faster by thirty knots at cruising speed and by forty-five knots at maximum speed, as well as more heavily armed and better protected, McCain elected to use them in areas where Japanese fighters might be encountered and to reserve the PBYs, with their much longer range, for wider open-ocean searches. This factor would have an important bearing on events the night of 8–9 August.

Admiral Fletcher expected McCain to conduct operations by night as well as by day, using radar for night searches. On 20 July McCain suggested that this would depend on weather forecasts indicating favorable navigation conditions. Otherwise, the searches would be made by day. In fact, radars on both the B-17s and the PBYs were of little use, providing a search beam of only about fifteen degrees on both sides of a plane and a range of about twenty-five miles.

McCain's B-17s covered the Slot as far as the line dividing their area of responsibility from that of the RAAF Hudsons and for 120 nautical miles beyond. Since that line split the channel between Santa Isabel and Choiseul islands, the B-17s' area included the approach to the Slot immediately south of Bougainville straits and west of Choiseul.

The airfields in the New Hebrides and New Caledonia, soaked by tropical storms and lacking almost all facilities, were sorely inadequate for the task. Planes returning to base after dark had to be guided by burning gasoline-soaked rags or truck headlights. At Espíritu Santo, aircraft had to be refueled manually from drums. With the B-17s needing no less than fifty drums to fill up, this was a long, tedious task. Only by desperate effort had the strip been finished in time for Operation Watchtower. Planes could land and take off, but that was about all. Every facility was inadequate, from the harbor, where there was no wharf, along primitive tracks to the airfield, where there were no stocks of gasoline and too few service crews.

On both 7 and 8 August McCain's B-17s were to conduct a 750-mile search. Other surveillance safeguards that Turner had asked for he failed to get. He wanted six search planes to be based at Tulagi under his own hand as a backup for McCain's forces. He got none. He also wanted twelve flying boats to be based at Ndeni and Malaita. Instead, he had to be content with six.

Five marine air squadrons and the army's Eleventh Heavy Bombardment Group were sent to the South Pacific, providing in all 291 land-based aircraft, including thirty from the Royal New Zealand Air Force. Of the total, only 146 were immediately available to give direct support to Operation Watchtower. The rest were scattered throughout Fiji, Tonga, and Samoa.

It soon became apparent that, try as he might, Admiral Ghormley could not meet the D-day of 1 August. It was not until 22 July that the amphibious force, most of which was now assembled in Wellington, sailed for Fiji to practice the landings. Rehearsals began off the island of Koro in the Fantan area of Fiji on 27 July. Former Australian residents in Tulagi and Guadalcanal made a useful contribution in describing to the marines the terrain that faced them beyond the beaches. Detailed intelligence reports of Japanese positions and strengths radioed to Townsville by coastwatchers had made possible the preparation of sketch maps. Troops landed during each of two rehearsals. In the second, fire-support groups practiced bombardment and carrier aircraft dropped bombs on imaginary shore targets. Perhaps in this simulation the marines learned what it might be like to land at Guadalcanal and Tulagi, but landing craft were few in number and frequently they got snagged on coral reefs, which put them out of commission. The rehearsal did not include the landing of supplies, a serious omission that resulted in long delays on the beachhead when the operation began.

Curiously, target practice did not figure in the rehearsal program.[8] Neither the *Vincennes* nor the *Quincy,* which had only recently arrived from the Atlantic, had held night battle exercises or night target practice for at least fifteen months. The *Chicago* had not carried out a surface firing since October 1941. Only the *Australia* had engaged in target practice since May. And the only units that had operated together were those of the Australian Squadron.

A conference called by Admiral Fletcher in the *Saratoga* off Fiji on 26 July revealed even more dangerous shortcomings.[9] The U.S. Navy's surface and air role in the early period of the war had been to engage the Japanese fleet, to protect the main base at Pearl Harbor if the enemy attempted further attacks, and to protect convoys bound for the war zones. For the first time in the history of war, opposing fleets had engaged in major actions far out of sight of each other. Although the Imperial Japanese Navy had come off second best at Midway and the Coral Sea, U.S. losses had also been heavy. Yet another role for seaborne air, providing close support for landing forces, executed so brilliantly in subsequent operations in the Central Pacific, had not been fully developed in theory and had never been put to the test.

At the outset of the conference in the *Saratoga,* it was clear that Fletcher opposed Operation Watchtower. According to Vandegrift, Fletcher appeared to lack knowledge of or interest in the whole affair, and to be nervous and tired. Both Turner and Vandegrift had assumed that an essential role for Task Force 61 would be to ensure the success of the landing; the carriers with their aircraft would remain until the transports were unloaded and the beachhead was secure.

Fletcher had a different view. He wanted to know how long it would take to secure the beachhead. Turner replied five days.

"Five days!" Fletcher barked. "I'm going to take my carriers out in two days. I refuse to risk air attack against them for a longer period."

Burning with anger, but outwardly cool, Vandegrift remarked that the day was over when naval forces could land a small force and then abandon it. Not even five days was enough to guarantee the success of the landing.

Turner had been responsible as amphibious commander for the overall Watchtower plan, and Fletcher, who had not been available during the planning stage, disapproved. The operation would not have adequate logistic support, he argued, and it would be conducted by a task force that lacked training and fighting experience.

"Now, Kelly," Fletcher said to Turner, "you're making plans to take that island from the Japs and the Japs may turn on you and wallop the hell out of you. What are you going to do then?"

"I'm just going to stay there and take my licking," Turner replied.

Fletcher said he would stay until the third day, then dismissed the conference, insisting afterwards that there had been no friction between Turner and himself.[10]

A singular absentee was Admiral Ghormley, who sent in his place his chief of staff, Rear Admiral Dan Callaghan. Ghormley had the authority to overrule Fletcher and to insist that the carriers remain as long as they were needed or their fuel supplies would permit. No explanation for his absence has ever been given other than he "found it impossible to give the time necessary for travel with possible attendant delays." Nor has it been satisfactorily explained why, instead of taking over as task force commander to launch the operation, he delegated this authority to Fletcher. Despite his experience, Fletcher was still regarded with some doubt by the navy for his failure to go to the assistance of the Wake Island garrison in its hour of need, and by naval aviators for his loss, as a line officer, of the *Yorktown* and the *Lexington.*

At the *Saratoga* conference Turner again raised the question of moving six reconnaissance seaplanes from Tonga to Tulagi. Callaghan replied that no ship was available to transport them. He would have to be satisfied with short-range scouting to protect his force against the approach of surface forces.

Estimated Japanese sea strength in the Bismarck–New Guinea–Solomons area was eleven cruisers (Cruiser Division 6 and possibly Cruiser Division 8), thirteen destroyers (Destroyer Squadron 6 and Destroyer Division 34), fifteen submarines and possibly three more, twelve subchasers, one seaplane tender (at Rabaul), an unknown number of motor torpedo boats (eight or ten were reported at Tulagi), and fifteen to seventeen transport and cargo vessels.[11] Four small submarines were reported at Kukum, but this, intelligence thought, seemed doubtful.

The best available information put Japanese air strength at about 150 planes. From incomplete information it appeared that there were about six fighter squadrons (ten planes each), of which one squadron had new aircraft and one Zeros equipped with pontoon and wing-tip floats. Similarly, there appeared to be about sixty bombers and thirty transport planes. About eight fighters (float types) and seven to ten four-engine passenger aircraft had been operating from the Tulagi area.

On 7 July a coastwatcher, D. G. Kennedy, the district officer and a New Zealander who had spent most of his life in the islands, had reported from Santa Isabel Island that four large vessels and four floatplanes were anchored in Rekata Bay. This was confirmed by aerial reconnaissance on 9 July, when one transport and three destroyers were sighted. On 14 July the presence of four cruisers, one flying boat, and one floatplane in the Rekata anchorage indicated that a new base was being established there, a matter that remained clearly impressed in Admiral Turner's mind on 8 August when reports were received from the RAAF Hudsons of the approaching Japanese cruiser force.

The Japanese were consolidating and improving their bases in the Solomons–Bismarck Sea area, and further reinforcements would arrive soon. Additional reports indicated that the Japanese were also reinforcing their bases on the northern coast of New Guinea and expanding southward, inland from Gona, with Kokoda Airfield an initial objective. They had shifted aircraft between the Netherlands East Indies, the Marshall islands, and New Britain, and the air force in the New Britain–Solomons area had apparently been increased.

Information derived from sigint was highly accurate. Thus reports that the Japanese landing on Guadalcanal had been made by the Eleventh and Thirteenth Pioneer Detachments, supported by a marine or naval landing force, only marginally overestimated the armed strength the U.S. Marines were likely to encounter there; other reports indicating that more than four thousand Japanese troops had landed were serious overestimations. In fact, in addition to seventeen hundred unarmed

Martin Clemens with his Guadalcanal scouts. (Courtesy Martin Clemens)

construction workers, mostly Koreans and Taiwanese, the principal force consisted of only several hundred *rikusentai,* or naval landing force, sailors and navy officers trained at the army's infantry school. Their light armament came from the army, heavier materiel from the navy. The component units were named after three naval districts: Yokosuka, Sasebo, and Maizuro. Characteristically, the navy had not bothered to inform the army, which was soon to become so deeply and bitterly involved, that it was building an airfield on Guadalcanal or that it had stationed the *rikusentai* there.

The latest intelligence was available when Turner met Vandegrift and Crutchley and the task group commanders aboard the *McCawley* on 31 July to review the plans one final time.[12] Fletcher did not attend, nor did the Briton Crutchley have the opportunity to meet the captains of the American ships in his screening force. Even after long practice together, officers find it difficult to operate with navies other than their own, much less with officers they have not met. Crutchley, moreover, had barely had time to make himself known to the Australians, and he had never commanded a squadron in action.

From the beginning of the Pacific war the Allies had been underestimating the Japanese capacity not only to fight but also to surprise. As late as September 1944, Lieutenant General George C. Kenney, commander of land-based air forces in the Southwest Pacific, wrote that the Japanese would never make good airmen.[13] "The Japs can't do it," he said. "Too much of their population is peasant class–rice planters, fishermen, ricksha pullers–who are too dumb, too slow-moving and utterly lacking in mechanical knowledge and adaptability." The following month the kamikazes struck.

Senior British officers were no less mistaken. As Admiral Crutchley would well have known, on 13 February 1942 the Admiralty had promulgated a message from Vice Admiral Geoffrey Layton, Commander in Chief, Eastern Fleet, saying that according to the evidence the Japanese were not good night fighters.[14] It was essential, he believed, to exploit this weakness to the utmost.

The admiral had it all wrong. Because the Imperial Japanese Navy lacked the strength to match the Americans ship for ship and plane for plane, heavy emphasis had been placed on night fighting. It was more than a tactic, it was a tradition. Just past midnight on 9 February 1904, Japanese destroyers, in what was to prove a dress rehearsal for Pearl Harbor, sped to the attack against Russian battleships at anchor outside Port Arthur, thus launching the Russo-Japanese war. Three of the ships were crippled. This, Japanese sailors had it drilled into them, was the way to fight.

In the interim between world wars, hard training and night fighting were the twin pillars of naval preparation. Night fighting exercises were conducted in deliberately dangerous conditions, with accidents frequent. On the night of 24 August 1927, the light cruiser *Jintsu* sliced through the hull of the destroyer *Warabi,* while another light cruiser, the *Naka,* cut much of the stern off another destroyer. The casualties ran into three figures. After being brought before a court martial, the captain of the *Jintsu* committed suicide. This, however, did not put an end to the emphasis on night fighting. The training paid off. Sailors with superior night vision were trained as lookouts and supplied with vitamin A tablets. The best, using their powerful night glasses, could detect the movement of a ship 8,000 meters away on a dark night.

As for surprise, ever since the attack on Port Arthur, it had been the key element in Japanese military thinking. In the 1920s Lieutenant

General Toshio Tani had given a series of secret lectures on the lessons of the Russo-Japanese war at the Japanese War College. Tani repeatedly emphasized the need for surprise, both tactical and strategical, and bitterly regretted the six months Japan had spent negotiating with Russia.[15] In future wars, he vowed, Japan would shorten the negotiating period to prevent a hostile power from seizing the initiative. Pearl Harbor had its genesis at Port Arthur, and the flag that flew from the masthead of the *Akagi,* the Japanese carrier flagship on 7 December 1941, had flown from Togo's flagship thirty-seven years before. What was soon to occur off Savo Island had its origins in the same philosophical approach to war that Tani had drilled into his students at the War College and that the navy learned in those endless night exercises.

4

The Carriers Depart

For two years, Australian and New Zealand soldiers had been heading for war in luxury liners. No one who saw it, or who was in one of the ships, is likely to forget the sight of the *Queen Mary, Queen Elizabeth, Aquitania, Mauretania,* and *Île de France* in line ahead passing through Sydney Heads with thousands of troops bound for the Middle East. Now it was the U.S. Marines' turn, and the array of ships leaving Fijian waters for the Solomons was almost a who's who of American shipping. Two converted American President liners were fresh from the stocks, but there were old ships as well, including the former *City of Newport News,* now the *Fuller,* built in 1919, and the even older *City of Los Angeles,* now the *George F. Elliott.* For the U.S. Marines, the long journeys across the Pacific were anything but tropical pleasure cruises. Overcrowded quarters, sometimes in the holds, furnacelike heat during nightly blackouts, horrendous outbreaks of prickly heat, the constant danger of submarine attack, the nagging fear of those first vulnerable moments on the beach—all of this was aggravated by enforced inactivity.

For the First Marine Division, only partly trained and with the watershed of first action still ahead, it was a depressing introduction to war. Aboard one transport the daily ration had to be reduced to 1,500 calories. Rancid butter, rotten eggs, and no fresh food left a diet of soup and bread. Some men lost up to twenty pounds, scarcely the best preparation for the exhausting slog that lay ahead on Guadalcanal. Bakers ran out of shortening ten days out and had to use an oil substitute, with the result that almost half the marines aboard came down with diarrhea. An outbreak of mumps and shortage of medical supplies did not help. The heads were inadequate to cope with the number of men, and steel helmets had to be used instead. When the division sailed from Wellington, many of the marines had been aboard ship for a month.

Tensions ran high—at sea with the task forces; on Guadalcanal, where coastwatchers had begun to wonder whether a landing might not be too late; and in Washington, where the Joint Chiefs regarded two editorials in the *Sydney Morning Herald* recommending an immediate Allied offensive as a breach of security that imperiled not only the forces involved but the whole code-breaking operation. It had already been seriously endangered by articles in the American press after Midway, and by the *Dominion* article quoting the *New York Times* and the *Herald Tribune.*

To add to the Joint Chiefs' concern, naval communications intelligence reported on 1 August that a new Japanese operations force, D, might invade western or northwestern Australia, while a striking force had been created to disrupt Allied supply routes from India.[1] Every day the warnings mounted. Cryptanalysts had decoded one of the most important messages of the Pacific war—a signal from Tokyo to Berlin that it did not intend to open a second front against the Soviet Union unless forced to do so by extraordinary circumstances. If the Russians could breathe more easily, the signal left no doubt that Japanese pressure in the Pacific would continue.

Fortune was generous on 6 August, D minus 1, a high-risk day for the transports and their escorts. An overcast sky and mist made surface visibility poor and prevented reconnaissance by Japanese Tulagi-based flying boats. Crutchley put the *Canberra* on surface radar guard and ordered the escort force to assume the first degree of high- and low-angle readiness, though still permitting small parties to leave their quarters for meals.

The expeditionary force approached Guadalcanal and Tulagi from the west, a maneuver greatly assisted by moonrise in the early hours of the morning. Savo Island and the western end of Guadalcanal began to show up darkly as the squadron heading for Tulagi, with the *San Juan* in the van and including the *Chicago,* the *Canberra,* five destroyer minesweepers, and six destroyers, took the lead. Six miles astern came the *Australia,* the *Hobart,* the *Vincennes,* the *Quincy,* the *Astoria,* and nine destroyers. Four former destroyer transports and four transports accompanied the Tulagi force. Nine transports and six store ships completed the Guadalcanal contingent.

No glimmer of light had broken the predawn darkness when the

Tanambogo Island just before the marines landed on 7 August 1942. The Japanese seaplane base is burning, as are the tender and a seaplane in the harbor. (80-G-11896, National Archives)

carrier-based planes, thirty-six fighters and forty-four dive-bombers, blasted Tulagi, destroying the seaplanes there and working over the landing areas, the antiaircraft batteries, and the shore batteries.

Aboard the transports, marines heard the crump of bombs and saw the pyrotechnics of eighteen seaplanes bursting into flames and sinking in Tulagi Harbor. Close to Guadalcanal there was another fireworks display: destroyers opening fire on a motor auxiliary vessel. Fighters came in to complete the job, and the ship, which appeared to have been carrying gasoline, exploded in a fireball.

General Vandegrift had divided his force into two main groups. Brigadier General William Rupertus, assistant division commander, took charge of the force to take Tulagi, Gavutu, and Tanambogo. Initial resistance here was expected to be strong, and Rupertus had under his command the best trained and prepared units—the First Marine Raider Battalion, the First Parachute Battalion, two elite forces, and a battalion of the Fifth Marines. For the Guadalcanal landing, Vandegrift had the First Marines and the rest of the Fifth Marines, with the Second Marines in reserve.

First ashore was a small party of marines that landed at Haleta, on Florida Island, to secure the promontory sheltering Tulagi and to ensure that the Japanese could not enfilade the force making the major landing. The party landed without opposition.

The landing at Tulagi was set for 0800, one hour and ten minutes ahead of the Guadalcanal schedule. It was preceded by heavy bombardment from the *San Juan,* destroyers, and minesweepers. According to Crutchley's account, between 0740 and 0745 the *San Juan* fired a remarkable 560 rounds into a small hill on Tulagi, after giving the secondary landing at Haleta a 100-round bombardment. If the weight of shells delivered was impressive, the manner of their delivery was not. The shells sprayed Tulagi haphazardly, revealing a clear need for closer spotting and more accurate gunlaying to obtain a higher percentage of effective hits and to prevent shells from falling among friendly troops.

Twenty miles to the west, the 8-inch-gun cruisers *Vincennes, Astoria,* and *Quincy* and the destroyers *Hull, Dewey, Ellet,* and *Wilson,* working close along the north shore of Guadalcanal, had kept anticipated Japanese positions under constant bombardment. They were rewarded when big fires broke out at Kukum, where coastwatcher Martin Clemens had reported antiaircraft batteries and a supply dump.

Twenty minutes before the marines were to land at Guadalcanal, destroyers marked the line of departure for landing craft and aircraft outlined the limits of the beach with colored smoke. Between the two pillars of smoke there now descended a blanket of 8- and 5-inch fire from the *Quincy, Vincennes,* and *Astoria*. In five minutes the cruisers fired 45 rounds of 8-inch and 2,000 rounds of 5-inch fire, while the destroyers let off another 200 rounds.

At 0920, only two minutes after the first marines went ashore, a flare signaled that the landing had been made without trouble. No resistance was encountered, and the marines pushed on. What they discovered was astonishing: The Japanese, believing this was a naval raid, had simply disappeared into the hills, abandoning everything, including their breakfasts, and leaving the keys in the ignition of their vehicles.

Things were not going nearly so well on Tulagi. Although the landings at Haleta and Blue Beach had been unopposed, with the

From left, 7 August: Florida, Tulagi, Gavutu, and Tanambogo. (80-G-11899, National Archives)

marines quickly gaining control of the northern part of Tulagi, secondary landings had come under fire from shore guns. More difficult tasks lay ahead. The Japanese had concentrated in the south, which now came under intense bombardment from the *San Juan* and the destroyer *Ellet* as well as from the air.

Three hundred and fifty miles to the northwest, on Bougainville, coastwatcher Paul Mason, from his high lookout on Malabita Hill, had been listening to the traffic at Tulagi and translating it for his enthusiastic boys. "The bearded Yauwika pricked up his ears," he later wrote.

> Soon we all did. From the northwest we could hear the dull and ever-increasing note of a host of aircraft approaching our site. Some of the boys shinned to the tree tops, for our view was obscured in that direction. In a matter of moments the largest formation I had ever seen raced across a break in the jungle—twenty-seven streamlined Japanese dive-bombers, their blades glistening in the sun as they raced at high speed for Tulagi. And more were following closely on their heels—another packed formation of fifteen of the same type. They were passing only

The landing on Florida Island, before the main landings at Tulagi and Guadalcanal. (80-G-12645, National Archives)

> a few hundred feet over our high location. It was 8:40 A.M. They were still audible to the southeast as I flashed the [radio] report through to VIG Port Moresby, from where it was tapped out to station VIT Townsville and was in the hands of Tulagi ten minutes later. With such reports as this the time factor was all important: consequently they had to be transmitted in plain language to avoid the time entailed in encoding and decoding. The risk of enemy interception of the signal, and the location of its source, was one that had to be taken, for the risk was worth it.

The task forces all heard it.[2] Malaita picked it up and passed it on. Pearl Harbor rebroadcast it. In twenty-five minutes every ship in the invasion force got the word. Well before this, Turner in the *McCawley* had signaled Fletcher in the *Saratoga* requesting that for the rest of the day fighters over the area all be used against air attack. So, as the Japanese bombers and their escorts droned on, the U.S. carriers, some thirty miles west of Guadalcanal, turned into the wind and their fighters took off.

The coastwatcher network had demonstrated not only how effective it could be but also how well guarded it was. And the carriers' quick reaction clearly confirmed Plunkett-Cole's observation in the *Canberra* that air attack was considered the greatest danger. In contrast, the following day when Stutt, on another coastwatcher frequency, sent out his signal warning of the presence of enemy surface ships, it attracted some attention but caused little concern.

Rear Admiral Sadayoshi Yamada, commander of the Twenty-fifth Air Flotilla, had received the distress signals from Tulagi in the early morning of 7 August. He knew that many of his planes would be obliged to make forced landings on the long haul back from Guadalcanal. So important was the need to strike back quickly that this could not be allowed to stand in the way of the operation. Twenty-seven Bettys, each carrying two 250-kilogram and four 60-kilogram bombs, escorted by seventeen Zekes, took off from Rabaul at 0955 (Solomons time) to attack the carriers. Unable to find them, they attacked the transports off Tulagi instead. The Zeke pilots were shocked when they received their orders. They had never heard of Guadalcanal, and they could not believe that they were being asked to engage in combat with Grumman Wildcats 540 miles away.

The *Enterprise* launched two flights of Wildcats. The first flight's mission was to patrol at 18,000 feet over the carriers. At 1300 four planes were vectored to Tulagi, where they sighted a formation of Bettys protected by Zekes at a height of 12,000 feet. Lieutenant V. P. De Poix shot down one bomber and later made an emergency landing on the *Wasp*. One pilot failed to return. The second flight, with orders to patrol over the transport screen, sighted twenty-three Bettys and ten Zekes at the southeastern tip of Santa Isabel Island. The Zekes attacked immediately. While the Americans claimed one Betty and one Zeke shot down, three of the six Wildcats went down in dogfights.

A flight from the *Saratoga* apparently had the misfortune to meet the formation of Saburo Sakai, Japan's legendary fighter ace—he had already shot down fifty-six planes in China, the Philippines, the Netherlands East Indies, and New Guinea—at a height disadvantage. The four Wildcats, led by Lieutenant J. J. Southerland, saw a large flight of Bettys over Savo Island at the same altitude. The Zekes, flying above the Bettys, swooped down on the Wildcats. Three of the pilots, including

Southerland, failed to return. The fourth, Ensign D. A. Innis, came back with his plane badly shot up.

The Bettys arrived over the transports and their escorts in tight formation. The transports, which had remained at anchor, should have been sitting ducks, but the Bettys were too high. Much to the disgust of Sakai, instead of carrying torpedoes the Bettys were loaded with bombs that fell harmlessly into the sea. As for Sakai, his Zeke miraculously escaped. Half paralyzed from a wound, his windshield blown out by gunfire, the Japanese ace completed an incredible nine-hour round-trip journey back to Rabaul. After a year in a hospital and the loss of one eye, he was back in the pilot's seat, shooting down one of the last Superfortresses to be lost in action over Japan.

Sakai had emerged from the preparatory flight course at Kasumigaura Air Station tough in mind and muscle. A specialty of the training there was "pillar-felling," a strenuous and violent game that often required the services of nurses and doctors. The participants, barefooted, formed human walls on either side of a huge, flag-topped wooden pillar. When a bugle sounded "Advance" the two sides would rush forward, roaring war cries, pushing, beating, punching, and kicking in a wild rampage. Only biting was forbidden. The free-for-all continued until members of one group grabbed the pillar and brought it down. Trainees needed to be tough to survive, and Sakai was tougher than most. He could hang by one arm from the top of a pole for half an hour and swim fifty meters in under thirty seconds.

Sakai and the other Zeke pilots were more than impressed with the Wildcat's high rate of survival under heavy gunfire. But the loss of the Wildcats to the Zekes sent shock waves through the carrier force. The carriers suddenly appeared to be dangerously vulnerable, an impression not lost on the ever-cautious Fletcher. There was general agreement that the Wildcat had proved no match for the Zeke in dogfights. Plane for plane, the Zeke was superior in climb, speed, maneuverability, and endurance. Only in firepower and in ruggedness, the ability to "take it," was the Wildcat superior. The Japanese had five planes shot down; two others made emergency landings.

Commander H. D. Felt, who commanded the *Saratoga*'s air group, eschewed pleasantries in his report on combat flight operations:

> Our fighter pilots operating the F4F4 [Wildcat] airplane are at a distinct disadvantage when in combat with the Zero-type fighter. Our naval aviator does have the advantage of excellent training, a good gun

> platform and armored and leakproof tank protection. However, if our VF squadrons are to be given a reasonable chance to destroy the Japanese VF, they must be operated as squadrons and be permitted to bring into play the team work which they have spent hours of study and flight time to develop. That team work can spell success. Lack of it results in a dangerous melee.[3]

Another serious weakness had also been revealed in air support. Five days before the Watchtower landings, three officers and three radiomen had been transferred to Turner's staff on the *McCawley* to set up communications for direct control of the air support force. In action, they were confronted with the overwhelming task of handling all radio traffic between the ground forces and the supporting aircraft overhead. This meant that there was no direct communication between the attacking ground forces and their air support. For this the marines on Tulagi paid dearly.

Advancing toward the southern end of the island, they encountered fierce resistance. By nightfall the battalion of the Second Marines, intended for the occupation of Santa Cruz, had been thrown in to reinforce the force ashore. Resistance was especially heavy on the small island of Gavutu, where preliminary bombardment was significantly less than effective in destroying Japanese caves and dugouts. The marines were to suffer even more heavily on the smaller island of Tanambogo. At nightfall the Japanese there were still in control, and no supplies had yet been landed in the Tulagi area. At 0135 on 8 August the Raider Battalion reported that it had suffered 22 percent casualties and the Parachute Battalion 50 percent casualties.

A second Japanese air attack by nine Val dive-bombers during the afternoon had been beaten off by fighters, but not before the destroyer USS *Mugford* had received a direct hit from a 250-pound bomb, which caused considerable damage to the superstructure and put out of action the two after gun mountings. This time the Japanese had escaped detection by the coastwatchers, and the task forces had no warning either by radar or from the fighter cover. Two of the attacking planes were shot down over the destroyer screen, and others were claimed as dogfights persisted beyond Savo Island. Only three of the Vals returned to base.

All had continued to go well on Guadalcanal. The only real resistance the marines encountered was from the thick rain forest in which one battalion had become bogged down. If the marines had secured less territory than Vandegrift had hoped, nearly eleven thousand were ashore and there had been no casualties from enemy fire, a better result than the rehearsal on Koro Island. There four marines had been left behind!

A much graver cause for concern than the situation on the ground were the bottlenecks that had developed in delivering materiel to the Guadalcanal beachhead. Crutchley noted that during the night the beach had become so congested with gear and equipment landed from the transports and store ships that unloading had to be suspended. In the absence of a rehearsal at Koro Island, major problems had not been anticipated. Marines allocated to unloading duties were too few in number, and combat commanders, though still not under fire, were reluctant to reduce their strength in the line and beef up unloading details because of what they regarded as an inevitable Japanese counterattack. The morale of unloading parties was not helped by driving rain and lack of shelter. Rations had been packed in cardboard containers, and these softened, swelled, and burst in an appalling mess of cereal, sugar, and canned goods.

Many of the boats carrying supplies to the shore were unsuitable for the task. In the absence of bow ramps, crews had to struggle in the water to lift packs over the gunwales, an exhausting and in some cases almost impossible task. Amphibious tractors, though few in number, demonstrated how invaluable they could be in operations of this kind, running supplies directly from transports offshore to inland dumps. While they shuttled back and forth, however, the beach bottleneck assumed disastrous proportions. As darkness descended at Guadalcanal, 150 landing craft, loaded with supplies, were either on the beach or standing off, waiting for hours for their turn to unload. The marines occupied the west line of the Tenaru River and on the east a security line about longitude 160°06′ East. No major contact with the Japanese force had yet been made.

The night of 7–8 August passed quietly on Guadalcanal. Intermittent fire, all outgoing, broke the silence of the jungle night. About daybreak a party of 150 Japanese passed close to a marine bivouac; instead of attacking, it moved deep into the jungle.

By noon on 8 August the marines had entered the main Japanese camp at Lunga. Although it had been subjected to naval bombardment, it was in good order, with large canvas tents set roughly seventy-five feet apart. They provided accommodation for about a thousand men, with latrines, stores, sick quarters, a wireless telegraphy station, refrigeration, a reticulated water supply, and all the comforts of a good camp, including electric power.

Soon after taking Lunga, the U.S. Marines occupied the airfield. Again, there was no resistance. One 5,000-foot runway and a control building had almost been completed. In another forty-eight hours the runway would have been ready to land the first Japanese planes. There were deep and well-protected shelters, and large quantities of food and other supplies in store.

Half an hour after taking the airfield, the marines moved to Kukum, where the Japanese had built a camp for fifteen hundred men. It showed every evidence of hasty evacuation. No attempt had been made to destroy the stores, and large quantities of building material, clothing, tools, guns, and general stores fell into the marines' hands. McCain's bombers had been less than accurate. There were good shelters against shelling and aerial bombardment. Most of the shells fired by the Allied cruisers and destroyers had fallen harmlessly among the coconut palms, although ten wounded men were subsequently captured, the only apparent casualties of the bombardment.

While the marines were pushing on, coastwatcher Jack Read heard the roar of approaching Japanese planes and saw red discs and propeller blades flashing as they passed only a few hundred feet over the Buka Passage. He counted them and called Malaita: "Forty-five bombers going south." The message reached the task forces at 1040, singularly unfortunate timing since about this very time, when Stutt's signal was received, everyone's attention was concentrated on meeting the air attack and not on the possibility of night action many hours later.

After suffering heavy losses on 7 August, the Twenty-fifth Air Flotilla had been reinforced overnight by an additional nine Bettys. Rear Admiral Yamada decided to throw everything into the attack against Fletcher's aircraft carriers, a decision that Fletcher himself had expected. Five reconnaissance aircraft set out to find the carriers in the early morning. Visibility southwest of Guadalcanal was poor, and two aircraft sent to search this area failed to sight the carriers. In the mistaken view, however, that the enemy invasion force came from east, or northeast, of Tulagi, and that that was where the carriers would be found, the Twenty-fifth Air Flotilla concentrated there, and of course failed to find their targets. The alternative was to attack the ships in the transport area off Tulagi and Guadalcanal, an operation that resulted in the loss of another eighteen Bettys.

At 1040 Admiral Turner received Read's warning. At last, stores were steadily landing on Guadalcanal. Now everything had to stop. Out went the order to cease unloading and for the transports to get under way. General quarters sounded, and the cruisers and destroyers maneuvered to provide antiaircraft protection. Carrier planes sortied for air cover now that the threat was real. There was no time to lose.

In the midst of this, the signal from the Hudson landed without a ripple. If it conveyed any sense of threat, it was far off. So little attention did it attract in the *McCawley* that Turner did not learn of it until after the Japanese air raid had ended. Even then it caused little concern. The Allies knew nothing of the Japanese navy's years of night training, much less of the special effort expended for the development of lookouts' night vision. The indicated size of the Japanese force, even putting both the Hudsons' sightings together, did not suggest that Mikawa would be bold enough to launch a surprise attack. The Allies would not have attempted such an attack against a force so much larger than their own. Inexpert in night fighting, they would not have dreamed of attempting a night attack. Most of the Allied ships had had little practice in firing, let alone night firing.

Not until after the air attack had ended and the surviving Bettys were heading back for Rabaul did anyone pay attention to the signal, and then the assumption of the flag officers was that the ships signaled a renewed air attack the following day.

That the Japanese scored near misses on both the *Australia* and the *McCawley,* two of the three flagships in immediate Guadalcanal waters, reinforced the view that attack from the air was much more likely to be effective than an improbable night attack by sea. Admiral Turner and his staff admitted to a contempt for the enemy. They simply did not believe that the Japanese measured up as fighting men. In the *Australia,* not only were Japan's night-fighting capabilities underestimated, they were regarded as a fundamental weakness. Along with this was the strongly held view of Admiral Crutchley's staff that intelligence derived by aerial reconnaissance was not to be trusted. Aircraft from the Southwest Pacific Command and the RAAF were held in ridicule.

Captain Riefkohl of the *Vincennes,* alone among senior officers, believed that there was a serious possibility of night action. Some junior officers in the cruiser force, marking the position of the Japanese ships on their charts and calculating time and distance, were also reluctant to discount a night attack. They played no part in the decision making. Although the Japanese had demonstrated the importance of surprise,

The attack by low-flying Bettys on 8 August. (80-G-17066, National Archives)

Captain Getting in the *Canberra* believed that in modern naval warfare surprise was no longer possible.

The *Saratoga* considered sending either a surface force or an air strike force to attack Mikawa, but all thought of offensive action was abandoned when the Bettys arrived with their torpedoes. This persuaded Admiral Fletcher to withdraw his carriers early.

The *Australia* saw the Bettys at noon. They appeared from the east, behind the cloud cover over Florida Island. Although the *Wasp*'s combat air patrol had returned just before the Japanese attack and the *Saratoga*'s aircraft were on call for emergency duty, the opening exchange was very much in the Americans' favor.

Wildcats from the *Enterprise* engaged the Bettys and shot down five in the first five minutes, two of them falling to the fire of Ensign W. M. Rouse. Between Tulagi and Guadalcanal Rouse made a stern run on one plane and set it on fire, made a run on a second and likewise set it on fire, then started after a third, which was shot down in flames by Machinist D. E. Runyon. Runyon had brought down another plane a minute earlier in a head-on run. Of the six Japanese planes encountered by the Wildcats, only one escaped.

The cruisers and destroyers, maneuvering into two independent squadrons between Guadalcanal and Florida, now launched a furious barrage against the low-flying Bettys as they came in to discharge their

A Japanese plane shot down by antiaircraft fire from the amphibious force. (NH 69116, U.S. Naval Historical Center, Turner Collection)

torpedoes. In five minutes the *Chicago* alone fired 142 rounds from her 5-inch guns and more than 2,000 rounds of small-caliber ammunition. The *Australia* claimed three of the Bettys, including one that launched a torpedo which missed the ship by about thirty yards. "A magnificent curtain of bursting high explosive was put up and enemy aircraft were everywhere crashing in flames," wrote Crutchley. "Torpedoes were dropped mostly at long range, but many of the aircraft continued to fly in towards the formation to strafe." The U.S. destroyer *Jarvis,* struck on the starboard side by a torpedo, was stopped dead.

During an attack by two or three Bettys, the elderly transport *George F. Elliott* made a 30-degree turn to bring them under effective fire. One of the aircraft flew directly toward the bridge. About a hundred feet from the ship's side, it began to wobble and changed course slightly, then crashed into the ship's starboard side. Plane parts and bodies scattered over the deck along with flaming gasoline and lubrication oil. About forty-five officers and men were wounded or killed. The burning gasoline started fires above and below decks, and within minutes the *Elliott* was a flaming torch without power, electricity, or steam. Two years later the Japanese, their homeland now threatened by the U.S. advance, would officially launch the kamikaze campaign that sent 3,917 pilots crashing to death on Allied ships. The trailblazer was the crippled Betty, alight and trailing smoke, that smashed into the *George F. Elliott.* Despite assistance from the destroyer USS *Hull,* flames reached the transport's engine room and she had to be abandoned.

The attack on the *George F. Elliott* was not the only incident to illustrate the determination of Japanese fighting men. When the *Jarvis* approached a rubber raft to pick up the survivors of one of the Bettys, the airmen fired pistols on the ship and then shot themselves.

The Japanese garrisons on Gavutu, Tanambogo, and Tulagi exhibited similar tenacity. Although a handful escaped to Florida Island, 737 of the original garrison of 750 died. Only 3 surrendered. The marines lost 144 killed and 194 wounded out of a total force of 4,000.

Another air raid alert in the afternoon again delayed unloading operations for a couple of hours, and the chaos on the beach at Guadalcanal that had existed at sundown on 7 August was in no way ameliorated. The original plan had envisaged all stores being ashore by the night of D plus 2, and transports sailing that night. The plan, it was now obvious to all those at the beachhead, had been excessively optimistic.

If this was bad news for Vandegrift, much worse was to follow. Admiral Fletcher was about to renege on his earlier agreement to remain for a third day. Shaken by the loss of the *Saratoga*'s fighters to the Zekes on 7 August, he also worried that a Japanese aircraft carrier might be in the area. That possibility, indicated by reports from Fortresses that had flown over Rabaul on 7 August, had been dismissed by naval communications intelligence, which believed the sighting to be the *Kasagi Maru* or a sister ship fitted with a flight deck but used only for ferrying planes. That the Japanese aircraft had been airborne when they passed over coastwatcher Paul Mason 350 miles to the northwest suggested that they were land-based, an opinion shared by Admiral Noyes and the American carrier pilots. Nevertheless, the use of Zekes so far from their base at Rabaul no doubt perplexed Fletcher as much as it had their Japanese pilots. On the night of 7 August, he ordered the *Saratoga*'s aircraft to be held in readiness as a striking force against a Japanese carrier the next day; Admiral Noyes was to direct the *Wasp* to conduct a morning search for carriers in the direction of Rabaul, and the *Enterprise* was to conduct a similar search in the afternoon.

So serious was Fletcher's concern that even Paul Mason's warning about forty-two bombers on their way to attack the transports failed to persuade him on 8 August that the *Saratoga*'s fighters should be released to meet them. On the contrary, he complained that the *Saratoga* did not

American ships burning off Guadalcanal after the Japanese air raid on 8 August. The USS George F. Elliott *is left center. (NH 69114, U.S. Naval Historical Center)*

appear to be complying with his orders. Twice he rejected Turner's appeal through Noyes to release eight fighters for combat patrol.

The weight of the torpedo attack on the transports at noon not only added to Fletcher's concern about the vulnerability of his forces but also raised again the thought that the planes might be carrier borne. The Japanese scored hits on the *Jarvis* and the *George F. Elliott,* and had near misses on the *Australia* as well as the *McCawley.*

Fletcher had a healthy respect for Japanese torpedoes. He had seen the torpedo attack on the USS *Lexington* during the Battle of the Coral Sea, when Japanese aircraft from as low as fifty feet had scored two hits on the carrier and sent her to the bottom. And he would never forget what happened at Midway, when torpedoes had sunk the USS *Yorktown* right from under him.

Thus two relatively short-range scouting patrols went in the general direction of Rabaul looking for a nonexistent Japanese carrier. The *Wasp*'s 0815 flight shot down a single-seat floatplane near Rekata Bay, reinforcing the notion later in the day that this might be the destination of the force sighted by Stutt and Willman.

Despite the *Enterprise*'s success in the noon attack, the screening force saw little of carrier-based air during the day. This was due in part to Fletcher's instruction to the *Saratoga,* in part to errors of judgment in the *Wasp* and the *Saratoga,* and in part to reduced demand for close support from the landings. The *Wasp* launched her combat air patrol over the transports and screen too soon to participate in the noon action. And by the time the Japanese arrived, her fighters were heading back. The *Saratoga*'s fighters arrived only to see dark clouds left by the cruisers' antiaircraft fire hanging in the sky. The Bettys were on their way back to Rabaul.

The *Saratoga* launched 240 sorties on 7 August and only 114 the following day.[4] She lost seven fighters and one dive-bomber during the two days. On D-day, the *Wasp* launched 223 sorties, on 8 August 89. Her losses over two days were a fighter and a scout bomber in action and two other fighters, one of which crashed on the flight deck and the other in the sea. The *Enterprise,* which lost four fighters in action and two in night water landings, launched 237 planes on 7 August and 135 the following day.

The daily bulletin issued by CinCPac to all subordinate task force commanders continued to indicate a high-level surface threat. The Eighth Base Force, the Fifth Air Attack Force, and the Sasebo Fifth Special Landing Force were all at Rabaul, along with fifteen warships and a dozen transports. On 4 August the bulletin had noted that Cruiser Division 6, Cruiser Division 18, and Destroyer Command 6 were all in the New Britain–Solomons area. The following day it revealed that the *Chokai* and the *Aoba* were in the Rabaul area, a clear indication, given Admiral Mikawa's presence, that an important Japanese operation was about to take place.

On 6 August, a day ahead of the marine landings, the bulletin again gave notice that the *Chokai* and Cruiser Division 6 were in the Rabaul area. Little activity passed unnoticed by radio traffic analysts, and all Japanese movement was noticed in the traffic of 7 August. It was obvious that the enemy was receiving urgent operational orders.

Because of yet another Japanese code change, one signal intercepted on 7 August was not deciphered for another two weeks. It said that on 7 August the *Chokai,* Cruiser Division 18, and another unidentified unit would depart from Rabaul for a rendezvous with Cruiser Division 6 in the vicinity of Bougainville, then proceed to Gaudalcanal, where subsequent operations against the enemy convoy would be based on reconnaissance reports.

The author of *The Role of Radio Intelligence in the American-Japanese Naval War* wrote that, despite the vital missing link, it was "evident that most operational authorities were aware of the presence in the Solomons of the enemy cruisers which were eventually to destroy four allied warships in the night of 8–9 August."[5] Nonetheless, Admiral Crutchley, with the concurrence of Admiral Turner, divided his force of heavy cruisers and thus gave lowest priority to the possibility of a surface attack.

The assumption that surface attack was not likely rested on a fragile foundation. Even before Allied task forces left Fiji, a change in call signs indicated that the Japanese were increasing communications security. At the same time, Admiral Mikawa reached Truk in the *Chokai.* Naval communications intelligence reported that enemy strength had increased tremendously around Rabaul. The Fifth Air Attack Force had received many reinforcements. Additional destroyers and submarines were also being sent to the region, leading to the conclusion "that a new assault would be made by the enemy at the opportune moment."

In considering the disposition of the screening force, Crutchley, before reaching the Solomons, decided to divide into two groups the major surface forces available to counter enemy attack. Either or both groups might be brought against the enemy, depending on his size and composition.

The *Australia* group consisted of HMAS *Australia* (Captain H. B. Farncomb), HMAS *Canberra* (Captain Frank E. Getting), and the USS *Chicago* (Captain Howard D. Bode)—all heavy cruisers—and the destroyers USS *Patterson* (Commander Frank R. Walker) and USS *Bagley* (Commander George A. Sinclair). In the *Vincennes* group were the American heavy cruisers *Vincennes* (Captain Frederick L. Riefkohl), *Quincy* (Captain Samuel N. Moore), and *Astoria* (Captain William G. Greenman), and the American destroyers *Henley* (Commander Robert H. Smith), *Helm* (Lieutenant Commander Chester E. Carroll), *Jarvis* (Lieutenant Commander W. W. Graham), and *Mugford* (Lieutenant Commander Edward W. Young).

The disposition provided for the following: two destroyers, the USS *Blue* (Commander H. Nordmark Williams) and the USS *Ralph Talbot* (Lieutenant Commander Joseph W. Callahan), on radar and antisubmarine guard patrol, covering the entrance on either side of Savo Island; the two main groups, each with their 8-inch-gun cruisers screened by two destroyers, covering the approaches from north of Savo Island to the transport groups; close antisubmarine and anti–motor torpedo boat screens of destroyers and destroyer minesweepers around the transports; and two light cruisers, the USS *San Juan* and HMAS *Hobart,* screened by two destroyers, between the two transport groups as cover against light enemy forces entering the combat zone from the east.

Crutchley intended to meet any enemy force to seaward of the area between Savo Island, Sealark Channel, Guadalcanal, and Tulagi. Air reconnaissance, he expected, would give warning of the approach of enemy surface forces.

In the event of either or both groups being ordered away from the disembarkation area to meet the enemy, Rear Admiral Norman Scott, in the 5-inch-gun cruiser USS *San Juan,* was to direct the activities of the remaining vessels, including HMAS *Hobart* and the American destroyers *Monssen* and *Buchanan.*

The rationale behind the division of Crutchley's 8-inch-gun cruiser force was to cover the approaches to the north and south of Savo Island. Because Crutchley had not met or worked with the captains of the U.S. cruisers, both he and Turner believed that the scheme would work more effectively if Captain Riefkohl, in the *Vincennes,* had tactical command of the second group. Riefkohl notified the other group commanders of his planned operations. He was not in turn advised of theirs.

An hour before sunset each night, the destroyers *Ralph Talbot* and *Blue,* chosen because they were believed to have the best radar and radar capability of the nine destroyers, were to leave the disembarkation area and establish the antisubmarine patrol and radar guard. Their patrol area put the destroyers westward and northeastward of Savo Island; at times it was possible for them to be as much as twenty miles apart. Commander Gatacre, in plotting their patrol, allowed for a radar pickup of about seven miles, but their courses were not coordinated. In fact, at the time Mikawa passed through them, at 0110 on 9 August, they were fourteen miles apart.

The *Australia, Canberra,* and *Chicago,* screened by the *Patterson* and the *Bagley,* were to be under way south of a line drawn 125 degrees from the center of Savo Island and west of longitude 160° 04′ East. The *Vincennes, Astoria,* and *Quincy,* screened by the *Jarvis* and the *Helm,* were to be under way north of the line and west of longitude 160° 04′ East. The *San Juan* and the *Hobart,* screened by the *Monssen* and the *Buchanan,* were to remain east of longitude 160° 04′ East. There was also provision, if need be, for a destroyer striking force to concentrate five miles northwest of Savo Island; it could attack with torpedoes and then maintain touch from westward, engaging in gun action when the cruisers also engaged. At the same time, the dispositions made it almost impossible for Crutchley to concentrate his forces, thus raising the possibility that a cruiser force of the size indicated by naval communications intelligence could knock out both groups in successive blows.

Admiral Turner had examined the dispositions in detail and approved.[6] Captain Riefkohl, with flag authority thrust upon him, had not.[7] He pointed out that it was possible for the two groups to be as much as seventeen miles apart and also for them to be so close together that they could interfere with each other. To reduce the danger, Riefkohl decided to patrol clockwise. It was at this point that he asked Crutchley for his plan of operations for the *Australia* group and received no reply.[8]

Apparently unmoved by CinCPac's intelligence and reports of Mikawa's force off the east coast of Bougainville, Crutchley's dispositions for the night of 8–9 August were identical to those for the night of 7–8, with one exception: The *Wilson* replaced the crippled *Jarvis* on the *Vincennes*'s screen. The admiral knew that a Japanese task force could reach Guadalcanal during the night. He assumed that it would not be strong enough to risk a surface action, specifically a night action, with the powerful cruiser force under him. No provision was made in Crutchley's instructions for night action in the event of a surprise attack by enemy forces. If Willman's message, following so soon after Stutt's, had given cause for concern, Crutchley gave no evidence of this when he made his dispositions. He had received reports that Japanese submarines were heading for Guadalcanal. If carrier-borne aircraft were Fletcher's bête noire, Crutchley worried constantly about submarines. Ensuring the protection of the transports was his principal concern.

Another problem for Crutchley with his mixed U.S.-Australian force was to determine what degree of readiness should be maintained. British and American versions of first- and second-degree readiness differed. With officers and men exhausted, Crutchley wanted to keep his ships ready for immediate action while allowing some relaxation. Thus he had ordered that while first-degree of readiness was to be assumed, a limited number of men might be allowed to fall out for meals. The result was unfortunate: in the U.S. Navy this was equivalent to second-degree readiness, which allowed some men to go below and sleep in their bunks.

At 1350, the *Enterprise* had launched fourteen Avengers from Torpedo Squadron 3 to search a 220-mile area in a broad arc from a point just west of the northern tip of Guadalcanal. It covered New Georgia, the southeastern part of Choiseul Island, and Santa Isabel. The *Enterprise* had carried out a similar search over the same area on 7 August. At that time, however, the *Enterprise* had been some thirty-five miles west of Guadalcanal. In the intervening nineteen hours she had moved about a hundred miles to the southeast, away from the search area and close to San Cristobal. This added substantially to the Avengers' flight time. With a range of 1,020 miles, they could nonetheless have reached well beyond the Slot. Instead, they returned to the *Enterprise* without having sighted the enemy.

Twelve of the aircraft landed between 1741 and 1745. One landed at 1835 and another, the fourteenth and last, eight minutes later. The two latter aircraft had extended their search to 260 miles in the western sector, reaching the extremity of their flight at 1610. A third plane covering the western sector had stuck to the regulation 220 miles. Had it followed the example of the other two, it would have passed over Mikawa in Bougainville straits. The pilot missed contact by a mere thirty miles.

On 7 August Turner had signaled the following to McCain: "The plan for search for 8 August does not cover sector 240 degrees to 318 degrees from Malaita. South-West Pacific is responsible for this sector, but I consider a morning search by you is necessary for adequate cover." In compliance with Turner's request, McCain had had two B-17 aircraft installed with bomb-bay tanks to extend their range and had assigned them the sector 240 degrees to 318 degrees from Malaita for 8 August. They missed sighting Mikawa by about sixty miles.[9]

That same day Mikawa's own reconnaissance aircraft, catapulted at 0625, had returned at noon with a report that a battleship, six cruisers, nineteen destroyers, and eighteen transports were concentrated in the waters between Guadalcanal and Tulagi. Against all odds, he decided to press on and arrived in Bougainville straits, west of Choiseul, at 1600. Unobserved, and neither tracked nor attacked, he sped on toward Guadalcanal. There the approach of nightfall, though it caused new alarm for Fletcher, brought an ill-judged sense of increased security to the screening force, and there was some relaxation of general quarters.

Admiral Fletcher's state of mind at the time became apparent in a conversation he had with Lieutenant Commander Leroy Simpler, whose Wildcats had been heavily engaged with the Zekes on 7 August. Simpler had led the last flight of the day, a combat air patrol over the transports. He landed just before Fletcher sent his message to Ghormley indicating that he wanted to withdraw.

Fletcher asked him if he had been involved in any action on the flight. Simpler replied that he had not.

"You're lucky," said Fletcher. "It's just as well."

Recounting this conversation later to Lieutenant Roger Pineau, one of Admiral S. E. Morison's assistants, Simpler said, "Christ, . . . what kind of a way was that for a commanding officer to talk? It was tough enough for me to get Leroy [himself] to get a plane and go out after the Nips, and an attitude like that on the part of the skipper made it double tough to have to send my boys up to fight."[10]

Like others aboard the carrier, Simpler believed that warning of Mikawa's force had been received in plenty of time. "Intelligence officers told me that if the Japanese kept coming, they would be at Savo Island between 0000 and 0100 hours, but still the carriers withdrew," he said.

Fletcher had grown anxious to withdraw long before he spoke to Simpler. As early as 1630 he had sent a signal by blinker to Noyes: "In view of possibility of torpedo attack and reduction in our present fighter strength, I intend to recommend immediate withdrawal of carriers. Do you agree?" Noyes's approval came as Simpler was winging his way back.[11] At 1807, immediately after the return of all but two of the Avengers, Fletcher signaled Ghormley to recommend the immediate withdrawal of the air support group. In addition to his losses in fighter aircraft, fuel was running low, he said, and there were large numbers of enemy torpedo and bombing planes in the vicinity. Ghormley thought it over and at 2241 signaled his approval, a formality that Fletcher had not waited upon. At 1819 the carriers had begun to retire to the southeast.

Twelve minutes after sunset, Crutchley ordered the screening group to take up its night disposition. The situation at the end of the second day was not quite as favorable as he had expected. The air raids had delayed unloading operations, part of a night's unloading had been lost because of congestion on the beach at Guadalcanal, and at Tulagi the unloading had hardly begun. Losses to enemy attack had been one transport sunk and two destroyers heavily damaged. The Japanese were continuing to receive air reinforcements in Rabaul. Seaplane tenders were moving south, Crutchley noted, and he could expect heavier and more frequent attacks on the ships. The task force might not be so lucky as it had been the previous two days. Fletcher said the time had come for him to withdraw the carrier forces, and enemy submarines known to be in the area could be expected daily.

5

"We'll Catch Them Napping"

At 0625 on 7 August, across their broad fields of conquest, Japanese commands listened to the signal tapped out from the garrison on Tulagi: "Enemy task force of twenty ships attacking Tulagi. Undergoing severe bombing. Landing preparations under way. Help needed." Emperor Hirohito, who was at the imperial villa in Nikko to avoid the summer heat, thought that the landing was important enough to warrant his return to Tokyo.

"Don't worry, Your Majesty," Admiral Osami Nagano, chief of the Naval General Staff and the emperor's principal naval adviser, told him. "The landing is a reconnaissance. We can push them off with just our naval landing force, I believe. There would be danger if we let them consolidate, so we will move quickly to mount an operation against them. Please set your mind at rest and stay there."

Imperial General Headquarters was not unduly perturbed; the Americans, it assumed, were making nothing more serious than a reconnaissance in force and would withdraw in a couple of days. U.S. forces had landed on the Central Pacific islands of Makin and Tarawa about two months before and then withdrawn. They would probably do the same in the Solomons.

Rear Admiral Matome Ugaki, chief of staff of the Combined Fleet, was aboard the flagship *Yamato* at the Hashirajima anchorage in the Inland Sea, about thirty miles from Hiroshima, sweltering in a record-breaking heat wave that had lasted for thirty-two days. Otherwise the news was all good. Captain Masafumi Arima, commanding officer of the *Musashi* (the *Yamato*'s sister ship, with huge 18.1-inch guns and displacing a mammoth 64,000 tons), had come aboard on 3 August to

Vice Admiral Matome Ugaki

report that she had performed better on her trials than the *Yamato.* She would be commissioned on 5 August and go immediately into service.

On the New Guinea front all was going well. The force making its way overland had reached Kokoda, and an amphibious unit was seeking to advance by sea in concert with the advance on land. Difficulties might lie ahead, but prospects for taking Port Moresby, the primary target, had never seemed brighter. The staff had begun to debate the next step. Submarines had been raiding shipping off the Australian coast. There were suggestions that the Japanese navy should again concentrate on the destruction of the British fleet in the Indian Ocean as part of a plan to support the Indian National Congress in driving the British out of India.

The first signal from Tulagi gave no indication of Allied strength, but it quickly became apparent that the landing was not just a raid. Complacency soon gave way to serious concern. Ugaki noted in his diary: "At Tulagi all of seven flying boats were bombed and set on fire, while the garrison of 700 men fought back well. The last message sent by its communication corps was really tragic. At Gaudalcanal the air strip was completed only about yesterday. The garrison there consisted of about 1,200 and there are about 2,000 laborers in addition. They will not be captured easily, but the situation was unknown as no broadcast from that area could be heard."

By mid-morning all Japanese commands knew and appreciated the size of the Allied force. Ugaki made these comments:

> The enemy employed a huge force, intending to capture the area once and for all. It was extremely careless that the force should not have been detected until it attacked. A warning had been issued two days before, but we were attacked unprepared. Unless we destroy them promptly, they will attempt to recapture Rabaul, not to speak of frustrating our Moresby operation. . . . We should, therefore, make every effort to drive the enemy out first, even by putting off the Indian Ocean operation. We have made necessary arrangements accordingly.

Rabaul, at the northern tip of New Britain, now became the springboard for a Japanese riposte. The town had fallen to the Japanese on 23 January 1942 when a brief and hopeless defense ended in the massacre of 150 Australians who had surrendered. Surrounded by a ring of volcanoes, some of them active—the Mother, North Daughter, and South Daughter, with the Vulcan crater a few miles to the south—it had been the scene five years earlier of a disastrous eruption in which more than two hundred people were killed. The ground often shook when the volcanoes rumbled. This had not discouraged the Japanese, who, accustomed to earthquakes, had made it their headquarters for the twin-pronged drive to isolate Australia. Simpson Harbor, shaped like a horseshoe and around which the town had been built, provided excellent shelter and a seaplane base. There were two airfields, Lakunai, just outside the town, and Vunakanau.

As naval communications intelligence reported, Vice Admiral Mikawa had arrived there at the end of July. He was armed with the intelligence that the airfield being built on Guadalcanal had come under close air surveillance, and that there were heavy movements of shipping

Vice Admiral Gunichi Mikawa

from Hawaii. The Americans might be contemplating a counteroffensive. His initial reaction to the news, however, did not differ much from Admiral Nagano's. The fact that the Allied force had arrived undetected was at first thought to indicate that it was quite small and could be handled easily enough.

With Mikawa's arrival on 30 July, Rabaul became the headquarters not only of the Eighth Fleet but also of the Outer South Seas Force, responsible for the area south and west of a line bearing 280 degrees from the junction of the equator and longitude 180° East. As commander in chief of the Eighth Fleet, and temporarily of the Outer South Seas Force, Mikawa's task was to protect the amphibious force to be used in the occupation of Milne Bay and Port Moresby, and to care for the garrisons in Samoa, Fiji, and New Caledonia when these were taken under the orders issued by Imperial General Headquarters on 19 May.

Rabaul was headquarters as well for the Seventeenth Army, under

Lieutenant General Haruyoshi Hyakutake. He was responsible for the land operations against Port Moresby and would also command land forces in the invasions of New Caledonia, Fiji, and Samoa. Also in Rabaul were the Fifth Air Attack Force (Twenty-fifth Air Flotilla) under Rear Admiral Sadayoshi Yamada and an advance element of the Eleventh Air Fleet under Vice Admiral Nishizo Tsukahara, who, on his arrival 8 August, took over command of both the Inner and the Outer South Seas Force.

In less than eight months of war, Admiral Mikawa had crowded in a lifetime of experience. He had been second in command to Vice Admiral Chuichi Nagumo of the Pearl Harbor striking force and had himself commanded the support force. He continued in this command during the raids on Lae, Salamaua, and Ceylon. Following the Battle of Midway, he took over the Eighth Fleet.

A gentle, soft-spoken man, Mikawa found General Hyakutake in fighting spirit when they met in Rabaul on 7 August. Hyakutake told him that he was longing for the appearance of American soldiers in the area. The sooner they appeared, the more quickly Japan would win the war. Beating the Australians would have no impact on the general situation. The short way to end the war was to convince the U.S. Army that it had no possibility of winning. "Our force will shatter them in the ground battles," he said. "We are quite sure. We are therefore waiting for battles in New Guinea. Each of our missions is very important in order to get the war over as soon as possible."

Mikawa left the meeting encouraged by the army's confidence. He had not heard that the American army was strong, and like Hyakutake, he believed that the sooner they got to grips with the Americans the better. This view was heavily reinforced by another signal from Tulagi. "The enemy is powerful," it said. "We will burn our documents and fight to the last. We wish you good luck in the war." The call to arms that both commanders wanted had come.

Mikawa now knew that the American invasion of Guadalcanal was not a reconnaissance in force but a full-scale counterattack. The U.S. covering fleet, he had been told, consisted of two aircraft carriers, a battleship, three cruisers, and twelve destroyers, with a convoy of about thirty transports. Mikawa called in his staff to plan the naval countermove and at the same time asked General Hyakutake what land action he contemplated.

Hyakutake told him that it would be easy enough to drive the marines out with only a small army force, but the ground forces at

Rabaul were earmarked for the Port Moresby operation. As commander of the Seventeenth Army, he could not make the decision to divert ground forces to Guadalcanal. "We will communicate with the Imperial General Staff right away," he said. "But won't it be enough for the time being to use naval landing forces . . . to drive them out?"

Mikawa agreed, and hastily organized a group of 519 men, consisting of the Fifth Sasebo Special Landing Force and the Eighty-first Garrison Unit, both of which were at Rabaul. It was arranged for this small force, commanded by Lieutenant Endo, to board the 5,600-ton *Meiyo Maru* and the supply ship *Soya* under the escort of the minelayer *Tsugaru* and minesweeper 21.

The Japanese naval air force in the Southwest Pacific had been busy since the end of June building up its air bases in preparation for the seizure of the island groups intended to isolate Australia. The construction unit on Guadalcanal reported that fighters would be able to use the base runway by around 5 August, but the Eleventh Air Fleet and Twenty-fifth Air Flotilla Headquarters felt that the condition of the base should be confirmed before sending planes to land there. A base at Kavieng, New Ireland, had not yet been built, and the Buka base was thought to need more than a week to complete. Another construction unit had left Rabaul for Buka on 6 August.

Mikawa's principal staff officers were a study in contrasts. Rear Admiral Shinzo Onishi, his chief of staff since 14 July, was a passive officer who never made a move unless he could not avoid it. Mikawa's operations officer was Commander Toshikazu Ohmae. Born in January 1902, Ohmae had graduated from the Imperial Naval Academy in June 1922. Onishi and Ohmae were overshadowed by Captain Shigenori Kami, an eccentric but brilliant officer who was also the architect of the Savo Island engagement. After graduating from the Japanese Staff College, Kami had gone to Germany as assistant naval attaché. He remained there until February 1936, watching the rise of the Nazis with unconcealed admiration. In Berlin and Munich he was loud in his praise of Hitler. Promoted to commander after returning to Japan, Kami held successive posts on the staff of the Military Affairs Bureau of the Navy Ministry as well as in the fleet.

Kami had a role to play in Japan's signing of the Tripartite Pact. From 1937 to 1940, the country had been divided over whether to sign. The army was in favor, the navy against. The opposition was led primarily by navy minister Admiral Mitsumasa Yonai, vice minister Vice Admiral Isoroku Yamamoto, and the chief of the Military Affairs

Captain Shigenori Kami. (Courtesy of the monthly magazine Maru*)*

Bureau, Vice Admiral Shigeyoshi Inoue. The army was incensed by navy opposition, and there were rumors of ultrarightist assassination attempts on Yamamoto and Inoue. Finally the army minister, General Shuroku Hata, resigned, and the army refused to assign a replacement, thereby forcing the fall of the Yonai cabinet. An influential group of naval officers fascinated by Nazi Germany now put pressure on the leadership to conclude the pact after Yonai, Yamamoto, and Inoue had left their posts. Among them was Comander Kami. In September 1940, four days after the Japanese advanced into northern Indochina, Japan signed the Tripartite Pact. The tough, pro-German element in the navy had become increasingly powerful. Japan headed for war.

Kami, a former instructor in strategy and tactics at the Japanese Naval War College, was promoted to captain two months before the attack on Pearl Harbor. After serving in the war planning section of the Naval General Staff, he was posted to the senior staff of the newly established Eighth Fleet. He was already a legendary figure. A fitness fanatic, it was rumored that he had once done a handstand on the muzzle of a 16-inch gun on the battleship *Mutsu* when it was at maximum elevation. He was a *kendo* (Japanese fencing) expert, youthful in appearance, and hot tempered. His basic principle was that offense was the best defense. After the attack on Pearl Harbor, he had proposed in all seriousness an assault on the Panama Canal. Nearly three years after the Battle of Savo Island, Kami was to be largely responsible for sending the battleship *Yamato* on her reckless suicide mission to Okinawa.

Kami in Japanese means god, or divine, and at the Battle of Savo Island, Kami earned himself the nickname Captain Divine, Divinely Inspired. Even before the full significance of the American attack at Tulagi was appreciated, Kami had proposed a night attack. The American fleet would stay for two or three days, he said, with little regard for Japanese surface power. Kami's was a bold tactic, but typical. No one else on the staff would have proposed taking such a risk, for the Japanese had no knowledge of the Allies' organization and formation.

Kami's argument gained weight when it became obvious that the Allies were not engaged in a minor reconnaissance. Japan's position in the Solomons, the stepping stones to the South Pacific, was now seriously threatened. The Japanese, it should be noted, continued to attach much importance to the use of land-based air against ships at sea. Mikawa realized, however, that whatever air support he commanded would not be sufficient.

A final message had arrived in Rabaul at 0805 on 7 August. "The enemy was in great force. No matter what the odds, the garrison will fight bravely to the last man, praying for everlasting victory." After that there was silence. No word came from Guadalcanal, either.

Admiral Mikawa's greatest concern in carrying out the operation was that his fleet had never trained together. He was afraid of the confusion in formation of a scratch fleet making a raid into the unknown sea in the dead of night. Nevertheless, urged on by Kami, he approved. He decided to minimize the risk of confusion by limiting the number of ships in the force to five heavy cruisers with 8-inch guns. Before daylight on 7 August, the *Chokai* had been at anchor in Kavieng Harbor, New Ireland, together with the four heavy cruisers of Cruiser Division 6. For greater security against the B-17s, which had stepped up their attacks, the *Chokai, Aoba,* and *Kako* were under orders to go to Manus

Island some 300 miles to the northwest, while the *Furutaka* and the *Kinugasa,* for logistical reasons, visited Rabaul. All ships had weighed anchor and were close to the point where they would go their separate ways in St. George's Channel. They waited only on the signal from Rear Admiral Aritomo Goto in the flagship *Aoba.*

That morning, aboard the *Kako,* Captain Yuji Takahashi was told that the communications officer, Lieutenant Shinichi Kondo, was decoding an important message. Communications worked faster in the *Aoba.* Admiral Goto had already read the distress signal from Tulagi and decided to head full force to Rabaul. More dramatic messages from Tulagi put wind in his sails. The previous day Cruiser Division 6 had just finished practicing with its main batteries. All torpedoes had been adjusted. Fuel supplies were ample. If there was a fight ahead, Cruiser Division 6 was ready.

Originally, the ships to be left behind were the light cruisers *Yubari* and *Tenryu,* and the destroyer *Yunagi* of Cruiser Division 18. The Eighth Fleet had another light cruiser, the *Tatsuta,* and the destroyers *Uzuki* and *Yuzuki,* but they had been dispatched to escort a convoy for the Moresby operation. Mikawa eventually included the three ships he had intended to omit after an appeal from the commander of Cruiser Division 18, Rear Admiral Mitsuharu Matsuyama.

All concerned knew that the raid would be hazardous. By noon on 7 August the plans had been drawn up. Mikawa sought the approval of Admiral Yamamoto and informed Imperial General Headquarters in Tokyo. The navy division of the Imperial General Staff, still smarting from the defeat at Midway, opposed the plan as too hasty. There would be no support from an aircraft carrier, and no adequate support from ground-based air.

It was clear at a glance that the plan did involve tremendous risk. The Americans had more powerful surface forces around Guadalcanal. None of the ships in the Eighth Fleet had ever operated anywhere in the vicinity of Savo Island, or Guadalcanal, which was 560 miles away from the Japanese base at Rabaul. The Eighth Fleet did not even have complete charts. The essential precondition for such a night attack was to have a thorough knowledge of the area, its shoals, and its channels. The Eighth Fleet did not even know the location of all the coral reefs.

An even more serious problem was the ships' lack of training together. The four heavy cruisers of Cruiser Division 6, the *Kako* (Captain Yuuji Takahashi), the *Furutaka* (Captain Tsutou Araki), the *Aoba* (Captain Yonejiro Hisamune), and the *Kinugasa* (Captain Masao Sawa), and

Admiral Isoroku Yamamoto

two light cruisers of Division 18, the *Tenryu* (Captain Shimpei Asano) and the *Tatsuta* (Captain Masatake Yoshimura), had been under the command of Vice Admiral Shigeyoshi Inoue in the Fourth Fleet until the organization of the Eighth Fleet. As for the heavy cruiser *Chokai* (Captain Mikio Hayakawa), she had been the flagship of Vice Admiral

Jisaburo Ozawa, operating in the waters around Singapore. Like the Allied screening force off Guadalcanal, the Eighth Fleet included not only ships but also commanders who were unfamiliar with each other.

Many senior officers, among them Admiral Osami Nagano, continued to have grave reservations about the operation. Some staff officers, however, argued that the Combined Fleet had lost its morale after Midway, and that the Eighth Fleet's plan should be adopted primarily to restore the navy's fighting spirit. This argument impressed the more cautious officers, and eventually the Imperial General Staff agreed, mostly because Yamamoto had not come out strongly against the operation. "We cannot disregard the views of a Commander-in-Chief when he is on the spot," said Admiral Nagano. "Mikawa is present in the area and is aware of the facts. He is in the best position to determine whether the action is ill-advised and we should leave the decision to him."

The staff of the Combined Fleet were not so easily impressed. When the issue was put to a vote, forty were in favor and sixty against. Many were worried. Yamamoto's judgment was that Mikawa had always been a cautious officer. He thought that there might be some chance of success if the Eighth Fleet made a rapid assault and a quick retreat into the night, and he went along with the view that, if it came off, it could help to restore morale. He approved the plan, making it clear, however, that it was not an order from the Combined Fleet.

The *Chokai,* returning in haste from her intended sortie to Manus and accompanied by the destroyer *Yunagi* (Lieutenant Shizuichi Okada), entered Simpson Harbor at 1330. By this time, Admiral Mikawa and his staff had put the finishing touches on Captain Kami's plan of attack. The U.S. transports gathered off Tulagi and Guadalcanal were to be the primary targets. Since the Japanese force had not operated together, tactics would have to be simple. It would operate in line ahead, with the *Chokai* in the van. As soon as the raid was over the force would retreat in all haste to get beyond the range of carrier planes known to be operating in support of the forces off Guadalcanal. The lessons learned at Midway had not been forgotten.

Mikawa, his staff, and the war correspondents who had arrived with him from Japan boarded the *Chokai* as soon as she arrived. As she sailed with the *Tenryu* and the *Yunagi* to rendezvous with Cruiser Division 6, which had remained in St. George's Channel, Captain Kami explained the plan to officers in the wardroom. Going slightly bald, and with a small, Hitlerian mustache, Kami had lost none of his legendary aggressiveness. He said there were about fifty enemy ships in the anchor-

Commander and staff of the Eighth Fleet. Front row, left to right: *Commander Toshikazu Ohmae (torpedo staff officer); Captain Shigenori Kami (senior staff officer); Rear Admiral Shinzo Onishi (chief of staff); Vice Admiral Gunichi Mikawa (commander); Captain Hideyoshi Goto (fleet engineer officer); Surgeon Captain Hiroshi Uchino (fleet medical director); Commander Kenei Kondo (gunnery staff officer).* Back row: fourth from left, *Lieutenant Commander Torao Mori (communications staff officer);* fifth from left, *Commander Takashi Hashiguchi (air operations officer);* sixth from left, *Commander Saburo Kiuchi (engineering staff officer);* seventh from left, *Lieutenant Shigeo Takahashi (aide to the commander). (Courtesy Library of War History Department, National Institute for Defense Studies, Tokyo)*

The heavy cruiser Chokai. *(Courtesy* Ships of the World*)*

The light cruiser Tenryu. *(Courtesy* Ships of the World*)*

ages. Japanese guns were insufficient to cover all the ships; the force would have to use searchlights to illuminate the warships and attack them first. "If we don't do it now, we don't know when we will get another chance," he said. "We'll catch them napping."

Not all the officers in the *Chokai* were so optimistic. "It's an intrepid plan," said Lieutenant Commander Shigeo Naka, the gunnery officer, when he discussed it with Captain Kami on the bridge. "Your story is that no enemy shells will hit us, while ours never miss the mark. We ought to be ready to take some hits."

The heavy cruisers Furutaka *(*left*) and* Kinugasa. *(Courtesy* Ships of the World*)*

The heavy cruiser Aoba. *(Courtesy* Ships of the World*)*

"Don't worry," said Kami. "Even the devil will avoid us if we are bold enough. I'm sure the attack will succeed."

The shadows were lengthening over Blanche Bay at the entrance to Simpson Harbor when Mikawa passed by South Daughter and into St. George's Channel. By 1710, he had cleared the approaches to the harbor and ordered line ahead. About an hour later he signaled Cruiser Division 6 to place itself in the rear of the *Chokai,* with the *Tenryu* on the bow, the *Yubari* to starboard, and the *Yunagi* to port.

They formed a distinctive array of ships.[1] The *Chokai,* completed in 1932, had three funnels, the foremost trunked aft above deck into the middle stack to divert smoke from the bridge, a high, cluttered superstructure, ten 8-inch guns in three turrets forward and two aft, and four 5-inch antiaircraft guns. She carried eight 24-inch torpedo tubes and twenty-four torpedoes. The *Kako* and the *Furutaka,* sister ships, had been completed in 1926. They had three funnels sharply raked, powerful searchlights mounted with each group of turrets, six 8-inch guns, four 5-inch antiaircraft guns, eight 24-inch torpedo tubes, and a loading of sixteen torpedoes. The *Aoba* and the *Kinugasa,* launched in 1927, had six 8-inch guns, four 5-inch antiaircraft guns, eight 24-inch torpedo tubes, and a loading of sixteen torpedoes.

Cruiser Division 18 included the light cruiser *Yubari* (Captain Masami Ban), commissioned in 1923. She had a distinctive round stack with double bends in it, actually two funnels trunked into one. She carried six 14-centimeter guns, one 8-centimeter antiaircraft gun, four 24-inch torpedo tubes, and a loading of twelve torpedos. The second light cruiser, the *Tenryu,* the oldest of the bunch, commissioned in 1917, had four 14-centimeter guns, one 8-centimeter antiaircraft gun, and six 20-inch torpedo tubes. The only destroyer, the *Yunagi* ("Evening Calm"), completed in 1924, had two funnels, one banded in white. She carried four 12-centimeter guns, four 20-inch torpedo tubes, and a loading of twelve torpedoes. Between them, the Japanese had forty-eight main battery guns, thirty-four of them 8-inch, and fifty-four torpedo tubes, forty of them 24-inch.

As early as 1933, two Japanese admirals had perfected a giant torpedo using oxygen under high pressure as fuel. Superior to anything produced by the United States or Britain, it was first called Type 93 by its designers because it had been developed 2,593 years after the founding of the empire; later it was known as the Long Lance. With a warhead of over 1,000 pounds, high speed, unparalleled range, and almost complete lack of track, the weapon had been used with great success during the Battle of the Java Sea. It was about to be used in this new battle.

By the time the ships settled into formation, darkness had descended. Until this time, the *Chokai,* aware that U.S. submarines were lurking, had been zigzagging. With nightfall, Mikawa felt more secure and abandoned the tactic. He was lucky. Lieutenant Commander H. G. Munson, in USS S-38, was lying in ambush when the formation passed within a hundred yards of his boat, so close that he could not fire his torpedoes. Mikawa was unaware of the narrow miss. At 2030, twenty miles south of Cape St. George, he set a course to pass north of Buka Island.

During the night, as the fleet headed east of Bougainville, Mikawa studied reports of the air attacks against Allied ships. Some were highly exaggerated. The Zekes reported that on 7 August they had shot down forty-eight American fighters, five dive-bombers, and a medium-sized unidentified plane for the loss of five Bettys and two Zekes. The reconnaissance reports of Allied shipping strength were contradictory. One report said that anchored off Tulagi were two heavy cruisers, three destroyers, and twenty-five transports. Putting all the reports together, Mikawa's staff concluded that they would face a vessel that looked like a battleship (the *Chicago*), three heavy cruisers, and about ten destroyers protecting about forty transports.

After considering these reports, the *Chokai* signaled each of the other ships: "The main force will arrive at the point 5 degrees 40 minutes S 156 40 E [about sixty miles east of Bougainville] at 0400 [0600 Solomons time] on 8th and carry out air reconnaissance covering bearings from

70 degrees to 130 degrees with a range of 250 miles and also to include Guadalcanal." The force was to remain in the general area, out of range of attack by carrier aircraft, until the results of the reconnaissance were received. Then the formation would head for the night attack at Guadalcanal.

The night passed peacefully. Buka Island came in sight at 0100, some ten miles distant and well beyond the night vision of coastwatchers. From Buka Island the force ran southeast, parallel with the coast of Bougainville but well out to sea. Just before dawn, it reached the designated area off the coast of Bougainville.

The heavy cruisers catapulted five reconnaissance planes, four Jakes, and one Type 94 from the *Chokai* in an attempt to locate enemy aircraft carriers. From this time until the planes were recovered, the force operated with the heavy cruisers somewhat dispersed to facilitate the handling of planes. At times the ships were relatively close, at other times well apart though still within eyesight.

The *Aoba*'s plane reported from the Guadalcanal area at 0925 that a ship like a battleship had been sighted ninety-five miles southwest of Tulagi, and at 1000 that it had seen a heavy cruiser, four merchant ships, and three destroyers off Tulagi. Closer to Guadalcanal, it saw two cruisers, four destroyers, and fifteen transports.

Only the *Kako*'s plane failed to return. At 0815, on a scouting flight from the *Wasp,* Lieutenant Commander E. M. Snowden sighted the Jake forty miles from Rekata Bay and shot it down with a short burst. If this was a minor affair, it nevertheless was to have a major impact on Allied decision makers.

At 1025, while continuing to move in the area east of Bougainville, Mikawa saw Stutt's Hudson. A trumpet sounded standby for action. Packing his ears with cottonballs, Fumio Niwa, a well-known Japanese novelist and war correspondent, made his way up the *Chokai*'s ladders to her bridge. Immediately ahead he saw the Hudson. After opening fire, Mikawa feinted with a 90-degree turn in the hope of misleading the plane into believing that he was heading back in the direction of Rabaul. By this time, however, Stutt had seen the *Chokai*'s reconnaissance plane and was hurrying back to Milne Bay.

The *Chokai*'s search plane landed on the water and was hoisted aboard by derrick. No sooner was it aboard than the trumpet sounded again. Niwa, who was drinking a cup of water in the wardroom, returned quickly to the bridge to see Willman coming from the north and flying low. His bombing attempt brought all the cruisers' 8-inch guns into play. Niwa saw flak bursting around the plane and two columns of water as the bombs fell into the sea. The ships continued to follow a northwesterly course after Willman disappeared.

The Hudsons were bad news, made worse by the realization after the intercept of Stutt's signal that Mikawa had not only lost the vital element of surprise, but, with more than seven hours of daylight remaining, there was more than ample time for the Allies to react before nightfall. The prospect of an attack by carrier planes if the force headed for Guadalcanal was now very real. Admiral Mikawa weighed the chances. He was sure the carriers were somewhere in the vicinity of Guadalcanal but were not close to the transport area. He reassessed Allied strength in the target area, setting it at six or seven heavy cruisers, four light cruisers, and some ten destroyers guarding both sides of Savo Island. This did not differ greatly from the estimates made by the Twenty-fifth Air Flotilla the previous day. Although the Allied force was bigger than Mikawa's own, each Allied group was weaker than the Eighth Fleet. The relatively few fighters sighted over the transport area was a hopeful sign. The Zekes, he had been led to believe, had been devastatingly successful in their raid on 7 August. The risk was worth taking. The operation would proceed.

For more than an hour after Willman disappeared, Mikawa remained circling off the Bougainville coast. Anxious to minimize the danger of an attack by the carrier planes, he decided to delay the operation an hour. At a speed of twenty knots, the fleet headed southward for the Slot at 1300. The attack would be made on 9 August at 0130, not 0020 as originally planned, so that on its approach the fleet would be exposed as little as possible to the danger of daytime air attack.

At 1530 Mikawa passed through Bougainville straits. To the south, only thirty-five miles away, one of the *Enterprise*'s Avengers turned for home with nothing to report. Fortune, as it had in St. George's Channel, favored Mikawa again.

As the Japanese ships entered the Slot, they began to prepare for battle. The speed of the torpedoes was set so that they would reach a distance of 20,000 meters at a depth of 4 meters, and spares were transferred to starboard in anticipation that this was where the action would be. Because the ships were observing radio silence, orders were sent from the flagship to the *Aoba* and from the *Aoba* to the *Kako* and so on by flag, a time-consuming business, especially later in the day when Mikawa needed to give detailed instructions for his night-alert cruising disposition.

The danger of interception increased with every southward mile. Staff officers in the *Chokai* watched the sun moving imperceptibly toward the west and prayed for sunset, which seemed an eternity in coming. At 1600, *nisei* in the *Chokai* intercepted heavy Allied radio traffic and concluded that they were perilously close to the American aircraft carriers. There was much talk of flight deck conditions as planes went into their landing patterns.

During the afternoon, Mikawa fretted that he had not heard the results of the noon attack by the Fifth Air Attack Force on the ships in the Guadalcanal and Tulagi anchorages. He had to know the disposition of the Allied force and obtain the latest possible intelligence on its size. He dispatched another Jake from the *Aoba.* It took off at 1612 with orders to cruise at 212 knots, by way of Choiseul and Vella Lavella Island, to Tulagi. The pilot's flight course and designated speed would put him over Tulagi at 1725, and, if luck still held, return him to the *Aoba* by 1910, when there would still be some twilight.

Half an hour after the departure of the Jake, Mikawa issued signal order no. 25 with instructions for the approach. Changes could be made later if fresh intelligence indicated a variation in Allied dispositions.

There was to be a vanguard consisting of the *Tenryu* and the *Yunagi* to port and the *Yubari* to starboard, each separated by an interval of 6,000 meters. The main body, led by the *Chokai,* would be 3,000 meters astern the vanguard, followed by Cruiser Division 6, with 1,000 meters between all ships.

The vanguard's task was to deal with any small ships encountered while the main force headed for the night's real business. When the time came for action, the *Chokai* would take the lead, followed by Cruiser Division 6, the *Tenryu,* the *Yubari,* and the *Yunagi,* with 1,200 meters between ships. In this approach, the main force would pass south of Savo Island and torpedo the larger ships in the Guadalcanal anchorage, after which it would torpedo and shell ships in the Tulagi anchorage. The cruiser force would then withdraw north of Savo Island. Commanding officers were to determine their own gun and torpedo firings. The speed was to be twenty-four knots. Transports were the main targets.

It was a simple order, heavily dependent on the surprise Mikawa still hoped to achieve despite the Hudson sightings. As soon as the order had been transmitted, another followed requiring all flammable material on the decks to be thrown overboard.

A tense moment came at 1715 when a mast appeared on the starboard bow of the *Chokai,* about thirty kilometers distant. Fortunately for the Japanese, the ship was the 4,650-ton flying boat tender *Akitsushima,* hull down and positioned to rescue ditched air crews.

Sunset came at 1816. Just before, Mikawa signaled, "Let us attack with certain victory in the traditional night attack of the Imperial Navy. May each one calmly do his utmost!" Once again, a Japanese fleet on its way to battle invoked the spirit of Nelson.

Twilight began to fade and there was still no sign of the *Aoba* reconnaissance plane. Signal flares failed to guide it home. In fact, it would not return, having been shot down over Tulagi. Neither had word come in from the Fifth Air Attack Force giving the results of the daytime attack. News would not reach the fleet until 2100. When it did it would be both highly encouraging and grossly exaggerated, claiming that the force had sunk two heavy cruisers, one large cruiser, two destroyers, and nine transports and had badly damaged one heavy cruiser and two transports, all of which were left burning. The odds, Mikawa would have reason to believe, had swung heavily in his favor. All that he had against him now were one battleship, three cruisers (one of which was badly damaged), seventeen destroyers, and nine transports (two of which were burning). Oh, Captain Divine, so divinely inspired!

At 1954, the force turned southeast to pass between Santa Isabel and the New Georgia islands. Speed was now twenty-four knots, and readiness condition 2 had been set in all ships.

6

The Captains Retire

Admiral Crutchley was not surprised when, at 2045, he got a signal from Admiral Turner requesting him to attend a conference aboard the *McCawley* in Lunga Roads. "Please come on board as soon as possible," the message read. "I will send boat when you approach." The quickest way to get to Lunga Roads was to go in the *Australia*, and Turner's message clearly implied that this was what Crutchley would elect to do. Crutchley, before setting out, ordered Captain Bode in the *Chicago* to take command of the *Australia* group. His signal, sent by lamp, with a copy to go to the *Patterson* and the *Bagley,* read, "Take charge of patrol. I am closing ComTasFor 62 and may or may not rejoin you later." By radio, Crutchley advised Captain Cornelius W. Flynn, commanding Destroyer Squadron 4 from the *Selfridge,* that he was closing the transports. He did not send this message to either the *San Juan* or the *Vincennes* groups.

Early in the morning, Crutchley had signaled Turner, "When you have time could I [as second in command] have a rough outline of present situation and future intentions?" Preoccupied during the day with problems associated with landing stores for Vandegrift, and dismayed by Fletcher's determination to withdraw, Turner felt that it was imperative for him to talk to Crutchley and Vandegrift. The situation demanded a conference at which all three officers were present. After receiving Fletcher's signal to the effect that he would now to be denied all air cover, Turner tentatively planned to leave at daylight. The conference with his two subordinate commanders had to be held that night or not at all. Before he made a final decision about his time of departure, Turner wanted to know whether enough supplies had been

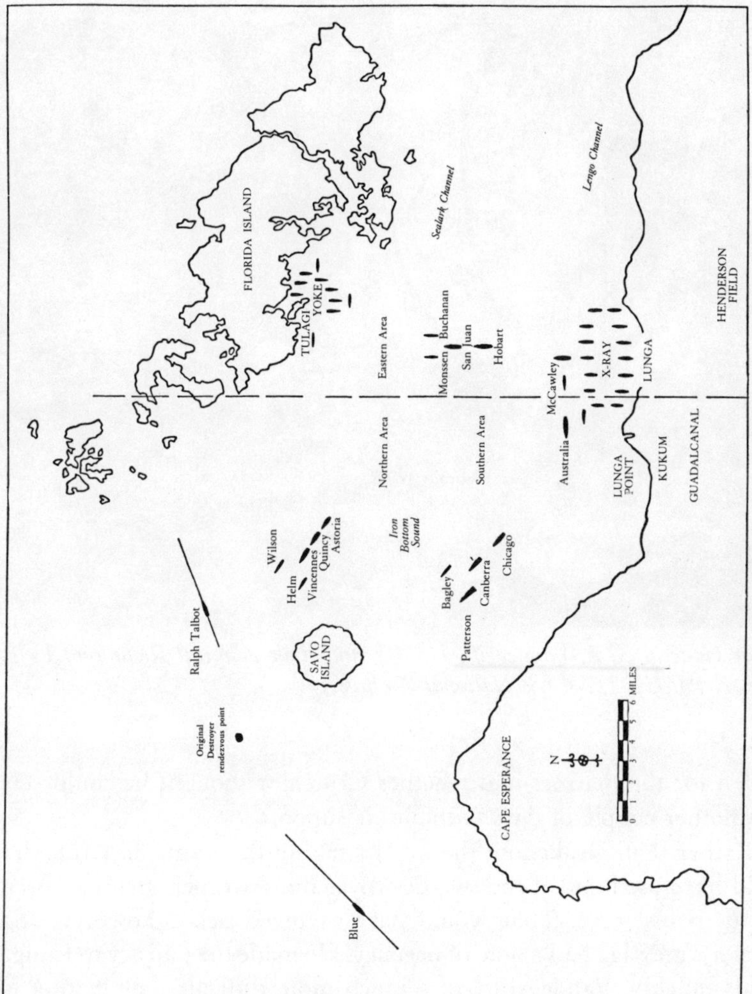

Allied Ships before the Battle

Major General A. A. Vandegrift, USMC, and Rear Admiral Richmond Kelly Turner. (80-GF-112-4-63, National Archives)

landed for the marines and whether Crutchley thought he could stay for another couple of days without air support.

Rather than weakening the line by taking the *Australia,* Crutchley could have used one of the two destroyer minesweepers that had been added to his force. That would have involved delay, however, and Turner's message had a note of urgency. He made the journey to Lunga Roads quickly. Vandegrift had a much more difficult time getting to the *McCawley,* and some hours passed before he arrived. Unaware of Fletcher's intentions, he thought that the conference was simply to discuss the unloading problem and was not unduly concerned.

This was a meeting of overworked men. Vandegrift recalled that "Jerry [Colonel Thomas, his chief of staff] and I were pretty tired, but these two looked ready to pass out." Turner was bitter about Fletcher's decision to withdraw. "He's left us bare ass," he said.

Turner, like Crutchley, rated very low the possibility of a night surface attack. He was misled by the reference to seaplane tenders in Stutt's signal and to its omission in Willman's. His staff had looked up seaplane tenders in *Jane's Fighting Ships* and concluded that, with a maximum speed of seventeen to twenty knots, they were unlikely to be part of an attack group. He considered the capabilities of the reported enemy, but as he put it, "I didn't take these capabilities and multiply them by three of four and then dirty my pants."

By the time Crutchley reached the *McCawley,* the long-delayed confirmation of the sightings by the Hudsons of Mikawa's force off Kieta had been received by both that ship and the *Australia.* The *Australia* received Stutt's report on Bells, the regular Australian broadcast, at 1818, and the *McCawley* received it on Fox, the scheduled U.S. Navy broadcast from Pearl Harbor, at 1842. At 2135 the *McCawley* received the message relaying the results of Willman's debriefing. Extant records contain no clue of how the delays occurred. At the conference with Crutchley and Vandegrift, Turner reiterated his view that the "seaplane tenders" reported by Stutt were headed for Rekata Bay and foreshadowed renewed, and heavier, torpedo attacks the following evening. Since Fletcher was going with the carriers, Turner would have to go with the transports.

Vandegrift worried about the supply situation on Tulagi if the transports pulled out the following morning. He pleaded with Turner to delay the departure of the transports until at least enough supplies were ashore on Tulagi to ensure the security of his marines.

Back in the *Australia* group, Captain Bode, in the *Chicago,* having been ordered by Crutchley to take command of the southern column in his absence, decided not to alter the original formation. Crutchley had told him that he did not know whether the *Australia* would return. Bode directed the *Canberra* (Captain Getting) to remain ahead of him, conduct the patrol, and change course as previously ordered by Crutchley for the *Chicago,* thus avoiding a great deal of maneuvering if the *Australia* should return. Then Bode turned in, half expecting Crutchley to come back before 2400.

And so the scene was set for battle. Mikawa, now halfway down the Slot, had one more thing to do before the rush in. Three planes, one each from the *Chokai,* the *Aoba,* and the *Kako,* would be catapulted for tactical reconnaissance and to drop parachute flares over Allied positions. The pilots had no experience in night catapulting, but this was a risk that had to be taken. There was no time to spare for a water takeoff.

Lieutenant Fumio Kiyose was to fly from the *Chokai*. Correspondent Fumio Niwa met him in the wardroom, walking around with a roll of charts in his hand. Kiyose planned to leave at about 2300. He was confident of success. "I'll fly at a very low altitude in case the enemy is using searchlights," he said. "According to the *Aoba*'s reconnaissance plane, six enemy ships are burning off Tulagi." A supply officer, Lieutenant Shigenaka Ando, asked if the battleship mentioned in earlier reports had been among Allied casualties. Everyone was anxious to claim the USS *Chicago* as a prize. She had been taken for HMS *Warspite* on several occasions that year, in the Battle of the Coral Sea and during the midget submarine attack in Sydney Harbor in late May. Kiyose told Ando that ship types had not yet been identified.

Just after 2200, a coded message reached the *Chokai*. Lieutenant Commander Chikayuki Koya wrote the details on a blackboard: "Two heavy cruisers, two light cruisers and one transport sunk. Two destroyers and one transport burning." Lieutenant Ando added another line: "The following are our expected battle results tonight: One battleship, four cruisers, three to four destroyers and transports sunk." Soon afterwards, a trumpet sounded a rehearsal for the action ahead: "All hands to battle stations!" and a sign saying Sick Bay was hung on the wardroom door.

Meanwhile the *Saratoga* (Admiral Fletcher) was heading southwest—away from the action, not toward it. Crutchley had moved the *Australia* twenty miles from the southern force to the transport area east of Lunga Point on Guadalcanal. At twelve knots, the *Australia* group continued its patrol along a northwest-southeast line, reversing course every hour. To the east of Savo Island, the *Vincennes* group pursued its leisurely ten-knot course around a box, each side five miles long.

The meeting in the *McCawley* heated up. If Fletcher had left the marines on Guadalcanal "bare ass," as Turner suggested, Turner's own planned withdrawal at 0600 the following morning was an even worse blow for Vandegrift. While Turner remained, there was at least a chance of getting equipment ashore. With him gone, there was none. True, there had been no opposition on Guadalcanal, but on Tulagi there had been fierce resistance. Moreover, to hold Guadalcanal against the Japanese reinforcement he expected, Vandegrift believed it would be necessary to control the whole northern plain, about 300 square miles, and forty-five miles of coastline. He not only had inadequate supplies, he lacked the forces to do the job.

Turner remained adamant that without carrier air cover, he had to go. His one concession was that he would defer a decision on his actual departure time until Vandegrift had determined just how many additional stores General Rupertus needed on Tulagi to continue operations.

The thought of a night surprise attack against the transports was remote from everyone's mind as Vandegrift and Crutchley left the *McCawley*. The night dispositions were all in place. The *Blue* and the *Ralph Talbot* were the eyes and ears of the force, guarding the approaches to Savo Island. Vandegrift and Crutchley left the *McCawley* together, Vandegrift to board a destroyer minesweeper that would take him to Tulagi for a meeting with Rupertus and Crutchley to return to the *Australia*.

A gentle four-knot breeze scarcely ruffled the surface of the sea when the two pickets took up their patrol. There was no moon. The sky was partly overcast, with visibility about three miles. The *Ralph Talbot* had a patrol and search pattern of close to seven miles. The *Blue*'s beat extended five and three-quarter miles.

Crutchley, who believed it required a surface radar range of only six miles to ensure that nothing could get through undetected, had attached great but unwarranted importance to the surface warning radars. They would detect any hostile ships entering the area. His confidence was not shared by the destroyer captains. For most of the previous night, when the destroyers performed the same role in the area, their radar had proved useless in identifying ships approaching the entrance from seaward—this was because they were close to land—and the lookouts had had to maintain a high standard of alertness.

The antisubmarine detection range of the destroyers' sonar varied from a few hundred to about 2,000 yards. The radius from the cruiser screening groups on which the radar picket destroyers operated was insufficient. The *Ralph Talbot,* for instance, was not far enough from the *Vincennes* group to give adequate warning of enemy approach. When the group was at the northern point of its patrol line and the *Ralph Talbot* at the easternmost extremity of her patrol line, there was a scant five miles between them—no more than the limit of night visibility in prevailing weather conditions. Even if the *Talbot*'s radar had been working effectively, and with no interference from the land, she would have been able to give only a fifteen-minute warning before the Japanese got within gun range of the group from the north.

Commander H. N. Williams, the *Blue*'s captain, had no illusions about the limitations of the radar.[1] On several previous occasions his radar had failed to pick up surface targets the size of a destroyer at ranges of more than 5,000 yards, although much better results had sometimes been achieved. This vital information seems to have been unknown to Crutchley.

The results this night were to be both better and very much worse. Three times the *Blue*'s radar picked up echoes that it identified as the *Ralph Talbot* on her patrol to the northeast, probably more than eight miles distant. Another time, at much closer range, her radar failed to pick up the crippled *Jarvis* because Savo Island was in the background. Since at twelve knots it took the *Blue* approximately thirty minutes to reverse course, there were times when the two destroyers could have been separated by an hour's sailing time. If Crutchley was holding the pass, it was with a precariously thin detachment. Yet in his report on subsequent action, he commented, "It should not have been possible for an enemy force to get inside Savo Island without being detected either visually or with radar by *Blue* or *Talbot,* to whom I had allotted patrol beats with this express object in mind."[2]

After Crutchley's departure for the meeting on the *McCawley,* the *Chicago,* which the Japanese had taken for a battleship, remained 600 yards astern of the *Canberra,* the destroyer *Patterson* 1,300 yards on the *Canberra*'s port bow, and the *Bagley* 1,300 yards on the starboard bow. The northern group patrolled its box in a clockwise direction in line ahead, the *Vincennes* being followed by the *Quincy* and the *Astoria,* with destroyers *Helm* and *Wilson* in antisubmarine screening positions 1,500 yards on the *Vincennes*'s bow. The course changed 90 degrees to the starboard at ten minutes before and twenty minutes after the hour. Without knowing it, Captain Riefkohl, in command of the group, was now the senior officer of the Allied naval force.

Twenty minutes after Mikawa had dispatched his three reconnaissance planes, the Japanese formation changed. The *Chokai* now led the line, with the destroyer *Yunagi* bringing up the rear of the single column. There were about 1,300 yards between each of the eight ships. As a means of recognition, long white streamers, or sleeves, were hoisted from the signal yards of each ship. They were a reminder of the final kamikaze attack during the war with the Russians when Japanese troops donned similar sashes for purposes of identification. Though the Japanese had lost thousands upon thousands of men, they won Port Arthur.

Today there was no thought of kamikaze tactics. Every Japanese ship was confident of success. Just after 2320 a red glow appeared in the sky over Tulagi and seconds later a mountain took shape through the haze. Officers had studied it in photographs; now, 20 degrees on the *Chokai*'s port side, they saw Savo Island with the naked eye.

As for the Allied ships, nothing much happened until 2345. At that point the *Ralph Talbot*, on the northern radar picket patrol, sighted an unidentified plane flashing a light low over the island. The destroyer broadcast a message on TBS (talk between ships) and TBO (a portable voice radio), "Warning! Warning! Plane over Savo Island heading east," and repeated it to the *McCawley* for several minutes on each transmitter. Receiving no reply, the *Talbot* called Captain Flynn, commanding Destroyer Squadron 4 from the *Selfridge*.

The *Patterson* heard the warning and tried to get through to Admiral Turner. Her message was not acknowledged.

The *Talbot* was now about seven miles from Savo Island, the *Blue* a little over ten miles away, the *Vincennes* group four and a half miles, the *Chicago* group ten, and the *San Juan* group eleven. Repeated efforts by the *Talbot* to get through to the *McCawley* failed. Crutchley did not know of the warnings until the battle was over. The *San Juan* heard the message and passed it to the *Vincennes*. In fact, the *Astoria* had made a radar contact half an hour before the *Talbot*'s warning, but it was unclear whether this was a ship or a plane. The *Quincy* also received the warning, but static caused by the weather and the fact that the Allied ships were chatting effectively drowned it out. The *Blue*, with her recently installed radar, picked up the plane at the time it was sent out and subsequently heard the noise of the engine as it circled over Savo Island and Esperance Bay, departing to the south. Some aboard the destroyer reckoned they saw running lights.

All the Allied ships heard the sound of planes overhead during the late evening. Well before midnight Lieutenant Commander E. J. Wight, principal control officer in the *Canberra*, was told that planes had been heard and immediately reported by voice-pipe to Captain Getting below the bridge. Wight thought the planes might be "friendlies" and remarked to the officer of the watch, Sublieutenant M. J. Gregory, that one of their own reconnaissance planes had probably lost its way. The *Canberra*'s executive officer, Commander J. A. Walsh, had a sneaking suspicion that the planes were enemy and stationed himself at the searchlight platform, where he kept a "vague lookout."

In the *Vincennes,* Captain Riefkohl failed to associate the unidentified planes with the "seaplane tenders" reported by one of the RAAF Hudsons. Instead of assuming an attack might be imminent, he retired to his emergency cabin to rest.

The astonishing consensus that planes overhead were friendly contributed substantially to the disaster that followed. If they were not, everyone assumed, Admiral Turner would have sent a warning. The hints about Japanese intentions accumulated, and were ignored. Like the clues in a detective story, the plot was there to be read. No one in authority got it right.

After Crutchley ordered the *Chicago* to take over, the *Canberra*'s Captain Getting called Lieutenant Commander J. S. Mesley, her navigator, and suggested that they change course every hour. Savo Island lay seven miles ahead. Beyond the island, in the open sea, the *Blue* remained on the alert. Occasionally the *Canberra* saw the *Blue* and her escort on the radar, but if they came in too close they disappeared. The *Canberra* could not see any ships in the northern group. As radar-direction-finding guard ship, she used her type 271 set for surface warning. The set was probably the most efficient Allied search equipment, but it was extremely limited by the confined waters in which the ship operated and the large number of friendly vessels inside working range. It was practically impossible to tell friend from foe.

The night was dark and humid, with squalls kicking up. There was no moon. Visibility was moderate to bad, varying from 4,000 to 12,000 yards. The maximum close range of the *Canberra*'s radar was somewhere between 500 and 1,000 yards, depending on the seas.[3] Rough water obscured approaching vessels.

Sublieutenant D. J. Medley, the *Canberra*'s radar officer, had detected the approach of cruisers at a distance of 60,000 yards, but if they came in closer no one knew because they were not picked up. Neither Captain Getting, Lieutenant Commander John Plunkett-Cole, nor anyone else aboard put much faith in the radar in these landlocked waters.[4]

Medley visited the radar station at about 2300 and found everything going apparently well. Since sunset all six radar operators had been on four-hour watches, two men at a time working half-hour tricks. They were still having trouble because of nearby land, but the set was working normally. The water was calm, the range about 500 yards. After checking the set Medley returned to his station to rest.

There was no communication between ships in the *Australia* group at this time, except by lamp. For improbable reasons of security, the Royal Australian Navy avoided the very-short-range radios (TBS) used by the Americans. Communication between ships in the northern group was no better. Their dependence on TBS so overloaded the circuits that the tactical voice radio became more or less useless, delaying or completely preventing the dispatch and receipt of critical signals. When the attack began, panic took hold and nothing of importance got through.

In the *Astoria*, both the surface warning radar and fire control radar operated normally. Great attention had been given to the training of operators, but many were still inexperienced. In any event, because of the encircling land the northern group's radar was practically useless as far as identifying anything approaching from seaward.

In the *Canberra*, Lieutenant Commander Plunkett-Cole had finished his watch at 2230 and retired to his cabin. There was not one senior or experienced officer on the bridge, no arrangements having been made for either the captain or the navigation officer to be there at all times. Moreover, in discussion with his senior officers, Captain Getting had decided that as the ship might be engaged in this patrol operation until at least 11 August, the fatigued crew could not maintain a continuous state of first-degree readiness, which they had done since the sixth, by day but not night. B and Y 8-inch-gun crews were allowed to fall out and sleep at or near their quarters, leaving communication personnel awake in all turrets, one on each side, and sentries on duty in shell-handling rooms. The 4-inch-gun mountings were manned, one on each side. The fore control crew was closed up, but the torpedo tubes were maintained in first-degree readiness, with one tube's crew asleep. All guns were empty. The motorboats had been defueled at dusk, at which time the Walrus aircraft was loaded with four 100-lb bombs and also defueled.

On the compass platform, dark hours were split into three watches for control officers. Each would get about four hours rest a night. There had been so much activity during the day that Lieutenant Commander Wight, like everyone else, was exhausted. The night before he had turned in at 2200 and been on duty again at 0200. He, the gunnery officer, and the torpedo officer had split the dark hours.

Soon after Mesley retired Captain Getting went to his cabin. He always made a point of not switching on the light there because of the effect on his eyes. If he slept at all, he did so sitting in his chair beside the voice-tube, ready to go up to the bridge at any time.

When he took over from Mesley at 2250, Lieutenant Commander Wight had no standing orders but was confident that he would know what to do if an enemy ship appeared. He would call the captain while the officer of the watch called the navigator. Main armament would be loaded and on target. By this time, the captain should be on the compass platform; if not, Wight would open fire himself.

He found nothing abnormal when he took over the ship, although he was mildly surprised that the guns were not loaded. They were almost always loaded at night. He was not unduly worried, however, and imagined the reason was that they could not be simultaneously prepared for barrage fire against aircraft, bombardment, and action against surface craft.

Also on the bridge was seventeen-year-old temporary Midshipman Ian Johnston, RANR, one of the youngest men aboard, as well as the yeoman of the watch and lookouts, relieved every half hour. No officer was in charge of the lookouts; Wight generally sent the midshipman of the watch around at frequent intervals to see if they were doing their job. Johnston alternated as midshipman of the watch with Midshipman Bruce Loxton, whose station was the port enemy-bearing indicator. The twenty-year-old Loxton was also the captain's "doggie" who had had a grandstand view of much that had taken place on the first two days of the operation. Getting's chair was in the port forward corner of the bridge, just to Loxton's right. He had listened in on the captain's conversations with other officers concerning the possible approach of a Japanese force. As the *Canberra* approached Tulagi he had also heard Getting say that it would be impossible, in that day and age, to achieve surprise.

Loxton had been on the bridge or in the plot all Saturday, except for a visit aft during the last dogwatch to change into clean clothes and shower. The night, in his words, was "as black as the inside of a cow." At one point, when the cruiser reversed course, a screening destroyer lost touch with her. When turning in on the chart table in the chart house at 2300, Loxton was aware that steam had been ordered for full power at dawn, as there was the possibility of an encounter with an enemy force sighted during the forenoon. Midshipman Johnston relieved him on the bridge at this time.

When Mesley passed the ship to Wight at 2250, he had been handling her all day and been called at least every two hours at night since 6 August. He was due to be awakened by Sublieutenant Gregory at 0145 to check the ship's position before altering course. He turned in for a brief rest, dressed, apart from his boots, on top of his bunk in his sea cabin.

The *Chicago* had been in condition 1 readiness until about 2030.[5] After consultation with his officers, Captain Bode decided that a modified condition would give everyone time to recover from the exertions of the previous two days. All stations were fully manned, but the length of watches was reduced to rest as many officers and men as possible in case they had to return to condition 1. The entire crew was fully clothed. No lights except standing red lights were allowed in the living spaces, and no bathing was permitted.

Still uncertain whether the *Australia* would return that night, and unaware of the exact position of the *Vincennes* group, Captain Bode assumed that the three American cruisers were patrolling a line, as his ships were. He was tired but not unduly worried. He had no flag staff to assist him, but he knew that his tactical officers were all experienced heads of departments. Carefully trained and tested, they had proven their ability to act in an emergency.

Earlier in the evening Bode had noticed that Commander Cecil Clinton Adell, the executive officer, was exhausted and suggested that he get some rest. Adell retired to his stateroom, within easy reach of his battle station. Captain Bode considered remaining on the bridge, but on second thought believed it prudent to retire also, as he anticipated air attacks at early dawn. At midnight, after his gunnery officer had relieved the assistant officer in main battery control, he went to his emergency cabin.

The commanders of the other four cruisers, Captain Riefkohl in the *Vincennes*, Captain Moore in the *Quincy*, Captain Greenman in the *Astoria*, and Captain Getting in the *Canberra*, equally exhausted after the activities of the previous two days, had already retired.

Part Three

THE BATTLE

7

Luck All with the Japanese

At midnight sharp, the *Chokai*'s officers assembled in the wardroom for supper. "The battle will be over in twenty minutes," one officer said. "Ten minutes for Tulagi and another ten for Guadalcanal. The next day will be much more dangerous." "Not so," the executive officer, Commander Kenkichi Kato, corrected him. "We will have withdrawn at full speed by that time." After Kato left the table, everyone relaxed. Navigation officer Lieutenant Commander Shiro Shigeki ordered beer all around and he and the chief engineer, Commander Kishaku Yoshimura, proposed a toast in anticipation of victory. "What happens if we want to pass water during the excitement of the battle?" a young officer asked. "We can't very well go to the heads once we are at battle stations. If nature calls, we'll just have to piss standing at station." Someone suggested placing empty fuel cans at each battle station.

More serious matters concerned gunnery officer Lieutenant Commander Shigeo Naka. He and the torpedo officer, Lieutenant Commander Koya, stressed the importance of holding fire until the torpedoes had been launched. "My men were looking forward to putting on a variety show at the anchorage tonight," he told Koya. "This will be an even better show."

In the *Aoba* men set about replacing antiair fuse shells with 5-inch projectiles for the surface attack. The officer, in charge of antiaircraft batteries, Lieutenant Tatsuo Takubo, took charge. His assistant, Ensign Satoru Takemura, had a younger brother, a fire control director, aboard the *Kinugasa,* the third ship in the column, and was concerned for his safety. "Bullets can't hit me," he said, pointing to a charm on his left wrist. "Anyway, the *Aoba* is unsinkable."

The three reconnaissance planes took off from the cruisers at 2300, right on schedule. At 0038 the *Chokai*'s seaplane reported that Riefkohl's three cruisers were eight miles off the coast of Savo Island on a bearing of 140 degrees, course 290 degrees, speed eighteen knots. Three minutes later Mikawa sent the signal to prepare for fighting.

At 0043 Mikawa was heading for the south strait when a lookout shouted, "Ship approaching, 30 degrees starboard!" At a range of 10,000 yards, and through the darkness, the lookout had spotted the *Blue.* Mikawa changed course 20 degrees to port and ordered by radio that the fleet would attack through the north strait.

At 0050 a lookout sighted the *Ralph Talbot,* and to avoid her Mikawa once again ordered a change of course. Despite the extreme range, the lookout saw her stern steaming away from the Japanese fleet.

Mikawa was taken aback by the report of the two pickets. His planes had not previously reported the American destroyers, and now one of them, the *Blue,* was passing his line of approach. With every gun trained on her, Mikawa had to decide whether to attack. The *Blue* decided it for him. The lookout on the *Chokai*'s bridge shouted: "The enemy ship has reversed course. No change in its cruising speed." The southern channel was open. At 0108 Mikawa radioed, "We will enter from the south strait."

The *Chokai*'s sailors could see dim red lights shining ahead. Enemy ships off Tulagi were burning. Mikawa continued at 26 knots, with all ships at general quarters, their guns trained on the departing *Blue.*

Meanwhile, the *Ralph Talbot* reached the extremity of her patrol. Turning slowly, she made her leisurely way southwest. The guardians of the gate saw nothing, their radar as ineffective as their eyes. The Japanese slipped between the two American destroyers and disappeared into the dark. "It was a lucky escape," Commander Ohmae recalled, "but our emphasis on night-battle practice and night lookout had paid off."

For the next fifty-five minutes, the *Blue* and the *Talbot* continued their patrols, still oblivious of the fact that the Japanese force had passed between them.

The Japanese began their run toward the enemy ships. At 0131 Mikawa signaled "All ships attack!" Commander Ohmae stood beside him on the *Chokai*'s bridge and scanned the sea and the chart before them on which they had plotted the locations of the Allied ships. Each ship was to act independently. Mikawa broke strict radio silence, keeping in touch with his following ships by radio tactical circuits. This commu-

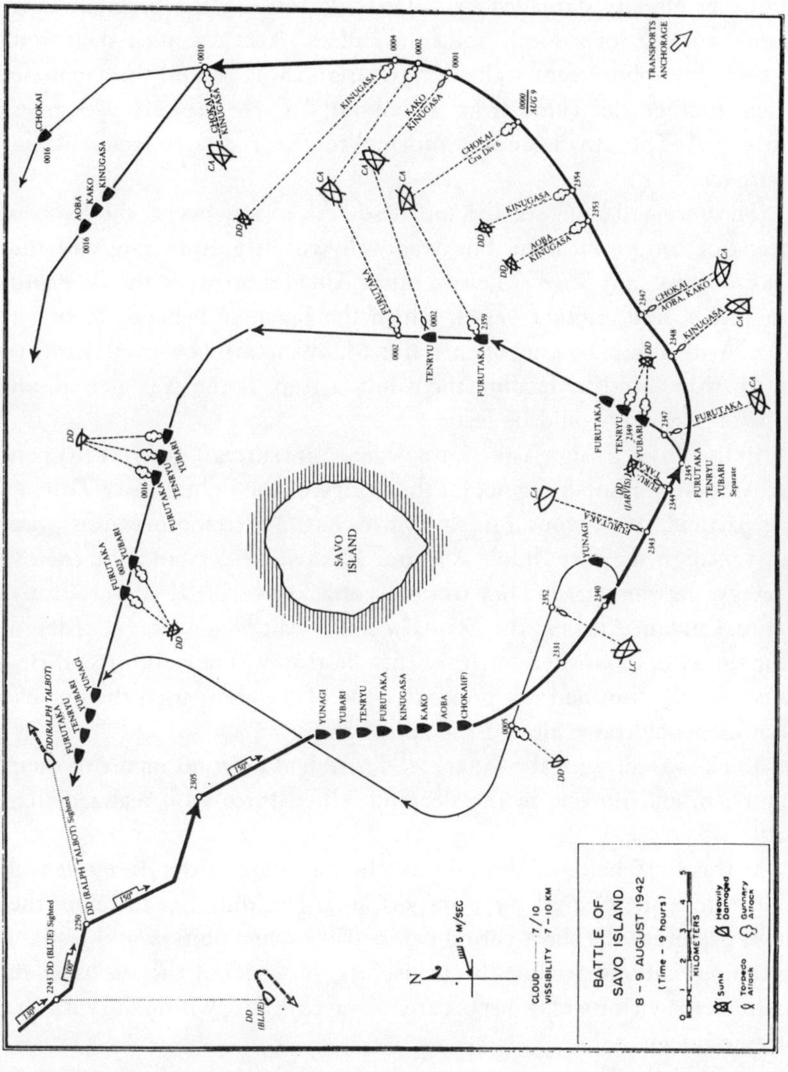

The Track of the Eighth Fleet, 8–9 August 1942

nication was limited to the heavy cruisers. The *Tenryu, Yubari,* and *Yunagi* followed the leaders without orders.

The *Chokai*'s tense silence was broken by the voice of a lookout: "Cruiser 7 degrees port!" This was the *Jarvis,* limping in the opposite direction, already damaged by a Japanese torpedo the previous day. "Look out for torpedoes!" someone called. "You can pick them out by their phosphorescent wakes." Savo Island was behind the Japanese when another call came from a lookout: "Three cruisers 9 degrees starboard! The small ship is moving to the right. It looks like a destroyer."

The *Jarvis* did not see the Japanese and, in any event, she had no means of communication. She was well within gunfire range of the *Chokai, Aoba,* and *Kako.* The two other Allied destroyers, the *Blue* and the *Talbot,* and another vessel, which the Japanese believed to be an Allied patrol ship, had not opened fire. Many Japanese believed that this fourth ship could be leading them into a trap. If she was alerted, all hope of surprise would be lost.

In the *Aoba,* Ensign Takemura ordered antiaircraft guns set to open fire. Captain Shimpei Asano, on the bridge of the light cruiser *Tenryu,* was particularly nervous. His ship's fire control director and guns were not yet aligned. Why didn't Admiral Mikawa understand the enemy strategy? he wondered. They would be attacked before they were ready to fire. Captain Araki in the *Furutaka* could wait no longer. He ordered four torpedoes launched at the enemy destroyer. They all missed. Because the flagship had not done so, none of the ships used their guns. Gunfire would have alerted the Allied ships.

Luck was all with the Japanese. There had been no report of their approach, and no one in the sleeping Allied force who realized that battle was close.

It was 0115 before Admiral Crutchley reboarded the *Australia* and 0130 before she cleared the transport area. Deciding not to rejoin the night patrol for the short period before 0500, when units would resume screening stations around the transports, he ordered the *Australia* to patrol in the vicinity of transport area X-ray, keeping within the antisubmarine screen.

At 0132 the *Chicago* group was still steaming at twelve knots, just over eleven miles from the center of Savo Island. The northern force sailed on in equally blissful ignorance, keeping formation in its square. The two forces were vaguely aware of each other's location, but Captain Riefkohl still did not know that he was in theoretical command of both groups. He had received no information from Crutchley and remained unaware that the *Australia* had been removed from the area.

Mikawa saw the *Canberra* and the *Chicago* in column, 12,500 yards away, at 0137. One minute later he sighted another cruiser bearing 060 degrees. This was the *Vincennes,* leading the northern group and heading toward the *Chokai.* The American cruiser was about 18,000 yards away—the greatest distance at which a visual sighting was reported during the action. She may have been silhouetted, or perhaps momentarily illuminated by a fire on Tulagi or by lightning, but Mikawa had already been advised by his cruiser planes of the presence of Allied ships east of Savo Island. He now had two targets in sight.

As soon as they sighted the Allied force, the Japanese ships slowed down to eighteen or twenty knots. In the *Chokai,* Captain Hayakawa shouted, "Torpedoes fire to starboard, fire!" and then "Independent firing!" The force was strung out in a long, loose column proceeding individually by division. This was the first occasion on which the heavy and light cruisers had joined forces. Since they had not maneuvered together, Mikawa knew that in a night action the control of his force from the flagship would be extremely difficult. His ships would fire independently whenever a target presented itself. Once more, he increased speed to twenty-six knots.

At 0140, as the Japanese ships skirted the tip of Savo Island, parachute flares dropped by the cruiser planes silhouetted the Allied ships. Large and brilliant, the flares came from high above the clouds, falling in a straight line without flickering, evenly spaced and about a mile apart. They lit up the transports and the entire area like a stage backdrop. The curtain was about to rise on Lieutenant Commander Naka's variety show.

From the *Chokai*'s bridge, war correspondent Niwa watched as one after another the brilliant flares lit up the sea, turning it the silvery color of the Milky Way. For a split second he saw the dark green shapes of ships through the flow of lights. "It seemed as if they were looking for a hiding place," he wrote. "It was a breathtaking moment." The American cruisers in the northern force also saw the lights but believed that they were star shell bursts from friendly ships in the southern group. The *Vincennes, Quincy,* and *Astoria* concentrated on getting men to battle stations while they waited to see what was happening.

As the Japanese dashed in, Captain Riefkohl sent out signals to the other two ships and the screening destroyers that, because of the current, they were to remain on course an extra ten minutes.

For the Americans, everything seemed to happen at 0140. The *Helm* sent a signal to say that a plane was flying over her, and a lookout in the *Vincennes* reported that a submarine had submerged 600 yards off her port quarter. When the ship felt tremors, it was thought that a destroyer was dropping depth charges.

The *Chokai*'s Long Lance torpedoes were on their way. Just before 0140 the flagship changed course, apparently to cross the T and at the same time unmask her battery. The other ships followed her signals by tactical circuit. Niwa heard splashes as the torpedoes hit the water and he was drenched as he ran, clutching his notebook and praying that they would hit their mark. Grasping the handrail, he craned his neck to look into the water and saw their wakes running like streaks of silver. Meanwhile, the Allied ships remained silent. "Almost immediately, the deadly weapons were heard smacking the water one by one," Commander Ohmae noted. "While we waited for them to hit, the radio announced that our following cruisers had opened fire with guns and torpedoes."

Because the TBS circuit was jammed, Captain Riefkohl had been having trouble trying to get the *Wilson* to take the place of the *Jarvis*. During the afternoon, he had had to act as the communication link between Admiral Turner and Admiral Scott, in command of the eastern sector.[1] The *McCawley*'s TBS had a short that seriously limited its transmission, and Riefkohl could contact Scott only indirectly, through the destroyer *Blue*.

At this time the *Yunagi,* last ship in the Japanese column, saw the *Jarvis* at about 3,000 yards on her port bow, on a roughly opposite course.[2] Rather than continue with the cruisers, her commanding officer decided to attack the American destroyer. Her orders had been to remain beyond Savo Island, acting as a picket and engaging Allied destroyers if they attempted to follow the cruisers. Instead, she chased after the crippled *Jarvis* and fired at her for about five minutes, knowing there was a gaping hole in her bow inflicted by an aircraft torpedo the previous day. In the war diary of Ensign Nakamura, aboard the *Yunagi,* no mention is made of pickets. Whether the Japanese ship obeyed orders or decided to act alone, she missed out on the battle of a lifetime.

Of all the Allied ships, only the destroyer *Patterson* was fully awake that dark Sunday morning. She was on the port bow of the *Canberra* just after 0140 when the Japanese first saw her, about 5,500 yards away. Around 0146, when the *Patterson* was about four and a half miles south of the western tip of Savo Island, Commander Walker saw a ship dead ahead, steering in a general southeasterly direction and very close to the western side of the island. She was about two and a half miles away, he thought. But the Japanese ship was actually closer. The *Patterson* had mistaken the heavy cloud bank off Savo for the tip of the island. That cloud bank also misled other Allied ships.

Commander Walker immediately sounded general quarters, tried to notify the *Canberra* and *Chicago* by blinker, and sent out a TBS broadcast to all ships—"Warning! Warning! Strange ships entering harbor!"—before changing course to port to unmask her guns and torpedo tubes, at the same time ringing up maximum speed. Seconds after sending out her warning, she saw one enemy ship change course to the east, hugging the south shore of Savo, then two more ships, one of which appeared to be a *Mogami*-type heavy cruiser, the other a *Jintsu*-type light cruiser. The *Patterson*'s bridge log recorded a cruiser of the *Katori* class as well. In fact, the ships she saw were the heavy cruiser *Furutaka,* with its oddly raked, mismatched stacks, and the two old light cruisers *Tenryu* and *Yubari,* clearly identifiable by their unusual-looking funnels.

Almost at once, a shell hit the *Patterson*'s no. 4 gun crew shelter, igniting rounds of ready service powder and enveloping the entire after section of the ship in flames. Guns no. 3 and 4 were put out of action. One of the crew was killed outright, two others died of wounds, seven were missing and thirteen wounded, including two men from the no. 4 gun who had been prevented from jumping overboard when their clothing caught on fire.

The *Tenryu* and the *Yubari* might have attacked the *Patterson.* The *Tenryu* reported that she fired on a destroyer at this time, "using searchlights, and sinking the ship," after which she was forced to follow the *Furutaka* because her gyrocompass had broken down by shocks from gunfire and she could not depend on the magnetic compass.

The *Patterson* was peppered by fire, causing hundreds of holes that were patched up with wooden or wax pegs, but all her casualties resulted from the shell that had hit her at the start of the action. She zigzagged at high speed, then settled on an easterly course, about parallel with the enemy, when a torpedo passed about fifty yards astern of her. The *Patterson* opened fire with star shells, following Admiral Crutchley's instructions to the letter: "In the event of an enemy surface force being detected, immediate report is to be made—the force is to be shadowed and frequently reported and when about to be engaged by cruisers, the destroyers may be ordered to illuminate the enemy force with searchlights."[3] She sent out her warning, and then receiving no permission from Captain Bode in the *Chicago,* refrained from using searchlights.

As the *Patterson* swung to port Commander Walker ordered "Fire torpedoes!" Her guns opened fire so quickly, however, that the order was drowned out, and by the time the reverberations died the opportunity was gone forever. Before anyone realized this, something was reported close on the ship's port bow. Walker ran to the port wing of the bridge to investigate but could not make out anything. The something was the wake of another torpedo, this one fired by the *Furutaka* at 0146. The Japanese cruiser's report states that several of her torpedoes "hit a destroyer that had advanced to the port side and sank it." The *Patterson* did not sink. By the time Commander Walker got to the port wing, the torpedo had missed and was running beyond her toward the *Chicago.*

Under heavy fire now, the *Patterson* was lit up by the powerful searchlights of the *Tenyru* and the *Yubari.* Presently the lights blinked out on one ship and the *Patterson* believed she had scored a hit; the ship appeared to be on fire. This was the *Yubari,* which had been hit several times and later admitted receiving "some scratches from the light fire of an enemy destroyer."

In the *Canberra,* Sublieutenant M. J. Gregory, officer of the watch, was very conscious of the fact that he had to call the navigator, Lieutenant Commander Mesley, at 0145. He had his eyes on his watch when, at 0142, he saw a flash and what appeared to be an explosion to starboard, almost due north. Principal control officer Lieutenant Commander Wight also saw the explosion and immediately reported down the voicetube to Captain Getting in his sea cabin. Midshipman of the watch Johnston was writing in the chart table. He heard a lookout shout "Ship ahead!" and emerged from the chart house. Then, hearing the voicetube answered, he went back inside.

The *Canberra* had received what should have been a last-minute warning of the approach of the Japanese force. Neither Wight nor Gregory saw the ship, but the acting yeoman of the watch, E. A. Johnson, looked through his binoculars when the warning was received and spotted the starboard screening destroyer and what he took to be Savo Island looming up in the darkness.

Lieutenant Commander Mesley, summoned by Gregory, jumped from his bunk and put on his boots. Gunnery officer Lieutenant Commander Hole and torpedo officer Lieutenant Commander Plunkett-

Cole, both sleeping in the admiral's sea cabin, also rallied to Gregory's call. It was a few seconds after 0143.

Wight saw the wakes of three ships passing south of Savo Island, fine on the starboard bow, moving from port to starboard against the blackness of the land. "They're not ours!" he shouted, and Midshipman Johnston came out of the chart house once again to get a better look. Wight already had the guns trained when he got the last wake of the three ships in the starboard enemy bearing indicator. "Starboard green two zero, load, load, load!"

In seconds, all four senior officers were on the compass platform. Mesley collected his steel helmet and antiflash gear from the portside table and took over the ship as Wight and Gregory raced to their battle stations.

Temporary Surgeon Lieutenant (Dentist) J. E. Newton, sleeping at his medical party station on B turret, was awakened by a flash and saw three torpedo tracks, one on the port side slightly converging, so that he thought it would hit the ship aft, and two to starboard, running parallel to the ship. He also saw one of the attacking ships when it was briefly lit up. "I formed the impression that it had two funnels, for'd thick and after thin. I placed it as a large destroyer or small cruiser. The distance was about 1,500 yards."

It was a cruiser, but it was not small. The ship, with her distinctive, oddly shaped forestack and slimmer after stack, was the *Chokai,* Yeoman Johnson's "Savo Island." The Japanese came in at high speed under cover of Savo Island. They cleared the island just as the *Canberra* approached the end of her patrol, about seven miles off Savo, and were bearing down on her for at least seven minutes before opening fire. This whole time they were vulnerable to Allied radar, but the *Canberra*'s surface warning set proved useless. Even the weather favored the Japanese. Their ships were on the edge of the cloud bank, whereas the Allied ships were some miles outside it. Silhouetted by the flares, they were clearly visible to the Japanese.

Meanwhile, the *Patterson* altered course to cross the *Canberra*'s bows and began signaling. From the Australian ship Sublieutenant Gregory saw the tiny wink of the *Patterson*'s signal, too small to be read. A lookout on the port side of the ship's after control heard the swishing of water and saw a number of ships moving about, one very close to the *Canberra,* signaling rapidly. He did not think that the signal was being made to the bridge, as the *Patterson* was abreast of the *Canberra*'s beam and the signal was facing her stern.

The *Chicago*'s action report makes no mention of the *Patterson*'s warning, but aboard the *Ralph Talbot* three of the crew reported a signal at about 0150 on the TBS: "Warning, warning, three ships inside Savo Island." And the *Talbot*'s gunnery report states that at 0200 Lieutenant R. D. Shepard heard the following signal on TBS: "All ships, warning, warning, ships coming in Lengo Channel." The voice he recognized to be that of Commander Walker in the *Patterson.*

The vital signal from the *Patterson* reached the *Vincennes*'s forward radar room TBS, and the operator reported it to radio control. Neither Captain Riefkohl nor Commander William Mullan, the executive officer, heard of it on the bridge. The *Astoria* and the *Quincy* also missed the message. All three ships were discussing the course change at the time.

The *Chokai* had launched her torpedoes at the *Canberra* and the *Chicago* at 0138. As the *Canberra* swung to port helm, one of them passed down her starboard side. Captain Getting ordered "Hard to starboard full ahead!" and someone, probably Yeoman Johnson, reported torpedo tracks and what appeared to be three cruisers fine on the port bow. "Tell *Chicago* three cruisers!" Getting yelled, whereupon Johnson dashed to the starboard side of the torpedo control platform and gave the signal to the American cruiser.[4] Armament was immediately trained on the targets.

At 0143, the *Chokai* had crossed the *Canberra*'s T at a range of 4,500 yards. Meanwhile the heavy cruisers *Aoba* and *Kako* were approaching bows-on. The range of all three enemy cruisers soon shortened to about 1,000 yards. Mesley shouted, "Torpedo tracks approaching the port bow, sir!" Through the dark, low cloud and the heavy rain, he saw at least two tracks heading across the *Canberra*'s course, apparently coming from one of the three enemy ships. This was the *Aoba.*

Getting shouted, "Load with anything!" Someone else yelled, "Torpedoes coming!" Midshipman Johnston, unfamiliar with enemy bearing indicator proceedings, decided to wake the action EBI officer and the action officer of the watch, Sublieutenant R. M. Dawborn. He raced down the ladder and alerted them, putting on his tin hat as he went. In seconds, both officers were on the bridge with the captain. The ship went to general quarters.

The wheel was hard over to starboard and the telegraph was at full speed. With luck, the *Canberra* would swing around in time to clear the tracks and miss the torpedoes. The officers on the bridge could see one ship ahead and another broad on the port bow, about Red 70 degrees.

Two star shells or flares were burning to starboard. Gunnery Officer Hole ordered "Open fire!" and Lieutenant Commander Plunkett-Cole crossed to the port torpedo control position to fire the tube there.

When the alarm sounded, Midshipman Loxton had been awakened by his relief, Johnston. "I asked him the time and was surprised that 'they' were early," Loxton recalled. He rushed up the port ladder to the bridge just as the ship began to swing fast to starboard. As he reached his battle station, gunnery officer Hole pushed him to one side, shouting "Out of my way snotty. Let me have a look!"

Captain Getting stood on the port side of the bridge, passing orders by voice-pipe to gunnery control. Midshipman Loxton stood close behind him. Within seconds, the gunnery control officer heard Hole call from the bridge, "All quarters stand to!" and then "Load, load, load!" Everything seemed to be going according to orders.

Down below in the engine room, machinery was running well. When the alarm sounded Commander (Engineering) O. F. McMahon went to the forward engine room. At 0144 the order "Full speed ahead" came on both engine-room telegraphs, and revolutions were increased rapidly on all units. Steam pressure was somewhere between 230 and 250, oil pressure between 100 and 140. The main throttles were being opened as McMahon arrived.

Mesley now noticed torpedo tracks on either side of the ship, very close, extending from abaft his limit of vision to the limit of visibility ahead, about a mile off. Air defense officer Lieutenant D. Logan, asleep in a deck chair on the platform above fore control when the action began, ran to B turret, where all antiaircraft positions had been given the order to stand to. His first action was to look over the top of the air defense position at the bridge and get bearings of the threat. He heard Captain Getting's order, "Hard aport and hard starboard," and seeing torpedo tracks pass down either side of the ship, reported this to the bridge. The *Canberra* then combed the tracks in what struck Logan as a perfect piece of seamanship. The radical turns saved her from being hit by the *Aoba*'s torpedoes.

The *Canberra*'s guns were still trained when the first shell hit her from port. Mesley saw flashes from both ends of one of the enemy ships and was temporarily blinded by an explosion on the port side abaft, just below the compass platform. Plunkett-Cole was knocked to the deck and also momentarily blinded as a shell hit the plot room immediately behind him. He was just picking himself up and was about to press the torpedo triggers when the ship received a second hit on the port quarter of her platform. The torpedoes did not fire. Nobody on the compass platform had had time to recover from the first salvo before this one came in. The shells hit both boiler rooms, and steam to all units failed. Electrical power failed throughout the ship.

Chief yeoman of signals, C. J. Gunthorp, was bending down to adjust his antiflash gear when he saw the flash of guns on the port beam. Next thing he knew he was sprawled in a starboard corner of the platform. Gunnery officer Hole was down on the deck in the other corner, with Midshipman Loxton lying beside him. There was a sudden lurch, and a voice calling "We've been hit!" Nobody, it seemed, knew exactly what was happening. Midshipman Johnston was conscious of a flash and a shock from the port side forward, and a second later, a blast of flame alongside him. He felt something hit his arm.

After her attack on the *Patterson,* the *Furutaka* began firing her guns and launched four torpedoes. She made no hits on the *Canberra,* but one or two torpedoes passed beneath the *Chicago* a little later. Her report states that she saw an enemy cruiser on fire about to penetrate the Japanese column. At this time the cruiser's steering started to falter. The *Furutaka* took left rudder to avoid the ship, then continued northward, still firing her guns.

Midshipman Johnston saw a lot of bodies and a fire lighting up the platform. He told someone to put out the fire near the forebridge clock, as it was illuminating the bridge. This was done. When Mesley could see again, he noticed several people lying on the deck of the compass platform. One was the captain, his head within two feet of the compass to which Mesley himself was clinging. Gunnery officer Hole was dead, as were several others on the platform. Many men had been injured, including Midshipman Loxton, who found himself sitting on the deck with his back to the standard compass. The phone to the fire control room rang and he crawled across the platform to answer it. There was no one on the other end.

Mesley shouted, "The steering's gone!" and someone else reported that the turret would not train. At this point Mesley ordered steering by main engine. "Get after control and tell the commander to come to the platform!" he shouted to Midshipman Johnston. Johnston took the wrong phone, the one to the forward engine room, and said, "Steer by main engine, the bridge is out of action!" There was no reply. He tried the exchange, whereupon the phone cut out and he decided to run to the flag deck. There it became evident that the ship had been badly shelled. There were bodies everywhere, and men screaming. The cat-

Captain F. E. Getting, RAN. (106675, Australian War Memorial)

walk was shattered and guard rails were twisted. The 4-inch-gun deck was a shambles. A huge fire was burning in the airmen's workshop and after control was on fire.

Johnston saw people lying in after control and yelled from the 4-inch-gun deck, "Commander, sir!" Commander Walsh emerged limping and bleeding from facial wounds. Johnston told him that the compass platform was out of action, everything was out of action, and the captain wounded.

Earlier, from the searchlight platform, Walsh had seen the flares on the starboard quarter and a ship ignite on the starboard bow. Spotting torpedoes coming down each side of the *Canberra* and ships' vague silhouettes, he had passed the alarm to damage control and after control. As he was doing this, ships on the port side opened fire. The *Canberra*'s Walrus plane caught fire; Walsh was struggling to put out the flames when the second blast knocked him out. He picked himself up and went down to the starboard waist. Fires raged everywhere. Nobody was on the 4-inch-gun deck. He managed to collect men elsewhere and had them run out hoses. There was no water pressure. He was giving orders to form bucket brigades when Midshipman Johnston found him.

Assisted by two men, Petty Officer R. W. Bevern and the chief boatswain's mate, Walsh made his way to the bridge to find Captain Getting, still conscious but obviously in great pain and growing weaker. His right leg had been shattered from the knee down, practically shot away. The bones were badly broken, and he had several large arm and head injuries, including shrapnel in the face. Getting refused attention, ordering Walsh to look after the other wounded and asking continuously what signals were being made and how things were going. Walsh took over command at 0148, nearly blinded by shrapnel hits to the face and still limping. "I think I'm going to faint," he told Mesley. He was encouraged to sit down on the portside gratings and soon, feeling better, told chief yeoman of signals Gunthorp to send off a message to Admiral Crutchley saying the ship's boiler room had been hit by a torpedo. This was passed to remote control, which had reported that the emergency set was working. Gunthorp ordered it passed in fleet code, prefixed "Immediate." There was no acknowledgment of its receipt.

Lieutenant Commander Plunkett-Cole reached the platform with a body full of shrapnel and several patches smoldering on the back of his overalls. "I've been hit in the bum like a bloody sparrow," he announced. Between them, Mesley, Midshipman Johnston, and Sublieutenant Dawborn put out the flames on his clothing. Plunkett-Cole refused further treatment, opting to climb to the bridge and find a life jacket for Captain Getting, propped up against the compass. Mesley ordered Johnston to make his way to the plot to get a first-aid box, as he wanted to assist Captain Getting. Johnston returned to say that the plot had been wrecked. A man was sent for the principal medical officer and a medical party. Blankets and sheets were brought from the pilot house to cover the wounded and dead, and medical officers arived to render first-aid to casualties on and near the compass platform.

Chief engineer McMahon appeared on the platform and bent over the still conscious Getting. "Sir, I'm afraid things are bad. We've been hit in the engine rooms." McMahon said that all steam and power were gone and that there was no main pressure water available. "Do your best, Mac," the captain whispered.

Walsh then had messages sent to Crutchley and Turner, giving details of damage and including news of the captain. These were relayed in fleet code and also prefixed "Immediate."

Surgeon Commander C. A. Downward arrived on the platform to find Getting propped against the compass, Commander Walsh, his face streaming with blood, standing on the port side of the bridge, and the body of gunnery officer Hole on the port side. Downward bent over the captain to look at his injuries but again Getting refused attention, telling the doctor and medical parties to tend to the other wounded.

Wounded were everywhere in the ship. When the alarm had sounded, the shell-handling crew of Y turret were playing cards on a makeshift table immediately above the shell-room hatch. Most men had stripped because of the intense heat, leaving only their shorts on. When the crash came no one had time to get dressed, although a few men grabbed their flash gear. Many men were blown off their feet.

Able seaman Stephen S. St. George was one of the cardplayers. Petty Officer Berry looked at his watch and remarked, "Quarter to two." Almost immediately the turret trained on the starboard beam. Then came the order "Load, load, load!" It was immediately executed on both port and starboard sides, then the turret swung to a bearing abaft the port beam. St. George asked what all the panic was about. "Think it's planes," someone said.

St. George was wearing only his blue turret shorts. He decided to "put the old blimp on." You never knew what might happen in the middle of the night. He dared not leave the clutch, but he considered putting on the rest of his clothes, including the antiflash gear, which because of the heat around the card table he had left on the deck. He was about to ask Berry to chuck his clothes over when the first crash came, accompanied by flashes of flame and dense palls of black smoke.

Petty Officer Berry was blown off his feet from his position at the ring control valve and St. George went to ground, "helped along no end by the blast." Almost immediately the turret pump died away, the lights went dimmer and burned out.

Stifled by the smoke, St. George was one of several who dived to the magazine door to free trapped men. He told of the situation inside:

> To the magazine crew I shouted, "Out of it, we've been whacked!" No sooner said then done, they poured up into the lobby. I went back and looked into the shell-handling room. Petty Officer Berry had released the shell room crew; he and somebody else were then opening the hatch to the cordite-handling room. I made my way to the mid study flat. As I emerged I heard a further crash in the shell-handling room, which sounded like another shell arriving, followed by a similar row in the mid study flat, which I think destroyed the bathrooms. We lifted the hatch above X and Y lobby to facilitate the exit of the men still below. To accomplish this, we had to clear the ladder to the wardroom flat, and lift it, thereby stopping the upward flow of traffic. There seemed

> to be no panic, one chap even apologised for bumping me, which seemed a trifle superfluous at the time. Able seaman Scott was standing next to me and said, "There's some wounded down here, let's get 'em." So I followed him to the engineer's office and found chief stoker Hunter with two wounded stokers. We carried them to the wardroom and laid them on the deck, informing Surgeon Lieutenant Warden of their presence. This done, we ascended to the quartermaster's lobby. As we attained this, we saw able seaman Halliwell making his way down, saying, "Let us through boys, I've only one leg." His left foot appeared to be doubled up and he was leaning on somebody's shoulder.

Continuing their search for wounded, St. George and chief stoker W. G. Hunter went to the wardroom hatch and found Petty Officer Haining lying on the deck. "Don't forget to tell my wife and child—and go and see her," he said, over and over again. He did not seem to mind the pain and protested when he was put on a stretcher, far too short for the wounded man, and taken with other men to join the doctor's patients. "That stretcher proved more difficult to assemble than a radio set," St. George complained.

All the well-laid medical plans for an emergency had gone astray. Surgeon Commander Downward, asleep in the sick bay when the attack began, had been awakened by one of his medical party keeping watch on the telephone. He heard a loud explosion, followed by screams of wounded. Among the first casualties to arrive in sick bay was a man whose left arm had been shot away. No sooner was a tourniquet adjusted and a morphine injection given to him and three other casualties than all power failed and the water supply stopped. With the ship listing and fires in the sick bay, men were moved to the forecastle. There they lay for hours in the pouring rain, under any available blankets, coats, or hammocks. From this time on, first-aid parties had to use their initiative and work as independent units. Stokers, able seamen, cooks, dental mechanics, stewards, butchers, and chaplains were all called in to assist with the wounded, who in the first five minutes amounted to more than two hundred.

Very early in the action the two forward medical stations were cut off from the after control party, where the operating theater was situated and supplies such as serum were stored on ice. Lack of fresh water added to the misery. Many wounded men were glad to get cold tea instead, brought to them in milk cans, all other receptacles having been destroyed. A can of tea was also taken to the bridge for Captain Getting.

There was a shortage of scissors. Needles tended to be blunt, and dressings were too small for the gaping wounds many men suffered. Broken bones, deep muscular wounds, and burns were the most common injuries. Splints, sulpha, and anesthesia were in short supply. The heavy, long-sleeved overalls that many of the crew wore gave little protection. The blast of the hits had even torn fastenings from their clothes. Able Seaman Stephen St. George seemed to be in half a dozen places at once. He lent a hand at bandaging and located cigarettes for the wounded. He also found some beer. Every man got a glass. He offered one to the Roman Catholic chaplain enlisted to help with casualties. The chaplain refused. Rather than see it go to waste, St. George drank it himself.

Fires were blazing on either side of both boiler room casings. Suffering from shock, mechanic F. H. Gorham nonetheless attempted to go below to boiler room A. Smoke, steam, and fumes were pouring out with a strong, sweet smell that made him vomit. He opened the airlock doors one by one, just enough to get a foot onto the gratings, but could only see about twelve inches through the haze, even with the aid of a strong torch. He shouted below. There was silence in the room.

Stoker P. C. Ackerman's station was B boiler room. He had been asleep in the recreation room when the alarm sounded. He went down to his locker with his boots on and found that he had left his life jacket and stoker's cap in the recreation room. He returned to get them and then went to the boiler room to collect his overalls. Ackerman made it as far as the fan flat and was about to enter the air lock when the explosion came. By the time he regained consciousness, it was dark and hot. All he wanted was to get out of the place. The doors had been locked when he went in, but the blast had knocked the clips off, making an exit easy. He had his shorts and boots on when he went in; now his boots were gone. He couldn't remember which deck he was on. His body and feet were burned from falling on the hot gratings, bits of skin hanging off him, his bit of beard was burning, but his hair was alright because he had been wearing his stoker's cap. He was the only man to escape from either boiler room.

Parties called to dump ammunition overboard struggled over buckled decks and burning debris. Star shells, high-explosive lockers, and forty-four-gallon drums of high-test aviation spirit were also ditched. The plane still had four 100-lb bombs on racks, which were impossible to reach.

The *Canberra*'s list had increased to about 15 degrees. Commander Walsh had the ship closed down amidships in the hope that the fires

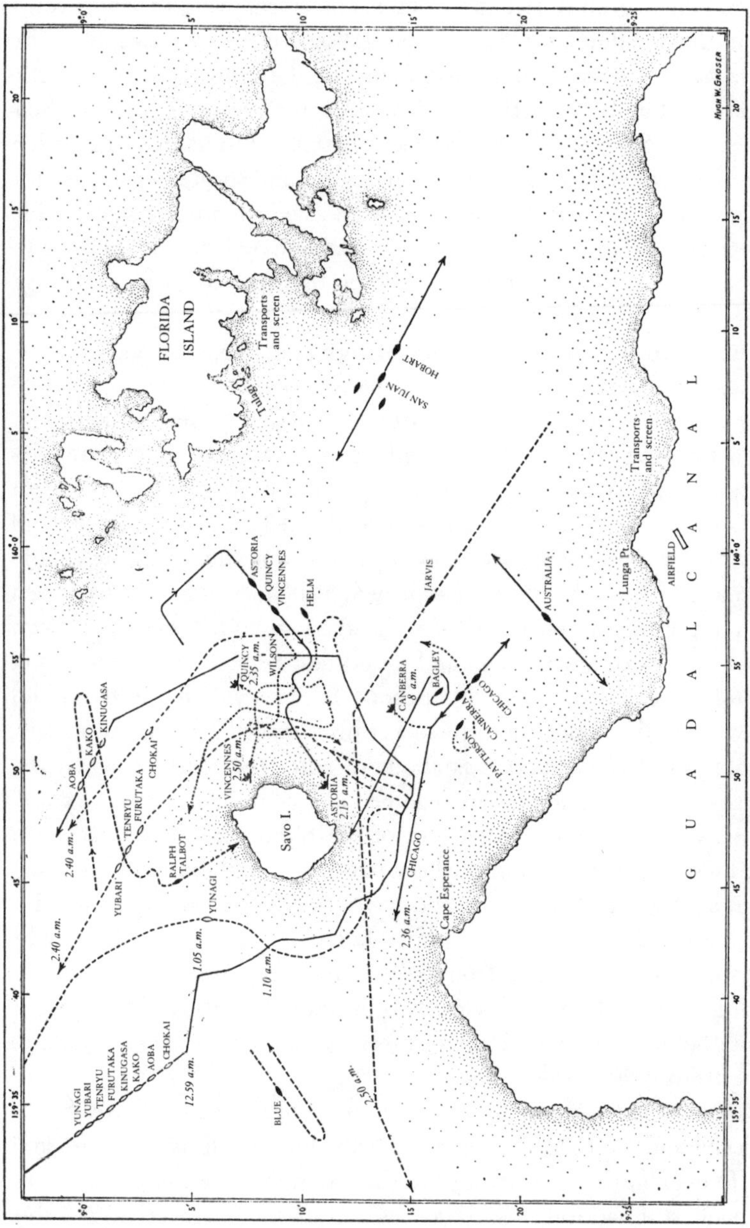

The Battle of Savo Island. (Courtesy Australian War Memorial)

would smother. They blazed out of control throughout the ship as bucket parties did their best with sand and water. Boats, rafts, and anything that would float were lowered over the side and secured, and orders were given to flood any remaining unflooded magazines.

Mesley recommended that Captain Getting have another signal sent out reporting the ship's condition. The message was dictated to the chief yeoman of signals and transmitted in code. There being no reply, it was transmitted a second time.

Captain Getting, growing weaker, still refused to be moved from the compass platform. All other wounded were patched up and taken to the forecastle. With every minute it rained harder and now it began to thunder and lightning too. The rain, at least, assisted the firefighting parties, and for a little while Mesley thought that the upper-deck fires might be bought under control. With more hands for the bucket parties, perhaps the ship could be saved.

Under attack for not quite three minutes, and without firing a shot, the *Canberra* was out of the fight. Between 0144 and 0147 she had received about twenty-eight large-caliber shells, all square amidships, ripping holes from eighteen inches to six feet in size. Shells from the first salvo alone had burst in the plotting office, in the port torpedo space, on the 4-inch-gun deck, and in sick bay, leaving the aircraft ablaze and igniting varnish on the catapult structures. After the attack the *Canberra*'s main guns were still trained in but she had no time to fire, for the dynamos had been hit. All power and lighting had failed. Eight-inch armor-piercing shells had passed through the ship below the waterline, and she was drifting and listing 15 degrees to starboard. Gradually she slowed down, until all steam failed and she came to a complete standstill. The *Canberra* was alone, about seven and a half miles from the center of Savo Island, apparently deserted by the rest of the force, and like her captain, only just alive.

8

Captain Bode's Lost Opportunity

All too late, the *Chicago* received three warnings of the enemy's approach. The first came at 0142, when she saw two orange-colored flashes near the surface of the water on or near Savo Island. These were from torpedoes launched by the *Furutaka*, and they were followed one minute later by the second warning—aircraft flares dropped over the transport area. The third warning came when the *Chicago* saw the *Canberra* swing to starboard at 0145.

As the *Chicago*'s officer of the deck considered this unscheduled change of course, two dark objects were seen between the *Canberra* and the *Patterson*, another off the *Canberra*'s starboard side. The first two were the *Kinugasa* and the *Kako*. The last was the *Aoba*, whose officers thought the American cruiser looked like a battleship. All of the enemy heavy cruisers were determined to claim victory over her.

Captain Bode, in his sea cabin fully clothed at the time the first flares were seen, heard the report through the door or port. When general quarters sounded at 0146, he received a report from the tactical officer and joined Commander Adell and Commander Irish on the bridge. The 5-inch director trained on the object off the starboard side and prepared to fire a star-shell spread.

In the meantime, the starboard bridge lookout reported a torpedo wake and Captain Bode began to turn the ship to starboard with full right rudder. Seconds later, the main battery officer sighted two torpedo tracks passing from port to starboard, bearing 345 degrees relative. Since the first wake to starboard was not seen from the bridge, while those to port were visible, the ship turned to port with full left rudder to run parallel to the wakes. The *Chicago* started to steady on course when

Bode, in an effort to adjust it more closely, saw what he believed to be a destroyer in position to discharge torpedoes further to port. He ordered a further turn to port.

The *Chicago* fired two four-gun star-shell spreads on the port bow and two four-gun salvos on the starboard side. These failed to function, so Captain Bode ordered illumination by searchlight. His order reached the gunnery officer in main battery control, but it was not carried out because the gunnery officer had meanwhile ordered a check to see whether that very order had been given. Bode repeated the order several times, putting his head into the conning tower door to check the talker's transmission of the order. After a minute or so, the order got through to searchlight control and a brief sweep was made to port. No target was disclosed.

The bubble track of the first torpedo crossed approximately seventy yards ahead of the *Chicago*'s bow, the second twenty yards ahead. Though Captain Bode did his best to comb the wakes, the enemy torpedoes were too close. The third track had just been seen by the foretop at about three hundred yards when, at 0147, an explosion came. A torpedo smashed into the *Chicago*'s port bow, well forward, or exploded under her bow, deluging her amidships with a great column of water well above the level of the foremast. A gash ripped the bow from about three feet above the waterline to the keel, and aft to frame no. 4. Mangled metal slewed about, still attached to the portside hull. Aboard the *Chokai*, correspondent Niwa watched as the column of water rose above the cruiser. For a moment it hung above the dark green shape of the *Chicago*, then cascaded down and out like a slow-motion movie until the cruiser was hidden from sight.

The wake seen from the *Chicago*'s bridge came from one of the four torpedoes, fired from the *Chokai*, which had passed the *Canberra* a little earlier—a dead wake on the smooth sea. The bubbling wakes to port came from one of four torpedoes fired by the *Furutaka*. Two other torpedoes that the *Chicago* had failed to see, launched by the *Kako*, hit her. The *Kako* claimed a hit on "what appeared to be a battleship." One of the torpedoes hit her bow, the other struck her on the starboard side but failed to detonate.

When the searchlight shutters closed, Captain Bode ordered further illumination to starboard and the firing of star shells. He repeated the order through the slots in the conning tower to check, once again, the transmission. The *Chicago* fired several rounds from the starboard battery on a ship, or ships, which were only briefly seen in flashes. Bode

The USS Chicago. *(80-G-462745, National Archives)*

thought that the *Canberra*, and perhaps the *Bagley* and the *Patterson*, were firing at enemy ships. What he was witnessing, instead, was the *Aoba*'s attack on the *Canberra*. The other ships were the *Tenryu* and the *Yubari*.

Five minutes after the action began, the *Chicago* was under attack from at least four enemy ships. Captain Getting's frantic signal, sent just seconds before he was wounded, had not reached the American cruiser.

A shell hit the starboard leg of the *Chicago*'s tripod foremast, above the base line. It detonated around the forward funnel, cutting cables and showering shrapnel over the communication platform, funnels, port catapult, after portion of the well deck, hangar, gun deck, and after portion of the boat deck. Commander Adell was wounded in the throat and arm, and many others were injured by shrapnel.

Seconds later a ship believed to be the *Patterson* illuminated two targets, resembling destroyers, on the port side. These were the two Japanese light cruisers. The *Patterson*'s report indicates that she did not employ searchlights. Rear Admiral Mitsuhara Matsuyama, commander of Cruiser Division 18, confirmed that the *Tenryu* used her lights while firing at this time.

The *Chicago*'s port battery opened fire on the portside destroyer at a range of 7,000 yards. The *Patterson* was crossing the line of fire at about 3,000 yards, on a course opposite that of the *Chicago*, and cleared without signaling. Two hits were seen on the target, which the *Chicago* believed were made by the *Patterson*. Shell fragments hit the after deck of the *Tenryu*, killing twenty-three men and injuring another twenty-one.

The *Chokai* had already attacked the *Astoria*, the last ship in the northern group at this time. The Japanese were no longer safe. The *Furutaka*'s steering difficulty caused her to sheer out of line to starboard, toward the American cruisers. The *Tenryu* struggled to keep up with the heavy cruiser, but her gyrocompass had been damaged by "shocks of gunfire" and she could not afford to depend on the magnetic compass. The *Yubari* had narrowly escaped collision with the errant destroyer *Yunagi*. She, too, reported that her gyrocompass had failed.

If the Japanese light cruisers were confused, the *Chicago* was even more so. Her report shows that at 0152 a ship was sighted bearing 270 degrees and established as friendly. This was probably the *Jarvis*. The friendly ship could not have been the *Patterson*, which at this time was heading on her opposite course. It was not the *Bagley*, the only other friendly destroyer in the area, and the *Blue* was too far away and much farther to starboard. One of the destroyers seen by the *Chicago* was the Japanese destroyer *Yunagi*, which had momentarily turned on her searchlights to assist her own light cruisers.[1]

As repair parties continued to patch up the extensive damage caused by gunfire and torpedoes, the *Chicago* slowed to twelve knots to relieve unnecessary pressure on the bulkheads. Captain Bode, having failed to take into consideration changes of course during the *Chicago*'s firing and maneuvering, believed his ship was still standing on course 315 degrees or thereabouts. He had not been informed of the *Vincennes* group's position, or that these ships were patrolling a five-mile square. Assuming they were patrolling a line, he had estimated that the group was probably standing out north of Savo Island, and that he could join them while covering en route the channel south of Savo Island.[2]

Six minutes later, Captain Bode observed gunfire between unidentified ships to the west of Savo. He went full speed—twenty-five knots—and prepared both turrets and broadsides for action. The ships disappeared behind the island as the *Chicago* continued on a westerly course, making no enemy report, and hurried off into the heavy blanket of cloud. This hid her from the *Chokai* and the *Kinugasa*.

The *Chicago*'s navigator suggested meeting up with the *Vincennes* group for an engagement northwest of Savo Island, but Bode decided, at about 0228, to reverse course, believing no enemy ships would be in the vicinity to follow the light forces he had earlier encountered. Soon after the *Chicago* reversed course, gunfire between two ships was seen abaft the port beam. The action appeared to cease almost immediately, and Bode stood on through the patrol area toward X-ray. What he had seen was the action between the *Ralph Talbot* and the Japanese light cruiser *Yubari.*

The *Chicago* strayed off in the wrong direction, not to be heard of for some time. She had been hit by one torpedo on the starboard bow, one under her bow, which did not detonate, as well as one 5-inch shell. She lost two men from gunshot wounds. Twenty-four were wounded, many seriously, including Commander Adell, whose throat wounds were stitched up on deck by the ship's dentist. Ensign Joseph Raymond Daly, USNR, a pilot from the *Saratoga*, was another casualty. He had been picked up badly burned after his plane crashed on 7 August. During this attack he suffered wounds to the face, neck, legs, and arms.

Half an hour after Crutchley's return to the *Australia*, Captain Farncomb had seen flares falling over the transport area. Between 0150 and 0153 more flares and searchlight beams were seen in the *Chicago* group's patrol area. At 0205 another ship on fire was spotted in the area. The glow from this ship, which was the *Canberra*, continued until daylight.

When the shell hit the foremast of the *Chicago*, that ship reported, the *Canberra*, now on her starboard bow, began firing at 0147. The *Bagley*'s commander also reported that the Australian cruiser opened fire at this time. Both were wrong. By that time the *Canberra*'s gunnery officer had been killed, Captain Getting mortally wounded, and most of the bridge personnel killed or disabled. The *Canberra*, a burning, helpless wreck, had nothing with which to fight. The flashes seen from the *Australia*, the *Chicago*, and the *Bagley* came from enemy hits on the Australian cruiser.

The destroyer *Bagley*, screening about 1,600 yards on the *Canberra*'s starboard bow when the action began, saw a number of unidentified enemy ships about a minute after the *Patterson*'s sighting. They seemed close to Savo Island, at a range of about 3,000 yards, and proceeding at high speed, perhaps thirty knots. These were the *Chokai, Aoba, Kako,* and *Kinugasa.*

As she made contact, the *Bagley* saw two or three salvos land short of the *Canberra,* followed by a heavy concentration of fire from the four

Japanese cruisers. The *Bagley*'s officer of the deck immediately ordered general quarters. Like the *Patterson*, the ship swung hard to port to fire torpedoes, but before the primers could be inserted in the starboard torpedo battery the ship had turned past safe firing bearing. As soon as safe bearing was reached, she steadied and fired four torpedoes in a northwesterly direction from her no. 2 torpedo tube.

The *Bagley*'s captain, Lieutenant Commander G. A. Sinclair, identified the targets as two light cruisers of the *Tenryu* class and two heavy cruisers of *Ashigara* class. They were the *Tenryu, Yubari,* and heavy cruisers *Furutaka* and *Kinugasa.* As the four ships of the enemy formation turned, they opened fire with their main and torpedo batteries. Three or four torpedoes passed thirty or forty feet astern of the American destroyer.

Visibility was extremely limited with the sky overcast and intermittent light showers, and soon after the *Bagley*'s torpedoes were fired the enemy, in follow-the-leader formation, was lost to view. No hits were detected by the destroyer's officer of the deck or by Sinclair, but the junior officer of the deck, Lieutenant John H. Gardiner, saw an explosion in the enemy area about two minutes after torpedoes were fired. Sound operator Edward Ryan traced the torpedoes and reported four explosions about two minutes after the tubes were fired, followed by two intense explosions in the same area.

The Japanese ships raced so fast to the northeast that the *Bagley*'s torpedoes had little chance of catching up with them. The *Astoria*, rear ship in the northern group of Allied ships, heard a distant underwater explosion at this time. It is possible that this was caused by the *Bagley*'s torpedoes, although the *Chokai* had fired torpedoes one minute earlier. The *Bagley*'s report shows that the enemy track was 1,500 to 2,000 yards abeam and that the time elapsed between the sighting and the firing of torpedoes was three to four minutes. It might have been longer. Had the *Bagley* fired in this time, in her swing to port she would have come close to a collision with the *Canberra.*[3] Actually, she swung in a circle ahead of the Australian cruiser, and clear of her. Although the *Bagley* and the other ships of the southern group had no information as to the movements of the *Vincennes* group, arguments that the destroyer's torpedoes hit these ships bear little weight.

Four minutes before firing her torpedoes, the *Chokai* had altered course radically to the north. Up to 0144 Mikawa's force had been steaming in a single column; now, having heavily damaged the Allied ships, it divided. Mikawa expected the rest of his cruisers to follow the

Chokai. This did not happen. American and Japanese sources differ as to the reason for the split. Mikawa said that everything went according to plan. However, it seems unlikely that he would have purposely divided his force at this critical time.

Just before 0144, the heavy cruiser *Furutaka*, fifth in the Japanese column, fired her guns and launched four torpedoes at the Allied southern group. To avoid collision with the *Kinugasa* ahead, she sheered to starboard and then decided to race toward the Allied ships in the northern group.

The two light cruisers *Tenryu* and *Yubari* turned to starboard at the same time. This move was not known to Mikawa until near the end of the battle. As mentioned, the shock of firing had damaged the *Tenryu*'s gun director, and the *Yubari* was experiencing trouble with a broken gyrocompass. In turning, the *Yubari* almost ran into the destroyer *Yunagi*, which had reversed course to pursue the damaged *Jarvis* and was now trying to catch up with the main part of the fleet. Lieutenant Shizuichi Okada, in the *Yunagi*, said that the destroyer had intended to follow the first ship in the column; instead, she lost her bearing. By this time she was short of fuel and could not run at high speed. She circled the tip of Savo Island to confirm her position.

As a result of the *Furutaka*'s steering defect, and the reversal of course by the two light cruisers and the *Yunagi*, the force now fell into two groups: an eastern group, comprised of the *Chokai* in the lead, and the *Aoba, Kako,* and *Kinugasa*; and a western group, comprised of the *Tenryu* and the *Yubari*, followed by the limping *Furutaka.*[4] The *Yunagi* was operating alone. After firing torpedoes at the southern group at 0148, the *Chokai* turned to port and sighted the northern force. The column broke up, but the divisions remained together. The *Chokai* and three of the cruisers passed to the east of the Allied force, while the two light cruisers and the *Furutaka* passed close to Savo Island, to the west. Rear Admiral Matsuyama, aboard the *Tenryu*, which was too far away to fire torpedoes, saw the *Vincennes* group by searchlight, and by the flares that silhouetted it, at a range of 14,000 yards. The flares seemed to reveal five heavy cruisers. The number of ships was correct, but not their composition: the *Vincennes, Quincy*, and *Astoria*, with the two screening destroyers *Helm* and *Wilson*.

After firing her torpedoes, the *Bagley*, having received no instructions from the commander of her group, turned to port, scanned the area between Guadalcanal and Savo Island, and proceeded toward the rendezvous five miles northwest of Savo. As she was passing close to the burning *Canberra*, the *Tenryu* caught sight of her from about a mile away and recognized her as a *Farragut*-class destroyer. The glow of flames from the Australian cruiser's fires kept the *Bagley* from seeing the enemy ship or the splashes of her shells, all of which missed. The *Tenryu* let her go. She was after bigger game.

Crutchley had decided not to rejoin the *Australia* group, "as there were but a few hours to 0500 when we would reform screen on the transport groups." In fact, there were about five hours of darkness, and he could have rejoined the *Australia* group in less than an hour. He had not notified Admiral Turner or the commanders of the *Chicago* or *Vincennes* groups of his decision.

Flares had been seen from the *Australia* at 0145, and Crutchley estimated that the Japanese were attempting an attack on the transports. He had seen, indistinctly, the start of the attacks on the *Canberra* and the *Chicago*, the action between the *Patterson* and the Japanese light cruisers, and a few minutes later, the beginning of the action against the *Vincennes* group. He reported very heavy gunfire: "I thought it must have been the *Vincennes* group coming into action against an enemy being engaged by the *Australia* group."[5]

Crutchley might have believed that the *Vincennes* and *Chicago* groups were coordinating for the defense of the transports, but he had not issued battle plans for coordination. His main concern at this time was the protection of Allied shipping at Guadalcanal. That was his objective, and he did not forget it.

A mere five minutes after the action against the southern group, the action against the *Vincennes* group had begun. The *Chokai* fired four torpedoes at the ships, then ahead of her, less than 10,000 yards away. Her Long Lance torpedoes and those of the *Bagley* were racing neck and neck through the water, with about one minute between them.

From 0132 to 0150 the *Chokai, Aoba, Kako,* and *Furutaka* had fired seventeen torpedoes at the southern group for a total of only two hits. Lieutenant Okada, in the destroyer *Yunagi*, reported that his ship had also fired half a dozen "Type Six-Year torpedoes at a cruiser with four funnels." He believed that one or two hit the fore part of the cruiser, near the magazine. The *Yunagi*'s war diary indicates that at this time she engaged an *Omaha*-class ship, "which went down with a great rumble." The *Canberra*, with three funnels, bore the closest resemblance to an "*Omaha*-class, four-funneled light cruiser." The *Chicago* had two funnels. Neither cruiser was sunk. Two torpedo hits were made on the

Chicago by Japanese ships, one causing damage and casualties; the other was a dud. The torpedoes the *Furutaka* fired at the *Patterson* missed. The southern ships had been finished off as a fighting force in under six minutes, mainly by gunfire, and there were enemy torpedoes to spare.

9

"We Are Friendly!"

The battle against the Allied southern group was what the Japanese heavy cruiser *Kako* described as a "tail-lashing." The leader of the attacking force was the *Chokai*, which would continue to indicate targets to the other Japanese ships. From this time on the Allied ships faced two equally strong and, so far, only slightly damaged opponents.

But for lack of information, the *Vincennes* and the two other American cruisers in the group would have had at least a chance of survival. As it was, they were left to fend for themselves on this blackest of nights for the U.S. Navy. In the *Vincennes*, Captain Riefkohl, leader of the northern group, had received the RAAF signal about an approaching enemy force during the day and its confirmation in the early evening. After studying the situation, he told Lieutenant Harry Vincent, communications and combat officer, that the Japanese might be planning to leave the two reported seaplane tenders at a Japanese base south of Bougainville while their cruisers and destroyers paid the Guadalcanal force a surprise visit. He had no further information about the Japanese force, but he assumed that if it had not been attacked and broken up by carrier air, Admiral Turner would alert his command to the possibility of attack that night.

The general location of the southern group was vaguely known by all three cruisers, but no one knew what the group was doing, or that the *Australia* had left it. No instructions regarding the night cruising of the *Australia, Canberra,* and *Chicago* were available to Captain Moore in the *Quincy*. Captain Greenman in the *Astoria* was "somewhat incensed" because Crutchley had not given him information as to the location of his ships. Uncertainty lent confusion to the *Astoria*'s radar operators, and officers of the watch frequently reported strange objects in the area where the Allied ships were supposed to be. It was presumed that the *Australia* and the *Canberra* were moving in and out of their patrols on the same stations they had kept the previous night. Information concerning the possible approach of a Japanese force had been received in the *Astoria*, either in the morning or early afternoon of 8 August. Another dispatch placed enemy submarines close to the area, and the *Astoria* had been warned by Captain Riefkohl.

The *Vincennes* was the first of the northern cruisers to be seen by the Japanese, at 0138, and the last to be attacked. Unaware of the absence of the *Australia* and that he was now not only the leader of his group but also commander of the entire task force, Riefkohl had no idea that the carriers had departed.[1] If the Japanese were on the way, they would be "chewed up" by carrier planes, or at least trailed. Riefkohl's main concern, then, was to keep his crew ready for a possible attack. Instructions were passed to fire control, damage control, the engine room, and all gun and lookout stations to be on the alert. He did not pass on warnings to the other ships in the group, believing they had received similar notice of the approach of enemy vessels.

Lieutenant L. P. Mooney promptly recorded the captain's instruction in the engineering department's night order book, signed it himself, and had it initialed by the chief engineer.[2] Mooney had heard that an enemy force was coming. It was rumored that Reifkohl had requested permission to take the *Vincennes* to sea. He reasoned that if the enemy force did attack, it would be during the midwatch. Consequently, he took over the main control midwatch himself.

Around 2350, the *Ralph Talbot*'s radio warning was received. A plane with running lights on, it said, was standing in toward Guadalcanal and the transport area. Riefkohl did not relay this report because he heard the destroyer squadron commander, who was near the transports, acknowledge its receipt. Surely Admiral Turner's flagship had received it as well.

When the *Talbot*'s signal reached him, Riefkohl inquired whether anyone had seen the lights of a plane. One man came to the bridge and was interrogated by both the captain and the executive officer, Commander William Mullan. The man said that he had seen a light on the port quarter for a moment. Captain Riefkohl could not believe that an enemy plane would fly over a force at night with its running lights on. The force commander must have received the signal, and as nothing further was heard, Reifkohl assumed that it had been a friendly plane sent in by the carrier group commander with a message. This had happened before.[3] Carrier task force commanders often sent messages to shore bases and other force commanders by plane, during daylight, to avoid using radio, which would disclose their position.

Just after midnight, Commander Mullan took over the bridge from Riefkohl and Lieutenant Commander Cleverland Dale Miller relieved the navigator, Commander A. M. Loker, as officer of the deck. Riefkohl, worn out after twenty-one continuous hours on the bridge, retired to his emergency cabin adjoining the pilot house. Before leaving, he told Mullan that since he had received no word from Admiral Turner, the Japanese force must have been destroyed by carrier planes. He gave orders to be called immediately in the event of any enemy contact or unusual occurrence.

At this time, Lieutenant Commander R. L. Adams, the gun control officer, was relieved by Lieutenant Commander R. R. Craighill. At the beginning of the watch, Adams had passed out word to all stations to be on the alert, for reports of three Japanese cruisers and three destroyers headed in their general direction had been received on 8 August. After being relieved, Adams went to the sky control platform to sleep.

The American command ship was in condition readiness 2, with six turret guns manned, two in each turret. Nine turret guns had been loaded ever since the appearance of low-flying torpedo planes that day. The broadside antiaircraft battery and heavy machine-gun batteries were fully manned. Main, secondary, plot, and damage control central were also manned. All boilers except nos. 7 and 8 were fired, and there was a watch standing in three. Two men stood watch on the searchlights. The radar was manned continuously and searching. The officer of the deck and the executive officer were both authorized to initiate action without direct orders from the captain.

Captain Riefkohl had had no opportunity to conduct night battle practice since taking command on 23 April 1941, though exercises simulating night action had taken place by day and night, and he was unaware of the state of night training in the other cruisers and destroyers. Captain Greenman in the *Astoria* and Captain Moore in the *Quincy*, however, were well known to him. He had the utmost confidence in their ability.[4]

During the time Riefkohl was in command, operating under different task force commanders in the Atlantic and the Pacific, various methods of maintaining condition readiness 2 had been tried. He considered his present one the best, as it permitted all turrets to commence firing at the same time, merely requiring personnel in the turrets to drop to their stations in the handling rooms as they were relieved by condition 1 crews. All turrets were manned with enough conditon 1 personnel to operate them before action began.

During the day, scuttlebutt about the Japanese force spread through the *Vincennes.* Chaplain Robert Schwyhart heard it during evening mess in the wardroom, when executive officer Mullan talked of the sighting and reasoned that at their rate of speed, the Japanese would probably arrive about 0830 the next day. Mullan confided to the chaplain that he and other departmental heads took the news casually. If the Japanese *did* come, he said, they would fall into a death trap.

Earlier, the chaplain had come to the assistance of *Life* photographer Ralph Morse, a young American war correspondent who had been aboard the *Hornet* for the Doolittle raid and later had witnessed the battle at Midway. During the landing at Guadalcanal and the capture of the air field there, he had shot countless pictures and needed to find a way of getting the film back to the States. When he heard that the *Vincennes* was returning to San Francisco for a five-year overhaul after the operation, Morse hiked back to the beach, pleaded with a landing craft sailor to take him to the *Vincennes*, and arrived at about dusk. Chaplain Schwyhart, pleased to be of help, placed the correspondent's film in the ship's safe. The ship's officers persuaded Morse to stay for the night instead of returning in the dark and perhaps landing near the enemy on the beach. They promised to get him ashore in the morning. After a meal with some of the junior officers, and a hand or two of bridge, the correspondent prepared for bed, secure in the knowledge that his film was locked in the cruiser's safe.

"What a day!" he wrote later. "I had been in many battles as a war correspondent with the Pacific Fleet, but never a land battle, digging down and eating dirt."

Chaplain Schwyhart, the guardian of Morse's precious film, sat for a while with Commander James D. Blackwood, the *Vincennes*'s chief medical officer, talking over the events of the day. On the beach a fire burned brightly, and from one point to another the two men could make out flying tracer bullets. Presumably the marines were still fighting. Blackwood was proud of the medical teams he had in the ship's three battle dressing stations. After the last couple of days, he told the chaplain, he could say that they had been thoroughly tested and not found wanting.

It was late before they decided to go below. Chaplain Schwyhart wrote another page of his journal, kept faithfully each day for more than a year since he had been aboard, said a prayer for the ship, and was in his bunk by about 2330.

In the plotting room, Lieutenant Donald Hugh Dorris also kept a diary. When he heard of the Japanese attack at Pearl Harbor, he had noted: "The Pacific Fleet certainly fell down on its intelligence work. . . . The ships certainly were not under the condition of readiness we have always been in when away from the United States." In another entry he expressed his eagerness for "a chance or several chances" to use the training he had acquired.

Lieutenant Dorris's chance had come. At 0140, the *Vincennes* sent out a warning to the *Quincy, Astoria, Helm,* and *Wilson* that she intended to remain on course an extra ten minutes because of the tides. A minute or so later, quartermaster Hans Petersen reported a signal from the *Helm* saying that a plane was flying over her. The *Vincennes*'s lookouts also heard a plane. At the same time, a lookout on the main deck aft sighted a submarine on the surface. Petersen felt a tremor and remarked to Commander Mullan and Lieutenant Commander Miller that he thought a destroyer was dropping depth charges.

The lookout's sighting was reported to the pilot house, but it is uncertain whether the report was acknowledged. Almost immediately, one of the sky lookouts reported to gun control officer Lieutenant Commander Craighill a shape he thought he saw broadside to the port bow. Craighill searched the entire area with binoculars but could make out nothing except the left tangent, so he believed, of Savo Island.

At 0145, by TBS, the *Vincennes* ordered course to be held until 0200. Also at this time came her first warning. Off the ship's port side, Lieutenant Commander Craighill spotted lights and what he thought looked like gunfire. A moment later, four star shell bursts were seen broadside to the port quarter, about eight miles away. From the bridge executive officer Mullan saw the great display of lights and recognized the silhouettes of a group of ships as the southern Allied force. They were on approximately the same course as the *Vincennes*, which was northwest.

Lieutenant Commander Adams, asleep on the sky control platform, was called and told that suspicious events were occurring off the port side. He looked and saw a burst of three or four star shells in the direction of Lunga Point. His first thought was that a ship was firing star shells to illuminate shore installations in that area. Shortly afterwards he saw flashes of gunfire to the right of the star shell lights.

The flares seen from the *Vincennes*'s bridge were high over the *Canberra* and the *Chicago*. Called by the officer of the deck, Captain Riefkohl picked up his binoculars, put on his cap and slippers, and joined his officers on the bridge to discuss the situation. He saw lights at a considerable distance off the port beam and a ship firing toward the southwest. This was the engagement between the Japanese light cruisers *Tenryu* and *Yubari* and the American destroyer *Patterson,* which was firing star shells toward the northwest.

At 0148, on Mullan's advice, quartermaster Petersen passed the word for all hands to man their battle stations. The *Chokai* saw the three Allied cruisers at this moment, changed course to the northeast, and launched four torpedoes from her starboard tubes.

If enemy ships were sighted, Captain Riefkohl expected, the *Australia* group would illuminate and engage them, clarifying the situation. Understandably, he was confused. Time after time he asked his chief signalman if any word had come in from Admiral Crutchley in the *Australia*. He seriously considered going to the aid of the southern group but, without action reports, instead signaled an increase of speed to fifteen knots. He would hold course temporarily while awaiting word from the admiral. To avoid disclosing himself to an enemy approaching from seaward, Riefkohl withheld orders to fire star shells. He also feared that the Japanese had sent in a destroyer force to divert his three cruisers south, away from the northern approach to the transports, while the main enemy force went around the other side of Savo Island.[5]

About this time, the *Patterson* broadcast its warning of three ships entering the harbor. The *Vincennes*'s forward radar room TBS operator received it and reported it to radio control as "Warning to all ships—three ships coming in at table end." The message reached neither Riefkohl nor Commander Mullan on the bridge, possibly because at the time the change of course was being broadcast to the other ships in the group.

Soon after the alarm sounded, officer of the deck Miller reported that gunfire had been seen in the sector near Guadalcanal where the southern group was operating. Squalls and the low cloud ceiling were making it difficult to determine the source of gunfire. There was still a distinct possibility that the *Australia* group was firing on Japanese installations on Guadalcanal.

The TBS for increased speed had just been set at 0150 when searchlights trained on the three cruisers. Lights from the *Kako* focused on the *Vincennes,* correctly identified by the Japanese as an *Astoria*-class cruiser, those from the *Aoba* on the *Quincy,* which they mistook for a *Portland*-class heavy cruiser. The *Chokai* illuminated the *Astoria,* the rear ship in the line. Captain Riefkohl presumed that the lights came from the *Australia* group, heading in to locate the enemy force he believed to be firing near Savo Island.

The Japanese ships had been ordered to proceed independently, but now they followed instructions from Mikawa in the *Chokai* to open fire. She used her lights for the double purpose of picking up targets and for informing the other ships of her location. The lights pinpointed ship after ship, controlling the performance of the other cruisers like a symphony conductor, calling in the heavy guns, the 5-inch guns, the antiaircraft guns, and the torpedoes.

Captain Riefkohl sent out a message on the TBS requesting the ships to turn off their lights. "We are friendly!" he signaled. As a precaution, gun control officer Adams trained on the nearest searchlight. Star shells were bursting over the port side and it appeared to him that two ships were firing at each other. Riefkohl's message went out to all ships, but only the screening destroyer *Helm* acknowledged the transmission. In desperation, Riefkohl ordered control to put out the searchlights with their guns, ran up a set of colors at the yardarm, and illuminated so that the friendly vessels could see his ship.

Chief yeoman L. E. Stucker's first message to Adams, on the captain's orders, was "Open fire on target of opportunity!" He heard Riefkohl ask Adams, "What do you suggest now?" The gun control officer replied, "Let's get out of here until we can see what we are doing. I'm not sure of my targets." Stucker then delivered Reifkohl's second message to gun control: "Cease firing. I am going to swing around. When we come back in we'll give them hell!"

The American cruiser's early-model radar was of little use because the Japanese ships were sweeping in a great horseshoe curve against the landmass of Guadalcanal. Her radar picked them up just as they opened fire, at which point, of course, it was too late. The *Kako*'s first salvo landed about 75 to 100 yards short. The *Vincennes* immediately returned fire with a full 8-inch salvo, using a radar range of about four miles, and followed this with a burst of star shells. The shells all missed their target. The second salvo from the *Kako* landed 100 yards short. The next raked the *Vincennes*, scoring amidship hits with both 8-inch and 4.7-inch shells. Gunnery officer Haruyoshi Mishimura reported that the Japanese cruiser's 8-inch shells had little trouble scoring on the American ships, as the range was so short and the *Kako*'s guns were firing at almost level trajectory. "We saw the shells penetrating the sides of the enemy ships," he said, "and watched through the shell holes as they exploded inside."

One of the first enemy hits on the bridge killed Lieutenant Commander Miller, standing close to Captain Riefkohl, and two men in the pilot house. Other shells exploded in the carpenter shop, the hangar, and the antennae trunks. Planes on the *Vincennes*'s hangar deck burst into flames. All gun control electrical power failed, except for communications, and a shift was made to auxiliary. The *Kako* dispensed with her searchlights and took advantage of the cruiser's fires.

The *Chokai* could clearly see all three Allied cruisers and could also make out gunfire from the *Helm*, ordered by the *Vincennes* to open fire at this time. The *Chokai* did not fire on the destroyer because crossfire would have interfered with that of Mikawa's other cruisers. From this time on, the Japanese flagship concentrated on the *Astoria,* while the *Aoba* poured her fire on the equally unready *Quincy*.

Another shell from the *Kako* hit the *Vincennes*'s main battery control station aft, killing the control officer and most others there. Riefkohl was now in the difficult position of trying to guide his task group and wage battle at the same time.

Circumstances dictated an immediate turn. Any delay would allow the enemy ships to pass under his stern, thus threatening the transports in the Tulagi anchorage. His forward guns would no longer be able to bear on the enemy. He decided to increase speed to twenty knots and have each ship make a simultaneous turn to port, continuing on a reverse course if the Japanese headed for Tulagi. But, owing to the loss of all intership radio communication, Riefkohl's attempts to signal the other two cruisers failed. Even his blinker signals had been lost in the blast on the bridge.

Just after 0153, with all hope of a simultaneous turn now lost, Riefkohl himself changed course to port, expecting the other captains to understand his plan and follow his lead. They did. "They turned beautifully," he recalled.[6] "They knew what I wanted. That had been my intention—turn reverse course. Then things got too hot and for some reason or other the *Quincy* balled things up."

The *Vincennes* was being hit continually by 8- and 5-inch shells. They set her on fire amidships and heavily damaged antiaircraft stations both forward and aft. Firefighting was ineffective, because mains had been ruptured and there was no water available topside.

By the time power had been restored, another enemy ship appeared.

This was the *Kinugasa,* returned from attacking the southern group. The *Vincennes* immediately trained on the new target and fired a second full salvo from her nine 8-inch guns. There was an explosion in the *Kinugasa* and her searchlights went out, followed by a burst of flame. The flame died down quickly, the ship made a radical turn to port. In the words of Lieutenant Commander Craighill, "She staggered off and went down immediately."

Craighill was mistaken. Both the *Chokai* and the *Kinugasa* were hit at this time, but neither sank. The *Kinugasa* lost some of her normal steering control and was forced to rely on her main engines as she struggled to remain in column. While she continued to come under heavy fire from the *Vincennes,* she was hit again on her starboard side near the waterline. This hit came from either the *Vincennes* or the *Astoria.* Meanwhile the *Chokai,* out of control, fell to the rear of the column, her turning circle being greater than that of the other Japanese vessels.

The *Vincennes*'s turn to port had placed the Allied group in an even more precarious position. She was being heavily hit, and Riefkohl could see the *Quincy* on fire off his port quarter. He orderd a change of course to starboard with a radical turn, intending to increase speed to twenty-five knots. As the *Vincennes* turned, she continued to be hit by both large- and small-caliber shells. She could make no more than eighteen knots and was being illuminated by a ship on her starboard quarter. This was the *Aoba,* now dividing her main battery between the *Quincy* and the *Vincennes,* close together and both on fire.

At 0155, the *Vincennes* was hit in the no. 2 fireroom by two or three of the torpedoes fired by the *Chokai* at 0148, just one and a half minutes after the Japanese flagship turned on her searchlights. Riefkohl thought the torpedoes were fired by a submarine, as no torpedo tube flashes were seen in the vicinity of the enemy searchlights before the hits.

Dense clouds of smoke, reeking of paint and rubber, poured from the fire control tube under the main battery director and all power was lost in forward control. Gun control officer Adams directed the turrets to go to local control, then went to the sky control platform, also shrouded in smoke. Obstructed by dead bodies, wounded men huddled together, and an unexploded shell, he made his way to the next lower level, where things were no better. Because of the smoke he could not reach the ladder leading to the bridge, so he made his way to the after side of the platform, climbed over the rail, and dropped down to the signal bridge. There he reported to Captain Riefkohl that he no longer had control of the ship's armament.

The first shell had hit the ship's movie booth and flung burning material on the well deck. The next explosion occurred in the vicinity of the no. 8 gun, scorching and injuring dozens of men. Executive officer Mullan found the first casualties on his way down the ladder to his battle station, and spent some time trying, without success, to get water to put out the fires. He went up the forward gun deck, starboard side, crossed between the stacks, and found a fire hydrant turned on. There was no water. Dead and wounded men lay everywhere.

Deciding to remove ammunition from the ready service boxes, Mullan had advanced only a short way to the port side when another explosion knocked him down, breaking a leg and an arm. Lieutenant R. J. Badger cleared him of the passageways, and in great pain Mullan was able to direct firefighting. The few survivors from the 5-inch guns, together with Badger and the ship's photographer, worked among the carnage, jettisoning burning debris, twisted remnants of guns, and whatever ammunition they could remove from the ready-service lockers. Mullan, unable to move, watched as badly burned men under Badger's supervision carried the flaming wreckage to the rails. "I observed the calm and efficient manner in which Lieutenant Badger went about his duty," he recalled. "His behavior must have been a bright flame of inspiration to those men working with him." One thing not lacking aboard the *Vincennes* was courage, and a spirit to save the ship from the disaster that already appeared to have overtaken the blazing *Quincy*.

Soon after the torpedoes hit, the *Vincennes* lost steering control on the bridge, but she was able to rely on the steering engine room. She also lost all main battery power. A hit in main battery control aft killed most of the personnel there and wrecked the station. Power for turrets nos. 1 and 3 was provided by auxiliary diesel generators. The crew had to operate turret no. 2 by hand.

From the *Australia,* Crutchley had seen that the ships under his command were in trouble. He made the following comments later:

> Then there began a general night action which at 0156 appeared to move to the right and to increase tremendously in intensity. I had received no enemy report from either of our guard units, or from any ship in our cruiser night patrols, and although a fierce night action was being fought, I had absolutely no knowledge of the number or the nature of the enemy force involved or of the progress of the action being fought. I conjectured that the *Australia* group had made contact with an enemy force of some sort, which would explain the firing in their

> general direction at 0150, and when at 0156 the action distinctly shifted to the right, I considered it probable that the enemy had turned to the eastward by contact with the *Canberra* and the *Chicago* and had then run into our other patrol containing the three 8-inch cruisers *Vincennes, Astoria,* and *Quincy*. I felt confident that our five 8-inch cruisers (and four destroyers) then on patrol immediately inside Savo Island could effectively deal with any enemy force likely (from our intelligence and reconnaissance) to have been [sent] against us.[7]

In the *Vincennes,* Lieutenant Commander Craighill found the bridge a mass of wreckage and incapacitated and dead men. He went to sky control and saw that all hands in that station got down below, ready to abandon ship if the order came. Heat, smoke, and steam were gushing up from below. When he reached the forward machine-gun platform, one deck below sky control, he told the men to make their way below as best they could. The heat here was much more intense, with thick black smoke pouring from the clipping room.

Craighill tried to open the hatches where men were trapped, but fire always drove him back. Then he returned to the bridge. Ladders being all torn up and on fire, a few survivors were rigging lines with which to lower themselves down. After a while he managed to clamber down one of the broken ladders to the conning tower deck. A large-caliber shell, probably 8-inch, had torn a huge hole in the port and after bulkheads of the port stateroom and taken a large section out of the fire control tube, which was burning inside. On the communication platform he found scores of dead and injured; with the help of others, he moved some of the wounded down to the next deck. The worst fires seemed to be at the after end of the searchlight platform. Attempts were made to put them out with pieces of canvas. Two men found a bucket and began dipping water from over the side. Life rafts, planes, and boat deck were all ablaze.

"Time seemed to be standing still, and everybody was dying," *Life* photographer Morse recalled. He had been asleep for a few hours when the alarm sounded. He grabbed his clothing, his life preserver, his camera, and lots of film and made his way to a spot he had already picked out, just in case the ship engaged in battle. It was a good position for photographs, just below the bridge: "What a scene! The sky was lit up with shelling and fires on ships. Ships were shelling ships and ships were sinking around us. I kept shooting like mad. Sailors were being hit all around us, and sailors were being killed just next to me." After a while Morse found a safe place for his camera on a hook near the bridge and joined sailors throwing wounded men into the water. Everyone was slipping and sliding on the bloody decks.

The aft battle dressing station was hit early, probably by one of the *Chokai*'s torpedoes. It had been quiet at first. Chaplain Schwyhart was at his station with a junior medical officer and the chief pharmacist's mate, Warrant Officer Frederick Moody, when the first casualties arrived, men mainly suffering from heat exhaustion or minor lacerations. About ten minutes later, the first seriously wounded men arrived, some with fearful burns, severed limbs, and broken bones. The chaplain tried to get in touch with Commander Blackwood, senior medical officer, in the forward battle dressing station. His phone rang at the other end but there was no reply.

Commander Blackwood was busy sewing up the slashed jaw of a black mess attendant when a shell exploded in the forward station. He and every member of the medical team were killed. The patient toppled from the operating table and escaped without serious injury, holding his broken jaw with one hand. The midships battle dressing station continued to tend patients, but in the aft station, corpsmen and patients were being knocked down every few seconds. They didn't know the ship was settling until a huge refrigerator toppled over and rolled thunderously toward the port side. "Then we knew the shape the ship was in," Warrant Officer Moody said. "We took the wounded, the one fellow in the bunk room and the other five and got them through a small hatch." There was no one left below in that part of the ship.

Gunnery officer Adams, making his way along the gun deck, saw many hits in the vicinity of the 5-inch battery. Dead and wounded lay at each gun. Only the no. 1 gun was still firing. After the rest of the crew had been wiped out, platoon Sergeant R. L. Harmon, USMC, and Ensign R. Peters manned the gun and reported scoring a hit on the conning tower of a submarine.

Some time after 0200, searchlights from two destroyers illuminated the ship. Riefkohl at first thought that these were friendly and tried to signal them, only to find that his colors at the gaff on the mainmast had long since been carried away. He ordered another large set raised on the foremast of the starboard signal yard and illuminated. Although the side of the ship was badly damaged and the signal flags in the starboard rack had been burned to shreds, chief signalman Moore soon had the new colors flying high on the one remaining halyard on the starboard yardarm, plainly visible in the glare of enemy searchlights.

The Japanese mistook the big red-striped flag for an admiral's and increased fire on the ship. Riefkohl sent a messenger to pass the order for fire on the lights. There were no guns left with which to fire. Then the captain pleaded for funnel smoke to hide his dying ship. None could be made.

When lights were trained on the *Vincennes* once more, Riefkohl believed that they also came from friendly ships: "One destroyer was then observed crossing our starboard bow from port to starboard, while the other was crossing from starboard to port. The one crossing from port to starboard may have been an enemy, but as the two vessels barely missed colliding and did not fire on one another, it is believed that they were both friendly. One DD [destroyer] on our starboard hand, probably the *Wilson,* was observed firing star shell and what appeared as heavy anti-aircraft machine-gun fire."

Neither of the American destroyers in the group was using searchlights. Their commanders held fast to Admiral Crutchley's rule to illuminate only if specifically ordered to do so. Captain Riefkohl believed that these "inexperienced skippers" took the instructions too literally: "Counterillumination was not attempted as enemy searchlight was believed to be on a destroyer and illumination of enemy by our destroyers was expected."[8] He had no means of communicating an order to his destroyers to illuminate, nor did he know where they were. He had last seen the *Wilson* just before 0158, when he turned to starboard.

And now the *Vincennes* was hit again, this time by fire from the *Furutaka.* Three or more shells, none of which penetrated, hit turret no. 3. The new attacker was joined by the *Tenryu* and the *Yubari,* which had come around the other side of the *Vincennes* group, between it and Savo Island. Up to about 0200 they had both withheld torpedo attacks on the group, but now the *Tenryu,* smarting from her encounter with the *Chicago* and *Patterson,* maneuvered to launch her still plentiful supply. The *Yubari,* slightly ahead of her, was followed by the *Furutaka,* which had already sent off her complement of eight torpedoes at the *Chicago* group.

The *Tenryu,* having launched six torpedoes at the *Quincy* at a range of about 3,000 yards, believed that the American cruiser had sunk. Minutes later the *Yubari* had fired four torpedoes toward the *Vincennes.* Rear Admiral Matsuyama said that from the *Tenryu* he could clearly see the silhouettes of the northern group. Each of the American cruisers was under fire for some ten minutes, so seriously damaged as to make close-range operations "reasonably safe." They appeared to be operating without direction.

At least one torpedo hit the port side of the *Vincennes*'s no. 1 fireroom. This was the *Yubari*'s "low-order detonation torpedo." It put the room out of action and killed everyone there.

Lieutenant Commander Edmund Phillip Di Giannantonio, assistant engineering officer in the after engine room, felt the ship rise out of the water and lurch to starboard. "She shuddered, shook, throbbed and quivered like a man with a malarial chill, staggered momentarily and then slowly rolled to port." He got to the phone and called the fireroom. There was no answer. He now had only one channel open for communication, the forward engine room, and was about to contact the officer in charge there when another, much closer hit occurred. It wasn't muffled this time, more like a blast. His eardrums bursting, Di Giannantonio found himself still on the phone circuit. He called the forward engine room. That circuit was also dead.

As soon as the lights came back on, he called, "Anyone hurt?" Chief machinist mate Baker bellowed back, "No, everyone's okay!" Each man was in the same place, manning the same pieces of machinery, as though nothing had happened. Di Giannantonio looked at the men on the lower grating. Their faces were covered with soot, obstructed by smoke and steam, but he could see the whites of their eyes looking up at him, waiting for his next command. Their training had paid off: the idea was to keep the engines going as long as there was steam.

As the western group of Japanese ships "went out on the starboard side and headed right out to sea," Captain Riefkohl saw that his ship was listing heavily to port as a result of the last torpedo hit. He directed that all life rafts still serviceable be put over the side. There were about eight of various sizes. Most of the others had been burned and could not be launched. He sent a messenger to damage control central to ask if the list might be corrected, but the man could not get through.

Steam pressure had dropped as the firerooms went out of commission and now, in Di Giannantonio's engine room, there was a terrific crash and then the hissing of a leak. Scalding steam engulfed the space, swallowing up the supply of air. All communication went dead and engine room control instruments were put out of action. "Close the throttles halfway and stand by to abandon the engine room," Di Giannantonio called. No one rushed to get out. The ship was listing to port now. Someone tried to open the port escape but found it jammed tight. The others waited while he climbed the ladder to open the starboard hatch. Then, in single file, they proceeded to freedom and fresh air. After making one last round of the engine room, yelling out for stragglers, Di

Giannantonio got topside to find it ablaze with fire. He was above the waterline, "in hell."

Men held flashlights so that others hanging on lines could jump and, if fortunate, catch a raft as it went by. Craighill, with Lieutenant Badger cutting down rafts high above the searchlight towers, watched as men flung themselves after the rafts into the sea. He went to the starboard side to look for wounded and found Lieutenant Commander Mullan prostrate from broken limbs and other injuries. With Badger's life belt, Mullan was lowered into a raft.

The last hits on the American command ship came from the *Chokai,* which fired a few desultory shots at the ship and then changed course. Mikawa reported that the three American cruisers had suffered direct hits by shell fire and torpedoes. "They burst into flames which enveloped the ships, gushed black smoke, slowly listed and sank." It was a premature report. None of the cruisers sank at this time.

Those able to walk helped the wounded and put life jackets on them as they were lowered to rafts in the water. But there were not enough life jackets for all hands. "A few men who could not swim and who had remained among the last," Riefkohl wrote, "when no life-jackets were available, were helped by others, but it is believed some of these were lost by drowning."

With the list increasing, it became apparent that the ship could not remain afloat and Riefkohl gave the order to abandon ship. At about 0240 he left the bridge with his talker, chief yeoman Stucker, and his marine orderly, Corporal J. L. Patrick, and went down to the upper deck to pass the word along.

The ship's whole superstructure was on fire and she was rapidly rolling over. Gun decks were awash. Medical officers Lieutenant Commander Samuel Isquith and Lieutenant W. A. Newman got the wounded into life jackets and helped open the doors so that one by one men could go over the side. By this time, the blazing superstructure was crumbling. Flaming beams tumbled to the deck, cutting off all escape on the port side. Isquith went off to the starboard rail and poised for a dive. As he went over, something hit his knee, and plunging into the water, he narrowly missed the after propeller blade.

Men were swimming for life rafts, yelling and screaming as they clutched at floating debris. Chaplain Schwyhart inflated his life belt and stepped over the rail on the port side, then remembered that he should take off his shoes. He leaned over the rail and with one hand attempted to undo the laces. At that moment, a terrifying sound erupted as if the ship was being twisted. There being no freeboard, Schwyhart simply stepped into the sea and began to swim.

Riefkohl, too, literally walked into the sea, ten minutes after he had given the order to abandon ship. "The ship went over and her mast hit the water near me," he wrote in his action report. "She turned turtle and went down by the head at about 0250."

Lieutenant Commander Craighill had left just before the captain. "The top decks," he wrote, "particularly amidships, were brightly lighted by the numerous fires, and, as we kicked away, I could see no signs of life about them, except one man on the well deck, who eventually made his way to the starboard bulwark, just forward of the catapult tower, and climbed over the rail. When we were about 200 yards off the ship, she finally reached her beam ends, seemed to hesitate before the stacks went under, and with burning planes and cranes crashing to port and into the water, . . . turned slowly over and went down bow first."

Men struggling in the water saw her propeller shaft rise high in the air, as though in final salute.

10

"Give Them Hell!"

The *Quincy,* center ship in the line of American cruisers, was the first to go to general quarters, but misfortune dogged her from the start. Owing to lack of information about the southern force, misunderstandings, the belief that submarines were the main threat, and sheer bad luck, she received the worst battering of all the Allied ships. In return, she inflicted the heaviest damage on the Japanese.

The cruiser had recently arrived in the Pacific after a tour of convoy duty in the Atlantic, where the danger of submarines was a major concern.[1] There main battery defense was regarded as less important than torpedo defense. Captain Moore had additional reason to regard submarines as a serious menace. He had had two contact reports of submarines approaching Tulagi. The first, received at 0710 on 8 August, stated, "Enemy submarine reported near. May enter area today." The second, "There are possibly one or more submarines in the transport area," was received at 1207. Other ships reported the presence of submarines during the night. HMAS *Hobart,* in the *San Juan* group, illuminated one on the surface, only to find that it was the wreckage of a Japanese torpedo bomber shot down the previous day.

On 8 August the *Quincy* was at general quarters from about half an hour before dawn until after sunset, and in condition readiness 2 during the night. Four boilers were in use, the other four hot. Ammunition condition 1 was set in main and antiaircraft batteries. All 8-inch guns were loaded and ready to fire, but not primed. Task force instructions required four antiaircraft director crews for condition 2, but there were not enough officers or fire controlmen.[2]

Many men who should have been on watch in their regular battle

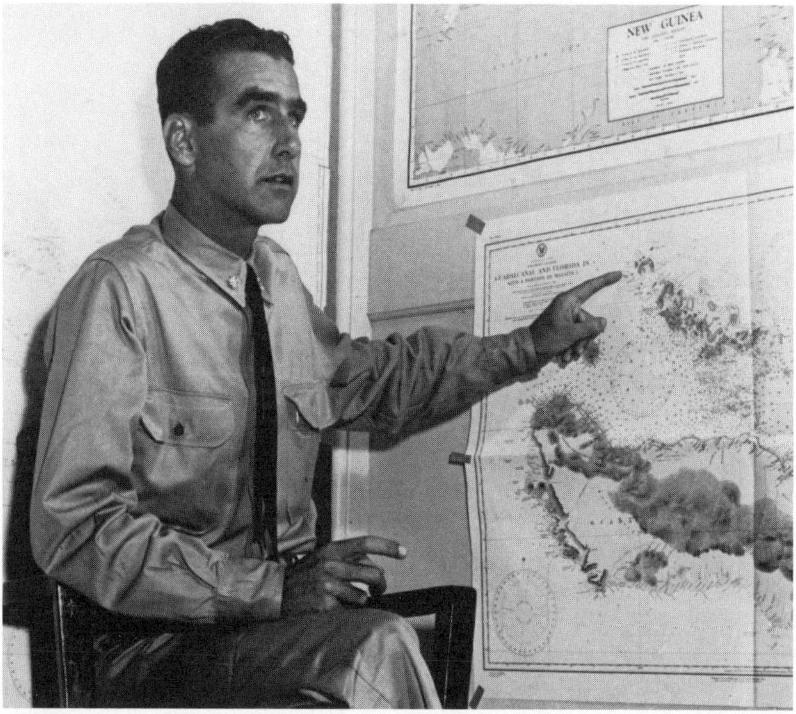

Lieutenant Commander Harry B. Heneberger, USN, the Quincy's *gunnery officer, describes the action at Savo Island. (80-G-16521, National Archives)*

stations were on watch in other stations, often in distant parts of the ship. Three-hour watches were being stood. Watertight doors and hatches had been battened down, part of the procedure for attack against submarines.

At midnight, Captain Moore was in his emergency cabin on the bridge. The navigator was in the chart house and the assistant gunnery officer, Lieutenant John D. Andrew, was supervisor of the watch, due to be relieved by Lieutenant Commander Edmund Billings. A junior officer, Lieutenant Charles P. Clarke, USNR, was acting as officer of the deck. Just before he took over, the bridge had sent word to control that radar contact had been made with a plane coming over Savo Island. Clarke told control radar to pick it up, but they were unable to do so. The executive officer, Commander William C. Gray, talked to him about the plane but decided that it was one of their own. Clarke protested, saying all their planes had been recovered by dark.

Gunnery officer Lieutenant Commander Harry B. Heneberger, off duty, was called to the bridge to confer with the two officers. The executive officer told him that Clarke's report was in error, information that Heneberger passed to gunnery officer Andrew. The ship had been fighting off Japanese plane attacks for two days, none of which were conducted by cruiser planes, so there was no reason why Andrew should believe this plane came from a Japanese cruiser. Five or so minutes later, instructions from the bridge said to disregard the contact. The *Quincy* would not go to general quarters. "The remarks of the executive officer at the time," Clarke recalled, made him "feel like a jittery schoolboy."

Soon after midnight sky control reported another plane. Once more, radar did not pick it up. At about 0120 an order came from the *Vincennes* by TBS that the next change of course would be at 0150 instead of 0200. Ten minutes later another plane was heard passing starboard, flying forward, and shortly afterwards a plane was heard on the port quarter. None of these passings was close aboard. Lieutenant Commander Billings went to the signal bridge to investigate but on his return said he had seen nothing and heard nothing. These contacts were not reported to Captain Moore.

The *Patterson*'s warning of three strange ships inside Savo Island came over the TBS about 0145, just as Clarke was relieved by Lieutenant (j.g.) Josiah Baldwin as officer of the deck. Forward control saw shell bursts astern at a distance of about 9,000 yards and, thinking these had been fired by destroyers in the vicinity of Tulagi to locate the planes previously heard, reported to the bridge. Billings sounded the general alarm, and Baldwin told the bugler to sound general quarters. Clarke sent the quatermaster to wake the captain. In the confusion the *Patterson*'s vital warning was not received in gunnery control stations.

The next warning came when the silhouettes of three ships were seen in the illumination provided by the searchlights of the two Japanese light cruisers engaged with the *Patterson.* The ships were rounding the southern corner of Savo Island, or so the *Quincy* thought, mistaking the massive cloud bank south of the island for land itself. The enemy was actually much closer.

Lieutenant Clarke had a brief glimpse of the ships—three cruisers and what he believed to be a destroyer, obviously enemy. The cruisers had three turrets forward and two aft, the center turret being the highest, towering superstructures, high bows, and long forecastles. Captain Moore was on the bridge by this time, but he did not broadcast the sighting of the ships to the *Vincennes,* nor did he alert his gunnery department to their presence.[3]

The other ships of the *Vincennes* group, with the exception of the *Astoria,* were in the process of assuming condition 1 as the searchlights came on. This usually took about five minutes during daylight, a minute or so more at night. But, as mentioned, watchstanders in the *Quincy* were not all stationed at their regular battle stations. Lieutenant Andrew later wrote:

> Condition of readiness two is worse than useless when the stations manned are such as to require a shift of personnel when general quarters is sounded. Absolutely no shifting of personnel from one station to another should be necessary. In most cases duplicate stations exist, for example control forward and control aft. Where this is not true, as in plot, half of the personnel regularly assigned should be alert, the others sleeping on or near the station. Such a system would permit opening fire at any instant, and fire would only be augmented, not interrupted or delayed, by going to general quarters.

Quartermaster second-class Lawrence L. Morris had stood the 2000 to 2400 watch with the officer of the deck. No sooner had he settled in his bunk and dozed off when general quarters sounded. "The whole ship's crew was in a turmoil, going here, going there, rushing to their battle stations," he recalled.

Men standing watch on the no. 4 5-inch gun when the action started broke open the locked ready service boxes and climbed over the hangar to get to the no. 3 turret, which had already been hit and was out of action. Just before the action began some general quarters stations had been changed, and many men were killed at stations where they had been earlier. It was the same in the forward engine room.

The *Quincy*'s shifting of stations took so long that many officers and men never reached their battle stations. The glare of the searchlights from the *Tenryu, Yubari,* and *Aoba,* which took the *Quincy* by surprise, was so brilliant that Japanese lookouts could see her guns trained in, fore and aft.

When Heneberger arrived on the control platform Andrew did his best to acquaint him with the situation, but by this time the first shells were landing off the *Quincy*'s bow. During the hubbub of going to general quarters, Heneberger and Andrew tried to identify enemy positions and get the battery trained out to port, toward the lights about 6,000 yards away.

At this point, two orders came from the *Vincennes:* "Steam at standard speed, fifteen knots!" and "Fire on the searchlights!" Captain

The USS Quincy *illuminated by Japanese searchlights. The picture was taken from a Japanese cruiser. (NH 50346, U.S. Naval Historical Center)*

Moore immediately ordered fire, but on reflection decided that the ships might be friendly. He ordered recognition lights turned on, thinking an enemy submarine had been found on the surface and that friendly ships in the southern group were illuminating it.

"Which way should I turn?" Captain Moore asked Clarke.[4] "To starboard," Clarke replied. From the bridge they saw the *Vincennes,* on fire, turn to port, forcing the *Quincy* on the port beam. One of the quartermasters handed Clarke a helmet and he ran to the starboard side of the bridge. Shells were flying across the signal bridge and he yelled to the signalmen to lie down. Then, crawling to the port side of the bridge, he witnessed one of the cruiser's planes catch fire on the catapult.

The *Quincy* carried five planes, each holding 135 gallons of gasoline. Whereas the *Vincennes* and the *Astoria* had drained their planes, the *Quincy* had not. To empty them would have taken at least three hours per plane, plus another hour per plane to refill them. Oil would also have to be removed. During this period and for the entire night, they would be out of commission. According to at least five of the nine aviators aboard the *Quincy,* the planes were not worth the hazard. As it turned out, planes on all three cruisers, drained of fuel or not, burned like bonfires, giving the Japanese perfect firing aim.

An order came from the bridge, "Shoot off the plane!" It was too late, so valiant efforts were made to toss the burning aircraft over the side. It couldn't be hoisted across the rails on fire, but before hoses with foamite could be rigged, the water cut off. Two junior air crew, Lieutenants L. H. Reagan and H. W. Smith, ran with others to don their flying suits. Another, Lieutenant T. A. Chisholm, was already dressed for taking off when an order to warm up the planes was countermanned.

Just before plot reported ready to forward control, the ship's 1.1-inch gun mounts were hit on the main deck aft. This was immediately followed by a nine-gun salvo from the *Quincy*'s turrets. After no more than two salvos had been fired, the *Quincy* swung rapidly to starboard, thus preventing turrets nos. 1 and 2 from bearing on the enemy. Another hit prevented the use of the main battery and turret no. 3. The two other turrets were trained out to starboard and resumed firing, but receiving further damage, they only got off one or two partial salvos.

During the change of course, the fabric-covered wings of planes on the well deck burst into flames, apparently from a salvo fired at one of the other American cruisers. For the next four minutes the heavy cruiser *Aoba,* having found her range, poured salvo after salvo on the *Quincy*. Shells from the fourth salvo went straight through the bridge house, killing or wounding several men, including the supervisory officer of the watch, whose battle station was with one of the repair parties. Conferring with the captain, Billings had been delayed until after the setting of condition 1 and had decided to stay on the bridge rather than open doors and hatches. This impaired the ship's watertight integrity while under fire.

With bullets and splinters flying around the bridge, Lieutenant Clarke pushed his chief signalman to the ground and then dove down himself, flat on his face. Water from the 1.1-inch-gun cooling tank gushed through a hole in the shield and drenched him. When he reached the pilot house he found that Lieutenant Commander Billings had been badly wounded, one side of his face practically blown away. He kept on saying, "I'm all right." Clarke grabbed him by the arm and asked if he wanted first-aid. "No," Billings repeated. "I'm okay, tell everyone to keep calm." He died later of his wounds. Then the JX talker was hit, and went down by the pyrotechnics locker. Clarke pulled him away from the locker, thinking it would explode. The man appeared to be dead, or at least unconscious.

Soon after the hit on the bridge, star shells were placed in the fuze pots of the port battery and the ship sent off two salvos above the low-hanging clouds. They burned out before dropping through the heavy overcast.

Then the *Aoba*'s fifth salvo hit, knocking out the *Quincy*'s four antiaircraft guns and killing most of the gunmen. Ammunition in the ready service boxes exploded and flying fragments cut the cartridge cases of star shells so that they burned like Roman candles. The port battery, too, was put out of action. New fires started in the mess hall, library, log room, sick bay, and supply office. All but one man was killed in the forward repair station. All around these spaces, glowing granules of incendiary material the size of Grape Nuts burned everything with which they came in contact.

A further heavy explosion somewhere below deck knocked down nearly everybody left on the guns. A sight setter was thrown clear of his gun and landed inboard on the deck. This was the first torpedo hit. There were more to follow.

Captain Moore saw that the *Vincennes* was making a radical turn of about 40 degrees to port. He had received no instructions and, not knowing what Captain Riefkohl had in mind, decided to change course to port as well so that he could bring more of his guns to bear. By now all the planes were on fire. With gasoline spraying everywhere and the hangar curtain removed because of blast damage received at Guadalcanal, fire had enveloped the planes in the hangar within seconds. The Japanese no longer had need of searchlights—the flames from the *Astoria* and the *Quincy* were enough.

When quartermaster Morris reached topside on his way to conning control 11, he saw flares overhead. "The ship was lit up like a city," he said. "Gunfire was going off when I reached my station and put on the earphones. It was exactly 0145. As the remainder of personnel reached Conn 11 the boat deck, well deck and planes were on fire. The executive officer, Commander Gray, never did arrive and the senior man, chief petty officer Leslie, asked me to contact the bridge to see if they were aware of the whereabouts of Commander Gray. The answer was that he was on the bridge."

Distress calls came from quartermaster Warren Clegg to say that water was coming into central station and the men there were trapped. With the deck buckled and warped, the dogs on the hatches could not be pried open. "The last I heard were screams of agony and prayers for help," Morris recalled. "Then we lost communication with them. No one, including quartermaster Clegg, survived that area of the ship."

Some men topside cut the dogs off a nearby hatch, allowing men to escape from below decks. One or two men who had to go through escape hatches on their way to battle stations, because of their size, could not get through and were trapped.

At 0204, at least two torpedoes from the *Tenryu* struck the *Quincy*'s port side, one in the vicinity of central station, the other near the two firerooms aft. They had covered the 3,000-yard distance in two minutes flat.

No men escaped from firerooms nos. 3 and 4. Exactly what had happened in no. 4 was unclear, except that it had been hit and was on fire. Men trying to enter found the deck raised several feet. They could see little through the flames and the smoke, nothing moving. Radio 1, also hit, was filled with shrapnel. Both of the ship's stacks had been perforated, the galley was on fire, the hangar and well deck were an inferno, boats on the boat deck were ablaze, and fires on the fantail were out of control. Steam roared from the stacks, scalding everyone in its path. On the gun deck, boiling water from broken pipes showered down on the few remaining gunners as they tried to escape.

After firing her torpedoes, the *Tenryu* swung back to starboard and rained fire into the port side of the *Quincy*. Then she left the cruiser and chased after the screening destroyer *Wilson*, shelling her with 5.5-inch guns for about a minute. It was a temporary change of target. She returned to the *Quincy*, this time to assess the damage her torpedoes had done, and decided the cruiser was sinking. But the *Tenryu* was mistaken. The *Quincy* had another thirty minutes or so before she gave up the fight.

One torpedo had hit the port side of no. 4 fireroom, smashing it to bits. The last words from gun plot, via telephone, told of the explosion. From the engine rooms Lieutenant Commander Eugene E. Elmore sent a message to the captain that the ship would have to stop dead in her tracks. He was not heard of again. All communication from the engine rooms was lost and they became sealed traps from which no man escaped.

Sick bay and the battle dressing stations were practically wiped out. Many patients were engulfed in flames and choking smoke, some being dragged, carried, and pushed along by the able-bodied. Men passed over their life preservers to the wounded and yanked laces from boots to make tourniquets. Shirts and other clothing served as dressings.

The *Quincy,* blazing from stem to stern, was about to come hard up against the *Chokai.* Shells dropped all around the American cruiser, sending up great columns of water. She continued to fight back, running as though out of control, disappearing beneath the columns only to reappear seconds later.

According to Captain Masao Sawa of the *Kinugasa,* his ship had to take full rudder to avoid the blazing cruiser. Captain Takahashi saw the *Quincy* sweeping toward his ship, the *Kako,* and ordered everything, even 13- and 25-mm machine guns, unleashed on her. Lieutenant Tsuneo Yonei, the torpedo officer, fired two torpedoes. These fell short.

Shortly afterwards, the *Quincy* saw two searchlights off her starboard quarter to the southeast. She trained on the target at short range and at 0205 fired her third—and last—main battery salvo, employing the six guns of her two forward turrets. One officer followed the tracers in flight and saw them go close to what appeared to be an enemy cruiser. Smoke rose up through the searchlight beam, and he felt certain the *Quincy* had made a hit. A second officer watched as the ship burst into flames, silhouetting another ship closer to her on the same bearing, possibly the *Kako.*

The *Furutaka,* astern of the *Kako,* made a sharp turn to port and separated from the leading Japanese ships. According to her gunnery officer, Lieutenant Nobuyoshi Komatsu, this was necessary because men on the bridge were blinded by the flashes of gunfire from following ships.

The western group of Japanese ships, the light cruisers, now decided to attack all three American cruisers with torpedoes. The *Tenryu* readied her mounts and maneuvered to fire.

Trapped between the *Chokai* and *Furutaka* groups, the *Quincy* was doomed. At least one enemy heavy cruiser was moving northward, on her starboard quarter, and one or more ships were on her port quarter. Captain Moore realized that the *Vincennes* group was no longer coordinated. Each commanding officer had to fight his ship independently, and whichever way he turned he ran the danger of colliding with either the *Vincennes* or the *Astoria.* For a time, the two Japanese forces divided their main battery fire between the *Quincy* and the *Vincennes,* now fairly close together in bearing and each self-illuminated.

On the *Chokai*'s bridge, Commander Ohmae, one of Mikawa's staff officers, stood amazed as tracers wafted back and forth between ships:

"Such counter efforts merely made a colorful spectacle, and gave us no concern. Second by second, however, the range decreased, and now we could actually distinguish the shapes of individuals running along the decks of the enemy ships. The fight was getting to close quarters."

While the *Chokai* continued her relentless fire on the *Astoria,* Captain Moore decided to steer the *Quincy* roughly parallel to the mean track of both Japanese groups as they came down on either side. His speed was only about fifteen knots, and he reasoned that that of the two Japanese ships was about twenty-six. He would sell his ship for a price. "We're going down between them—give them hell!" These were the last words control heard from the bridge. Soon afterwards, forward control lost communication with most parts of the ship. The forward sky director lost power. Director 1 was jammed in train. Investigation revealed that the forestay, carried away, had caught the radar antenna and the right arm of the spotting glass.

They were unaware of it in control, but a shell had ripped through the bridge house, killing almost everyone, including Commander Gray, the navigator, and the damage control officer. Battle station 2 took a direct hit in the conning tower, killing eight men. Quartermaster Morris, badly wounded by shrapnel, was the only survivor. He crawled through the flames, over the bodies of his shipmates, climbed over the gun shield, lowered himself on a monkey rope until it broke, then dropped to the top of no. 3 turret.

Several of the *Quincy*'s 8-inch shells scored on the *Chokai,* penetrating the operation room just aft of the bridge, killing thirty-four men, and burning all the charts there. Another 8-inch shell that hit near the aviation crane caused structural damage. Only the *Chokai*'s machine guns were still firing. Correspondent Niwa stepped over fallen men as he made his way down the ladder to the wardroom. As he went he pulled a splinter of shrapnel out of his arm and put it in his pocket as a souvenir. On every step there were sailors being treated for wounds. Others were already dead or dying. In the wardroom as he was being patched up, Niwa remembered the mess a couple of hours earlier at the long wardroom table, now turned into an operating bench. Every chair was occupied by a wounded man. The plush sofa covers were splashed with blood. Perhaps, after all, it had not been such an easy battle. He opened up his notebook to record last-minute impressions and found it stained with blood. His pencil had been cut in half.

Commander Ohmae attributed the hit on the *Chokai* to the *Quincy*'s last shot:

> From a group of three enemy ships the center one bore out and down on us as if intending to ram. Though her entire hull from amidships aft was enveloped in flames, her only forward guns were firing with great spirit. She was a brave ship, manned by brave men. . . . She certainly made an impression on our force. We were all shocked and disconcerted momentarily, but returned at once to the heat of battle, as the *Chokai* continued firing and directing fire at the enemy targets.

Ohmae entered the operations room and found it peppered with holes from shell fragments. "Had the 8-inch hit on the *Chokai* been five meters forward," he commented, "it would have killed Admiral Mikawa and his entire staff."

The heavy cruiser *Aoba* was not far behind the Japanese flagship. One minute after the *Chokai* was hit, she noticed that the *Quincy* had changed course to the northeast, and "although afire and penetrated by shells like a bee-hive, rushed to attack our battle formation from 20 degrees to port." The *Aoba* turned to port to make way for the two light cruisers and at about 0206 fired one salvo at the *Quincy*'s bridge. This "cleared out the pilot house."

Almost everyone on the cruiser's bridge was instantly killed. A junior officer, Lieutenant J. M. Mee, picked himself up from the deck and went to the bridge house to hear Captain Moore, collapsed beside the steering control, whisper, "Transfer control to battle 2." Mee, thinking Moore had breathed his last and finding himself unable to communicate with the damaged bridge, ran out to find a telephone still in commission so that he could communicate the captain's dying orders.

Battle station 2 had already been demolished, but this was not known in control. There Lieutenant Commander Heneberger and Lieutenant Andrew discovered that regular communication with the turrets had been cut off. They tried to establish auxiliary circuits, but to no avail. Since all other means of communication were lost, Andrew went down to the bridge to get information from Captain Moore and inform him of the damage to the battery.

The bridge was a shambles of dead bodies, with only three or four people still on their feet. According to Andrew, "In the pilot house itself the only person standing was the signalman at the wheel who was vainly endeavouring to check the ship's swing to starboard and to bring her to port. On questioning him, I found that the captain, who was at that time lying near the wheel, had instructed him to beach the ship and he was trying to head her for Savo Island." Andrew stepped to the port side of the pilot house to search for the island. The ship was heeling rapidly to port and sinking by the bow. At that moment, Captain Moore straightened up, fell back, and died without uttering any sound apart from a moan.

Other hits from the starboard side had damaged turret no. 1. Turret no. 2 was also out of action. By this time the eastern group of Japanese cruisers had ceased firing, and the *Tenryu* and the *Yubari* were firing only intermittently. The *Quincy*'s forecastle was awash, water sloshing halfway over the gun deck, and the list forced men to abandon the forward engine room. No one gave orders to abandon the after room, however, and it continued to operate as the ship slowly settled.

With all steering lost, it was impossible to carry out Captain Moore's dying order to beach the ship. There was no acting commander. Lieutenant Commander Heneberger, fifth in line below the captain, was convinced that some of his seniors were alive. He had no information on the fate of the damage control officer, the engineering officer, or the executive officer. Continuing to act as gunnery officer, and realizing the *Quincy* was doomed, he gave orders to gunnery personnel to prepare to abandon ship.

The *Quincy* drifted helplessly in the water, blazing and continuing to sink. Heneberger ordered his men to cut free life rafts, nets, and life preservers and throw them overboard. Anything at all that would float, including 5-inch-shell tanks, went over the side. At 0216, as the Japanese ceased the engagement and withdrew, all survivors in the gunnery area prepared to abandon ship. Four minutes later the *Quincy* was drifting westward, about 12,000 yards off the center of Savo Island.

Then another torpedo hit, on the starboard side below her 5-inch mount. A screaming blast of steam escaped from the forward stack and steam pressure dropped precipitously. The ship gradually slowed as salt water in fireroom no. 2 rose to the firebox of boiler no. 2.

There were far too few life jackets to go around. Those below decks were impossible to reach because of fire and smoke; those topside were out of reach, lashed high up on the hangar bulkhead, the searchlight tower, and the forward superstructure. Some men were dazed, others so badly wounded that it was difficult to find anyone to help remove rafts and floater nets, which were covered with canvas and securely tied. Some, however, were freed, and men tossed them along with shell canisters and mattresses over the side or climbed down lines and slings to the water. Without anyone in command, there was no general order to abandon. As the ship turned slowly over, bow first, rolling to port, hundreds of men crawled, ran, rolled, and slid down her sides into the depths. Some were blown over the side. Others floated off the ship. Many, some seriously wounded, jumped from the well deck and gun platforms with nothing in the way of support.

Lieutenant Clarke reached the gun deck and, for the first time, noticed how heavily the ship was listing. He clambered up to gun deck no. 2 to get a floater net, but the canvas around it caught fire before he could release it. The deck was burning, the whole ship on fire. Someone threw a lifejacket at him. He put it on and stepped into the sea.

Lieutenant Commander Heneberger, still unaware that he was the *Quincy*'s senior officer, walked into the sea, along with most of the other surviving offiers. Captain Moore would go down with his ship, his body later washing up on Savo Island to be buried by natives, one of whom kept his Annapolis class ring. All the other senior officers, the executive officer, navigator, engineering officer, watch supervisor, and first lieutenant would also go down with the *Quincy.*

Assistant gunnery officer Andrew, now the second senior line officer, reported that the spirit of the crew was excellent: "I did not note, either on board ship or in the water, any case of cowardice or any other lack of discipline." Heneberger said that, despite the suffering of many of the men, there had been no signs of panic or disorder. He remembered one man, Lieutenant W. A. Hall, the ship's dentist. Before the ship was abandoned, Hall, severely wounded himself, had made his way around the gun deck trying to help others. The last time Heneberger saw him he was sitting on deck, propped up against the bulkhead, holding the stump of the leg of pharmacist's mate Paul William Scott against his body in an unsuccessful attempt to prevent him from bleeding to death.

Just after 0235, a tremendous explosion ripped into the ship. She capsized to port, her mast ablaze like a huge burning cross. Heneberger saw a hole in the port side of her bottom, which he estimated to be three or four feet wide and more than fifteen feet long. The bow went under, the stern rose, and she slid from view for eternity.

11

The Coffin Boat of Friendship

In the *Astoria,* rear ship of the American line, Captain Greenman had received two reports regarding the possible approach of a Japanese force, one believed to have been sent out by a coastwatcher on Bougainville, the other from Honolulu. She had also heard from Captain Riefkohl in the *Vincennes* that submarines were in the area. With this information, and the general uncertainty of the situation in mind, night orders were prepared. Patrol areas and force locations were delineated on the chart and commander screening group instructions for night action laid out. These emphasized the maintenance of continuous radar watch, the alertness of lookouts, the possibility of submarine attack, station keeping, and general readiness.

The *Astoria* was an old Pacific hand. The Japanese called her the Coffin Boat of Friendship, a reference to the cruiser's journey to Japan three years earlier, when Admiral Turner, then commanding officer of the ship, carried Ambassador Saito's ashes back to his homeland. To the Japanese, Turner looked like a retired diplomat rather than a naval officer. Both he and the Japanese foreign minister had agreed that friendship between the two countries should last forever.

The *Astoria* had cleared Pearl Harbor with the *Lexington, Portland,* and *Chicago* two days before the attack there. She was escort to the *Lexington* and the *Yorktown* during the Battle of the Coral Sea, and at Midway was screening the *Yorktown* when she was sunk by torpedos and bombs.[1] Captain Greenman had been in command of the *Astoria* at Midway. More recently, she had accompanied the *Saratoga* to Pearl Harbor for fueling.

Greenman believed his ship was well trained. The only real weakness was night battle preparation, so during the week at Pearl he took the opportunity to conduct firing and battle drills, held almost every night before leaving for Operation Watchtower. The drills, conducted in both readiness condition 1 and 2, were discontinued on arrival at Guadalcanal, word being passed that the next time action was announced, it would be with the enemy.

The ship had been two days in the area, and Greenman was certain that the Japanese were going to do something about it. He knew they could arrive around 0300. The fact that a force was coming down made that clear. He expected to receive more information about it, confident that planes would pick up the enemy and he would be advised.

The *Astoria* was in condition 2 and material condition Zed, steaming on four boilers, with the other four hot. Her hull had been scraped during the stay in Fiji, and all interior paint had been removed from below-deck bulkheads and passageways. Greenman had received neither Admiral Crutchley's message regarding a change in the condition of readiness nor its later modification. All guns of the main battery were loaded, with two guns in each turret manned. All men were at their battle stations, except for a few in sick bay suffering from heat exhaustion and one who had just undergone an appendix operation.

Greenman did not believe his crew was particularly fatigued. They had been on edge for nearly forty-eight hours, but "it was a game to them," nothing that would markedly impair their efficiency. This also applied to the officers. He had closed living spaces below the second deck and had men bring up mattresses to sleep near their battle stations. Meals were served to men at their stations. When someone left his station, he had to get permission from the officer in charge.

Just after 2300, Captain Greenman retired, fully clothed, to his emergency cabin on the bridge, sparsely equipped with a small bunk and washstand. The doors of the cabin led directly to the bridge and were kept open at all times. The executive officer, Commander Frank Shoup, was asleep in his cabin. A little while later, damage control officer Lieutenant Commander J. R. Topper relieved engineering officer Lieutenant Commander J. A. Hayes as supervisory officer of the deck.

Before retiring, Hayes told Topper that the guns and all lookouts were being kept on the alert for submarines, and that the captain had directed the ship to keep close to the *Vincennes* in order to receive the maximum protection of the two antisubmarine screen destroyers, the *Helm* and the *Wilson.* As far as Hayes knew, the southern force and the *San Juan* group were in the same formation and patrolling the same locations as the previous night. The *San Juan,* Hayes also informed Topper, had reported to the *Vincennes* over TBS at about 2330 that a plane was sighted flying eastward from Savo Island. This warning had been given to the captain.

Topper made meticulous notes in his night order book. Washroom and toilet drains were open, and ventilation was provided to spaces where men were sleeping or standing watch. Hatches to central station and steering aft were open, with two men standing by each hatch so that they could be closed instantly. All hatches and doors above the second deck were secured, except those necessary for limited traffic. Half of the repair parties were on station, on the alert.

Of all the heavy cruisers in the Allied groups, the *Astoria* appeared best prepared.

Just before midnight, the fire control radar failed in main battery forward. The after control radar had also been out of commission for some time, owing to a short circuit in the transformer that could not be repaired. The ship's battery was completely lacking in fire control. Chief radioman John Joseph Datko, having made temporary repairs to the forward set during the evening, decided that rather than attempting to fix it during the blackout, he would resume work at daylight.

Ten minutes after he had retired to the radio room to rest, he was awakened and told that Lieutenant Commander W. H. Truesdell, the gunnery officer, wanted repairs made immediately. He found some spare tubes and made his way to control.

Both forward and after battle lookouts heard the sound of planes passing overhead after 0115. They reported to the supervisor of the watch on deck, who concluded that the sounds were caused by a blower. He listened but could not identify any noise as coming from planes. Captain Greenman was not advised.

Exactly at midnight, the *Vincennes* changed course to 045 degrees (T). About four minutes later the *Astoria* changed course to follow the lead ship. While on this leg of the square, Topper noticed firing in the vicinity of Tulagi and remarked to Quartermaster R. A. Radke that the marines were not having much of a picnic. "I feel sorry for them," Radke said. Intermittent firing from this direction continued for some time.

About 0120 word came over TBS from the *Vincennes* that the formation would continue on course until 0140, when the ships would change course to starboard by column movement. At the appointed time, the *Vincennes* changed course to 315 degrees (T), the *Astoria* following by column movement.

Soon after the *Astoria* had steadied on course Topper felt the tremor of an underwater explosion. This he put down to a destroyer dropping depth charges. As there had been so many warnings of submarines in the area, he went out to the starboard wing of the bridge to discuss the sounds with the officer of the watch, Lieutenant (j.g.) N. A. Burkey. Burkey said that he had heard nothing, and had had his talker inform the officer of the watch in central station to be sure the men there were on the alert. Word came back that they too had felt a slight shaking below. Captain Greenman was not notified. The explosion may have been caused by the *Bagley*'s torpedoes. On the other hand, it could very well have come from the *Chokai*'s torpedoes, fired a minute earlier, as they exploded after their run past the *Chicago* group.

Meanwhile one of the talkers in either sky control or the forward battle lookout reported that a plane had been heard, but not seen. Topper walked to the starboard side of the pilot house, thinking that a submarine was attempting an attack on the transports in the Tulagi or Guadalcanal areas. All he heard was the sound of blowers just aft of turret no. 1.

Four flares had already fallen through the clouds, but the *Astoria* did not yet see flares or ships, nor did she hear gunfire. However, the *Ralph Talbot*'s warning had the lookouts continually scanning the skies. Another plane was reported overhead. Then the *Vincennes* came over TBS with a message concerning the next course change. Set for 0150, it was now to be postponed until 0200. The *Astoria* did not receive the *Patterson*'s urgent report of three strange ships passing west of Savo Island, because at the time the group commander was discussing the course change with his officers.

For a while, all was quiet on the dark sea. The Japanese force had split and was well on its way toward the Allied northern group. In the *Astoria*, Lieutenant George Baker, radio officer, reached the main radio room and began to decode the signal about Japanese ships sighted east of Bougainville.

Chief radioman Datko had the forward fire control radar working in about twenty minutes and, just before 0145, went outside to look over the railings. Gunnery officer Truesdell was testing the radar, which Datko had fitted with a new tube using the ships ahead as targets. The set was working perfectly.

The first indication that everything was not right came when a lookout on the bridge reported star shells off the port quarter. Seaman First-Class W. H. Baker, on watch in the forward battle lookout, saw splashes that he believed were from depth charges way out on the horizon. Then he spotted a searchlight trained on the *Astoria* and flares on her port side. At the same time, three planes appeared flying in formation toward the port bow. "They were about 150 feet above the water," Baker said. "They were close enough so that I could hear them." The planes flew on the edge of the searchlight beam and seemed to approach from a point behind it. Baker did not see them cross the beam.

It was not at once clear whether the lights came from star shells or flares. In sky control, Seaman Second-Class Lynn Hager saw four or five lights at a distance of about 5,000 yards. They were obscured by mist and did not illuminate very well, but after dropping a short distance they turned brilliant. Hager thought they came from a plane. Yeoman Second Class W. F. Putnam, talker in the pilot house, saw what he thought was a flare on the port quarter, followed almost immediately by several more. He made no report because Topper had also seen the string of lights and recognized the star shells as in fact aircraft flares over Guadalcanal, about 5,000 yards away. They seemed to be lighting up the *Astoria*'s stern. Topper raced to the door of the pilot house and told Lieutenant Burkey, officer of the deck, to alert the captain and "stand by the general alarm." According to Burkey, he called the captain from the door to his special bridge cabin, then went forward to the starboard side of the pilot house.

Gunnery officer Truesdell, on watch in the upper director, knew at once that the lights were flares. Near the southern corner of the group's patrol square, they were being used to illuminate the cruisers. He immediately ordered all stations alert and returned to the control station. The bridge asked if the lights were star shells or flares; he ordered his talker to say "flares." He told the bridge to go to general quarters and asked permission to open fire. The flares had been dropped by enemy planes, he believed, which meant enemy action. Receiving no reply from the bridge, he opened fire immediately.

At about 0154 quartermaster of the watch Radke saw one flare, just dying out, followed by another four. They were quite a distance away, astern of the ship, all roughly the same height and in a line about parallel to the *Astoria*'s stern. He started into the pilot house to stand by for the general alarm when a ship to port opened fire. Without orders, he rang the alarm. Just before he pulled the switch, he heard the order "Stand by the general alarm!" Before the alarm stopped ringing, the *Astoria* opened fire.

Radioman Datko's repair of the forward fire control radar had worked. The set had picked up nothing until about the time the flares appeared, but now Truesdell got a definite fix on an object at a range of 5,800 yards.[2] Crews in all turrets were ordered to open fire on range from the newly repaired fire control radar, and the ship's six 8-inch guns poured fire on what turned out to be the *Chokai.* At this point Truesdell's spotter Lieutenant (j.g.) Carl Sander, reported a ship in flames to the southeast. This was the *Canberra,* already dead in the water. On the way to his battle station in radio 1, Datko stopped to look over the rails and saw two ships on the port side, about 2,000 yards apart. As the one on the left burst into flames, he heard the alarm go. The last thing he remembered as he ran to his station was Truesdell's order for targets to load. Then, as he said, "Hell broke loose!"

According to the *Chokai*'s records, she opened fire on the *Astoria* at 0153. Few records of time were kept on the *Astoria.* Most survivors had no idea of the time events occurred. Yeoman Putnam, talker on the bridge, did however look at the pilot house clock when the flares were first seen. Just before the hands reached 0155, the *Astoria* fired her main battery. Immediately afterwards, Putnam heard general quarters sound.

As damage control officer Topper was searching the area beyond the flares, he felt the main battery salvo unleashed. "This gave me quite a surprise, for I had not given any order about opening fire, nor could I make out any ships in the vicinity of the flares," he said. A second salvo went off as Topper turned and started for the pilot house. He came face to face with the captain. "Who sounded the general alarm?" asked Greenman. "Who gave the order to commence firing? Mr. Topper, I think we are firing on our own ships. Let's not get excited and act too hasty. Cease firing!"

Captain Greenman was not alone in thinking that the ships were friendly. In sky control, Seaman Hager spotted what he thought was an Australian ship bearing about 270 degrees relative to the *Astoria,* and in a second saw her open fire in the general direction of the *Astoria*'s stern. Ensign Raymond McGrath, officer in charge of turret no. 2, heard a message by telephone from main battery control, "Flares on the port quarter. The *Australia* is firing!" In fact, the *Australia*'s guns were silent that night.

Topper, who thought the captain seemed calm and collected, insisted that he had not directed the alarm to be sounded, nor given the order to begin firing. He too believed they were firing on their own ships. The guns ceased firing on Greenman's orders. Thus was set in motion a series of misunderstandings that destroyed all of the *Astoria*'s well-laid plans.

Someone on the port wing of the bridge now reported searchlights illuminating the ship to port and vessels far out on the horizon firing at her. Word came from main battery control that the ships the *Astoria* had been firing on were enemy cruisers of the *Nachi* class, which had a very heavy superstructure.

"Japanese cruisers!" Truesdell yelled from the upper director. "Request permission to resume firing!" Then from the phone talker on the upper director came an anguished plea, "Mr. Truesdell said 'Sir, for God's sake give the word to commence firing!' "

As the *Vincennes* gave the order for the group to increase speed to fifteen knots, Captain Greenman, fully awake now, saw the *Chokai*'s searchlights widely spaced through the rigging over the port catapult—one almost astern, the other pretty well abroad on the quarter—and flashes of fire from five different ships falling just short of the *Vincennes*. "Our ships or not, we have to fire on them!" he told Topper, and immediately gave the order. Topper believed the captain's decision was prompted by the splashes that had just landed ahead and on the port side of the ship. In sky control, Seaman Hager heard over the bridge circuit the order, "Fire every damn thing you've got!" followed by a second order, "Get those damn searchlights!" These were the last orders Hager heard from the bridge. Not much later, he lost communication.

After giving orders to resume fire, Greenman sent Topper to his general quarters station. In less than a minute, despite traffic on the ladders leading to the bridge, Topper was inside central station. As he entered, he felt a jarring motion and heard metal flying overhead. Almost at once there was a heavy hit followed by rattling metal. Men rushed about, shifting circuits and testing which lines were serviceable. Turret no. 1 had been hit by an 8-inch shell that passed through the paint locker. No fire was started, but all communication with the turret was lost.

Quartermaster Radke and boatswain's mate W. J. Brower believed that the first general alarm was sounded within thirty seconds of the flares being seen, and that the *Astoria*'s first shells were fired within fifteen seconds of the first alarm. Captain Greenman's impression was that the action began not more than sixty seconds from the time he left his cabin. The *Astoria*'s report, as we have seen, says Greenman was called between 0154 and 0155. He said that there was a delay in calling him at this most critical time: "I think, in going back, I would like to say that being as tired as one would be, I slept more soundly and was probably more difficult to awake. Had I been more rested I would have heard some of the confusion on the bridge and wakened myself. . . ." Greenman said that Burkey was busy answering the *Vincennes* over the TBS, and for this reason did not immediately call him. Greenman believed that the junior officer of the deck, Lieutenant (j.g.) J. J. Mullen, realized the delay and summoned him.

Later, Greenman praised Truesdell for acting "with commendable promptness in having his battery alerted, trained in the direction of the target, and guns loaded; and particularly is he to be commended for the fact that he opened fire at the instant an enemy cruiser was silhouetted against the flares and recognized as such." Quartermaster Radke was also commended for his promptness and initiative in ringing the general alarm without orders when he saw that action was imminent.

However much time had gone by between the sighting of the flares and the second general alarm, it seemed forever. When the *Astoria* resumed fire, the *Chokai* had fired four salvos without causing a great deal of damage, but valuable time had been lost to the Americans. The altercation on the bridge gave the Japanese time to find the range and close in. Mikawa could afford to be deliberate, taking time to get the range. For a while the Japanese flagship concentrated on the *Astoria*, the ship nearest her and the most vulnerable. Captain Kato, executive officer of the *Chokai*, could see that the *Astoria*'s main battery was not fully trained on either of the Japanese groups. "This fact was first reported by our lookouts," he said, "so we conducted the battle . . . without any worries." Mikawa disagreed with Kato. There were plenty of worries, he pointed out: target selection, shortage of time, use of torpedoes, and running aground.

The *Astoria*'s main battery salvo from turrets nos. 1 and 2 had missed its target, but her no. 2 1.1-inch mount opened fire at the same time, expending 190 rounds before it and the port 1.1-inch director were hit and several men killed. Many officers and men died on their way to battle stations. The *Chokai* reported receiving "a large number of machine-gun hits, but they did not do any harm."

The first salvos from the Japanese flagship had fallen short and too far ahead. The third and fourth also missed. The fifth struck the American cruiser with at least four 8-inch shells amidships, starting fires on the boat deck and on the planes in the hangar, and temporarily disabled power to turret no. 3. Again, the fires gave the Japanese a perfect target. The *Chokai* turned off her lights. (Mikawa said that she kept her searchlights on continuously. This is not supported by either Commander Ohmae or Captain Kato. The *Chokai* turned on her lights while directing the rest of the cruisers and while firing, and extinguished them between salvos.)

Captain Greenman had received no battle plan or orders from the *Vincennes* since the action began, except for the signal to increase speed to fifteen knots. He rang up full speed and swung the *Astoria* slightly to port to bring the targets as far forward as possible and still not interfere with the *Quincy*'s fire. About now, control advised him that turret no. 2 was at the limit of bearing to port. Could the ship swing further to port? It appeared that all three ships of the group were heading from 10 to 15 degrees to port of the base course, 315 degrees. The only move possible without disrupting fire, Greenman believed, was to port, although no signals indicated that this was the intention of the *Vincennes.* Engine and fireroom casualties delayed him in taking the turn.

Soon afterwards he turned slowly to starboard, shifting main battery fire that way so that the ship could draw ahead of the *Quincy*. The effect of this change, stern through enemy lines, was devastating. The *Astoria* crossed the enemy's T and masked all her batteries, repeating a mistake she had made at Midway. There she had turned with the *Yorktown*, taking her guns off target just when they should have been protecting the carrier.[3]

Soon afterwards, turret no. 2 would not bear, and gunnery officer Truesdell repeatedly called the bridge to come to port and keep the forward turret bearing. The course was soon changed and the turret was able to match in train. One more salvo was fired. Almost simultaneously, three armor-piercing 8-inch shells hit her no. 1 turret. Two roughly horizontal hits on the barbette exploded in the gun pit. All turret crews in the gun room and upper powder room, and all but two on the shell deck, were killed. More fires started, one in the well deck spreading to planes on the catapults. The five planes and the flammable equipment in the hangar and on the well deck ignited. Heat and smoke from this fire, drawn into the after engine room, made it unbearable and the room had to be abandoned. Thus the ship lost 50 percent of her power. Another shell hit the 5-inch battery, which was soon silenced.

From the *Chokai*'s flag deck, correspondent Fumio Niwa was watching. Every time the guns fired, he lost his footing. Long white lines streaked across the black sea as ship after ship in the eastern force fired at the American cruiser. "It is just like the fireworks display over the river at Ryogoku," he scribbled in his notebook. "Searchlight beams make marks across the water, shells fly in the light toward the target as if they were trying to race each other. The target is already burning. . . . the ships seem to be made of wood and paper. Wings on the planes on the rear ship drop to the deck, throwing off a wonderful display of sparks."

The *Chokai*'s next salvo was right on target. An 8-inch shell tore into the superstructure, killing navigator Lieutenant Commander Eaton and chief quartermaster Brom, who were helping the captain maneuver the ship. While all this was going on, Greenman repeatedly tried to zigzag the ship, using 10 to 15 degrees of rudder. She was losing speed, so he called the engineering officer, Lieutenant Commander Hayes, asleep in his cabin when the alarm went.

Hayes took his flashlight, tied to a lanyard around his neck, and proceeded to the demolished engine room. Making his way to the mess hall, immediately above the space where fires were burning out of control, he ran into Lieutenant (j.g.) J. T. McNulty, the electrical officer, wandering around dazed. Everyone else there was dead. No one saw McNulty again. He was killed soon thereafter while investigating conditions in the after signal room. There were no survivors from no. 1 fireroom. No. 2 fireroom was abandoned shortly.

Commander Shoup, the executive officer, had been asleep in his cabin when the alarm sounded. Pulling his pants and shirt over his pajamas, he ran to battle station 2 to find his talker, quartermaster Walker, the only man there. No one else ever arrived. Shoup stepped to the port side and was leaning over the splinter shield when a shell exploded nearby, burning his hands and face and momentarily blinding him.

This had been one of the first hits aft. Almost immediately, the planes in the hangar caught fire. Shoup's impression was that they had been drained of gas the night before, but they burned fiercely nevertheless. The boat deck was on fire, and Walker reported that there had been no contact with the bridge. The ladders on both sides were blocked; there was no chance of getting to the lower decks by ordinary means. Shoup ordered battle station 2 abandoned, and with Walker raced to the after part of the machine-gun platform, on the same level. A manila line, rigged from there down to the main deck aft, served to lower wounded men. All survivors from the mainmast stations, sky aft, control aft, and the machine-gun platform, were evacuated down to the same deck. Many 20-mm-machine-gun personnel had been killed at their station.

Shoup found about one hundred and fifty men on the main deck aft, including twenty-five or thirty wounded who had assembled around the fantail. Turret no. 3, still manned but without power, was trained on the starboard beam with guns elevated. "I could not understand why the enemy fire had ceased, and assumed that they were closing in to finish us with gunfire or torpedoes," Shoup wrote. The entire forward part of the ship was on fire, and it loked as if the magazines would explode. "The *Quincy* blew up with a tremendous explosion at about this time, which increased my apprehension. . . ."

Control parties and gun crews in exposed positions stood ground under a devastating rain of shells, shrapnel, and splinters. Almost all 5-inch-gun crews and a large number of the automatic-gun personnel were killed at their stations. Turret crews stayed at their posts and continued to fire, eventually under local power, until even that was gone. Many men in repair and ammunition parties died from shell explosions below decks, the implements of their trade still in hand.

Battle dressing stations and the dentist's office were hit early in the action. Lieutenant Commander Charles Flower ran down the ladders to sick bay and ordered everyone there to lie down. A man whose appendix had recently been removed jumped out of bed and onto the deck. Two men were in the operating room with Flower when large shell fragments bore through the starboard bulkhead about three feet above. With lights out, smoke and flames filling the room, and water sloshing in from the adjoining ammunition-handling area, Flower decided to abandon the station, and with the few dressings and medication available set up topside. Corpsmen and patients at dressing stations in this part of the ship were killed.

Absorbent cotton from guns, handkerchiefs, and undershirts had to suffice for bandages. There were few splints or tourniquets, not enough stretchers, no burn jelly for the scores caught in flash fires, no morphine, not even whiskey to ease the pain of the wounded.

One of the first hits forward had penetrated the armored door to the main radio room and exploded in the communication office. Radio officer Lieutenant Baker, who had been decoding the Fox schedule signal when action began, miraculously escaped injury. He did not finish decoding. Instead he lent a hand to care for the wounded, including the chief of communications, who was badly hurt. Another shell had pierced the armored bulkhead of radio room 1. The shack was blown to smithereens, the radio equipment wrecked, and most men on watch were killed. Chief radioman Datko's call to repair the forward fire control radar had no doubt saved his life.

Daylight was hours off, and the worst yet to come. Captain Greenman could see the *Quincy* and the *Vincennes* firing ahead of his ship, slightly off the starboard bow. Both were on fire amidships, the *Quincy* still almost in his line of fire. His radical change of course to starboard earlier had succeeded only in continuing to foul the range.

The *Astoria* now came under the heaviest fire, shells pummeling all sides from the foremast aft. Fires ranged out of control on the navigation bridge and in a hundred other places. All main hoses to the upper decks forward of the hangar were out of commission. Below decks, trapped men had little hope of escape. By the time doors were opened, most had lost consciousness and had to be carried out.

There was no word on the forecastle of conditions aft. Fires on the gun deck and below the galley, and another huge blaze in the wardroom, which could not be approached from either forward or aft, prevented access. Bucket brigades effectively attacked the gun deck fire and the starboard passage forward of that area, but all spaces opened below to allow men to escape had been closed after them and were impenetrable.

Greenman had as many wounded as possible moved to his cabin, where medical officers and assistants cared for the most seriously injured. Shortly afterwards the deck in the cabin heated up and the wounded were taken to the forecastle. In the meantime, brigades using buckets and helmets to dip water from the sea continued driving the fire aft on the gun deck. A gasoline hand-billy was rigged over the side to pump an inadequate trickle of water into the wardroom. Fire, having reached the ammunition in the lower hoists, set off frequent explosions below decks. Greenman ordered the forward 8-inch-gun magazines flooded. He was unsure of the situation in the 5-inch-gun magazine. If this exploded, everyone on the forecastle would be blown to bits.

By 0200, the gun deck was blazing away and the secondary batteries, with the exception of gun no. 1, were out of action. Gun no. 2 had been put out of commission by a shell that tore off the muzzle. The well deck and hangar were a mass of flames.

The next hit, striking the starboard side of the bridge structure, came from the *Kako*'s high-angle and 25-mm guns. Shrapnel knocked down the signal officer of the watch, who had been standing inside the door leading to the pilot house. Yeoman Putnam propped him against the bulkhead and gave him a lighted cigarette. Greenman intended to turn port rudder as soon as the *Quincy,* blazing fiercely from bow to stern, drew ahead, but just as the *Astoria* turned, helmsman Williams fell. For perhaps half a minute there was no one at the wheel. Putnam took it over briefly, reporting to the captain that he was unable to steer because compasses had been shot away.

He was relieved by boatswain's mate first-class J. Young, badly wounded, who staggered to his feet, stepped over the helmsman's body, and took the wheel. Immediately, he put left rudder on the ship and she began to swing back to port. During the confusion the *Astoria* had turned to starboard, to port, and amidships, leaving a net course much further to starboard than Greenman had intended.

As the wheel went over, the *Quincy* reappeared off the port bow, heading across at considerable speed. For seconds, it seemed that the ships would collide. Greenman yelled "Hard left!" and they scraped clear astern. Just before he passed out from his wounds, Young whispered to quartermaster Radke, who took the wheel, that the captain had ordered him to "steady her up." But the ship, making about seven knots, had lost control. Greenman ordered control shifted to central station; this was done immediately. Radke gave up the wheel and established communication with the forward engine room, asking for all possible speed. Word came back that eight knots was the best they could give. The engines were fast losing power. A few minutes later, the captain's talker asked what speed was available. None, came the answer. With power gone in the engine room, personnel there were ordered to leave.

As the cruiser swung by the blazing *Quincy*, a searchlight from the *Aoba* caught her just abaft the starboard beam. At an estimated range of 5,000 yards the 1.1-inch mounts on the *Astoria*'s after deck fired on the light, expending five hundred rounds—not a huge success, though the *Aoba* acknowledged that two of her torpedo tubes were rendered useless and that "fires in the launching tube chamber and elsewhere did great damage because of the wind."

Astoria's eleventh 8-inch-gun salvo, fired from turret no. 3 with a range setting of 4,700 yards, was unleashed on the *Kinugasa.* The shells fell short. This was the last director-controlled salvo fired from the *Astoria.* Now there was one chance in a million that the American cruiser would excape the fate that seemed to have overtaken the *Quincy.*

The *Kinugasa* ceased firing and returned to check the damage she had inflicted, awaiting further opportunity to train on her victim. When this came the Japanese ship fired four torpedoes, which, fortunately for the *Astoria*, missed. Great as her damage from gunfire was, she had not been hit below the second deck.

The *Astoria* was still illuminated by the *Kinugasa*'s searchlights. Men on the deck below the bridge were directed to get word to the turret to train on the enemy's lights. In a last desparate move Lieutenant Commander Walter B. Davidson, the communication officer, climbed to the trainer's window and coached the guns on the enemy cruiser. The range was about 4,300 yards when the *Astoria* got off one last salvo from turret no. 2.

Captain Greenman followed the shells in flight and saw the flash as they landed. It was a wild shot, well over the *Kinugasa* in range, but the *Chokai*, somewhere east of the cruiser now, received a direct hit on her no. 1 turret. "Four shells came from the leading ship in your [the Allied] column," Captain Kato recorded in his action report. "One shell hit the port side of the foward turret, killing ten men." When gunnery officer Lieutenant Commander Shigeo Naka ventured into that space, he saw that the right barrel of the turret had split in half. An 8-inch shell had penetrated the inside of the gun, twisting and turning until it pierced the rear wall. Twenty gunners lay in the shambles of the turret.

This twelfth and last shot from the *Astoria* was probably also the final salvo fired from any of the Allied cruisers. The *Chokai*, already hit by the *Quincy* and the *Vincennes*, had fallen behind until her encounter with the *Astoria*. The Japanese ships turned off their searchlights and were lost to view. At 0220 Mikawa signaled "All ships withdraw." For them, the battle was over.

By 0300 more than four hundred men, including seventy wounded and many dead, were on the *Astoria*'s forecastle, while on the fantail executive officer Shoup and his men worked slowly toward the well deck, making little progress. Separated by a wall of fire, neither group knew of the other's existence. Shoup kept turret no. 3 manned and loaded for a long time, without primers inserted, in case the enemy returned, but at last this also had to be flooded. With luck, he and his men would reach the forecastle and see if there were any survivors. But fire and smoke always drove them back.

Only designated men went over the side. There was no rush for life jackets. Most everyone aft was equipped with life jackets, and empty powder kegs from turret no. 3 were lashed together in pairs so that those without support would have it when they hit the water. All available rafts went over the side, secured to the rails, and wounded who could make it were lowered to the sea.

At 0400 the sound of the gasoline pump being used forward to direct water to the wardroom came to the men aft as a slow, faint throb, the first indication that there were others alive. The ship, Shoup began to think, might be saved. The list had been steady for some time at 2 to 3 degrees to port, and the fires forward were apparently not as bad as he had thought.

On the forecastle, Captain Greenman organized bucket parties under the direction of Topper, who reported up from central station, and preparations were made to gather the dead for burial. Topper sent several men to the sail locker to look for life preservers, as some people lacked them. All buckets, mattresses, life preservers, and first-aid materials were passed to topside. Returning to the forecastle, Topper had men cut up ropes for use as lifelines in case the ship had to be abandoned.

Fearful that ammunition would explode, Greenman and his officers and men were more than ready when at 0440 the destroyer *Bagley*, the only undamaged ship in the southern force, approached. The *Astoria* asked her to stand by. She came alongside at 0445, bow on bow. Greenman directed that only the seriously wounded be transferred to the destroyer, assisted by several able-bodied men. When all stretcher cases had been sent over, Greenman ordered the rest of the wounded aboard the destroyer. Little headway was being made with the fires, and it was impossible to flood the 5-inch-gun magazine. There was no sense in flooding the others, and gunnery officer Truesdell advised against trying. Finally, Captain Greenman ordered all hands remaining on the forecastle to transfer to the *Bagley*. This done, the destroyer backed away, stood clear, and was asked to stand by until daylight for an examination of the crippled ship.

Meanwhile, the party on the cruiser's fantail, blinking a small light unseen by the *Bagley,* believed they had been abandoned. The bucket brigades, having worked their way to the forward limits of the well deck, were blocked by a fierce oil fire in the starboard forward corner and by fire and dense smoke on the upper deck's port side.

As the brigade reached the forward part of the well deck, someone spotted a man between the starboard forward whaleboat davit and the break of the upper deck, hemmed in by the oil fire and another fire in the lumber stowage below. "At first I thought he was dead, but then I saw him move his hand feebly," Shoup records. He could not bring himself to order anyone to the man's rescue, but shipfitter first-class C. C. Watkins raced into the flames, reached the man, and started to work him out. He then called for help and two other men, shipfitter third-class Wyatt J. Louthrell and watertender second-class Norman Touve, plunged into the fire after him. Between them, they forced the davit up and the man was pulled free. As they dragged him to safety another man appeared pinned beneath the wreckage. They dragged him out, only to discover a third man over the side. They threw him a line and brought him in. Commander Shoup later called the rescue of these men the finest deed he witnessed in a night when high courage was commonplace.

Efforts to extinguish the oil fire with sand and carbon dioxide failed, as did repeated attempts by the engineering officer, Lieutenant Commander Hayes, and men of the after repair party to advance on the second deck. Dense smoke and flames always drove them back.

Before dawn a second destroyer started to come alongside the port side aft, then had to back off because of a reported submarine contact. Men on the *Astoria*'s main deck aft cheered and called "Go get him!" masking their disappointment. Once again, it seemed as if Admiral Turner's friendship boat had been deserted.

Hayes and a party of engineers were able to visit the forward engine room. They found it dry, and as they left they secured the battle hatches to both engine rooms. The trunks above the hatches had all been destroyed. Time had moderated the fires, and it was now possible to move over the gun deck on the starboard side of the forecastle. If only power could be provided, the *Astoria* might get up steam.

That hope came at about 0500 when the *Bagley* returned after reporting the *Astoria*'s condition. As the destroyer picked up survivors from the *Vincennes*, and a few who had been driven overboard by amidships fires, a flashing light appeared on the cruiser's stern. In the *Bagley* it was obvious that some of the *Astoria*'s remaining crew were still alive. No severe fires were seen aft, and the fire in the hangar and amidships seemed to be dying out. A squall blew in, adding further hope for the men stranded on the fantail. The *Bagley* signaled them.

On the *Astoria*'s starboard side, above the armor belt, there were about eight large holes, all a couple of feet or more above the waterline. The bridge had one gaping hole, and there were large holes on the hangar sides. The cruiser did not appear to be shipping any water.

Commander Shoup and Lieutenant Commander Hayes were waiting with their 150 survivors when, at dawn, the *Bagley* placed her bow alongside the starboard quarter of the cruiser. Both Shoup and Hayes told Greenman that there was a good chance the ship could be saved.

A salvage crew of two deck divisions, engineers, electricians, medical teams, and a ship control force, about 325 in all, returned to the ship, together with all the able-bodied officers and men present. Wounded and any personnel not required by the salvage party among survivors found on the stern were put aboard the *Bagley*, and she shoved off once more. It was just 0600.

12

The Phantom Battle

The parts played by the destroyers *Helm, Wilson,* and *Blue* in the Battle of Savo Island are confusing. The *Helm* and the *Wilson,* screening the three American cruisers, were anxious to assist but for most of the action could not find the enemy. They ran off in all directions, chasing after imaginary ships, or those that turned out to be friendly. Both destroyers saw star shells or flares and heard gunfire to the south at about 0145 but, because of fire and smoke, did not immediately spot the enemy searchlights and gunfire.

The *Australia* group's plan of operation was not known to Lieutenant Commander Carroll in the *Helm,* but it appeared as if that group, operating in the general direction of the lights and gunfire, was firing. The *Helm* opened fire at the same time as the *Vincennes,* but no target was visible. Only one salvo had been fired when a cease-fire was ordered. The *Helm* remained ahead of the formation for some minutes, then headed south, in the direction from which she supposed the enemy was firing.

At about 0200 she sighted a ship on the starboard bow, partly illuminated, it seemed, by a searchlight. Neither side, however, was using searchlights at this time. What the *Helm* had seen was a lightning flash. The ship appeared to be heading out to sea, passing close to the south side of Savo Island. The *Helm* changed course southwest and headed at full speed for the unknown ship, preparing to launch torpedoes. Before she could fire, lightning lit up the target once more and revealed the *Bagley,* from the southern group. Experiencing gyrocompass trouble, this ship was fortunate to escape attack from the *Helm.*

About 0150 Lieutenant Commander Price, in the *Wilson,* saw three ships on the port side of the Allied column lit up by searchlights and attacking the cruisers from astern. The *Wilson* opened fire, all four 5-inch guns targeted over the American cruisers on the starboard light, that of the *Kako,* in the enemy's eastern group. Price had not received the *Vincennes*'s order to attack, but he had picked up the *Patterson*'s warning that enemy ships were approaching, as well as the call from the *Vincennes* to increase speed to fifteen knots. Therefore he had a somewhat clearer picture of the situation than the *Helm*'s commander. The direction to increase speed was the last word Price heard from the command ship.

The *Wilson* continued fire over the *Vincennes* as several of the *Kako*'s "overs" burst between the *Wilson* and the nearest cruiser. The *Kako*'s first shot knocked the hands off the *Wilson*'s bridge clock, and from this time on the destroyer's report records no times. Meanwhile she tried to keep up with the cruisers, firing whenever her guns would bear.

So far, the *Wilson* had not been picked up by the enemy's western group, although the *Tenryu* and the *Yubari* were close by, busily engaging the Allied cruisers. She was never aware of their presence, though she was fired on by the *Tenryu* and heard shells flying overhead. One dud landed a few feet from her, without exploding. Meanwhile she identified one enemy ship, close off her starboard bow, as a *Monssen* type. To avoid collision, Price ordered an increase of speed to thirty knots and a hard turn to port. The *Wilson* continued on this turn until she was clear of the ship and her battery was unmasked to port.

But there was no ship of the *Monssen* type in the area. The *Monssen* herself was with the *San Juan* group. The enemy was the Japanese destroyer *Yunagi.* Neither ship opened fire.

On her new course the *Wilson,* anxious to relocate the enemy, saw only the *Astoria,* under heavy fire. At about 0210, using the searchlights of an enemy ship as guide, she fired on Japan's eastern group. Her control spotter noticed that this ship had the raked funnel typical of Japanese cruisers. This was the *Chokai.*

The *Wilson's* gun flashes partially blinded men on her bridge, but she continued fire on the *Chokai* until 0216, when the Japanese flagship turned off her lights. With no more targets in sight, the *Wilson* ceased fire, in the meantime losing sight of her own forces.[1] As she continued toward Savo Island a warning came over the TBS, apparently from the *Ralph Talbot,* that an enemy cruiser was standing out north of the island. Believing that she had been mistaken for an enemy vessel, the *Wilson* changed course south to avoid fire from her own ships.

The *Helm* records that she passed through the line of cruisers, between the *Vincennes* and the *Quincy,* both lit up by searchlights. A few shells fell close by. No sooner were orders given to fire on the lights from the *Furutaka* than they went out. Fifteen minutes later, a ship was sighted to the northwest, her searchlights combing the sky. The *Helm* chased her at about thirty knots and identified the ship as the *Ralph Talbot,* at which point the *Talbot* was illuminated by enemy searchlights.

The *Helm* fired four rounds of five-inch ammunition, no torpedoes, during the action that ensued. The *Wilson* fired 212 rounds of common antiair projectiles, no torpedoes. Her torpedo battery was set for firing, but with all the confusion, and doubt as to the location of friendly forces, Price believed it unwise to launch a torpedo attack.

About 0210, Admiral Crutchley sent out signals for all destroyers not already engaged with the enemy to concentrate on him northwest of the transport area. By 0230 all action had stopped.

While the Allied cruisers were blazing and sinking in the one-sided battle south and west of Savo Island, the destroyers *Blue* and *Ralph Talbot* continued to patrol the breached pass to the north, unaware that the gunfire they heard and saw came from ships their own oversights had allowed to go undetected.

The *Ralph Talbot*'s turn came around 0217. A single sweeping searchlight off the port bow lit her up for about ten seconds. The light was from the Japanese destroyer *Yunagi,* lost in the fog of battle since her chase after the damaged *Jarvis.* Instead of taking action against the *Talbot,* the *Yunagi* signaled the western group's *Tenryu* and *Furutaka.* Minutes later, another sweeping searchlight illuminated the *Talbot* and she was fired on. Six salvos were unleashed, five of which fell short. The one hit knocked out her no. 2 turret and killed two men.

Lieutenant Commander Callahan, the *Talbot*'s captain, believed one of the ships was a friendly destroyer from Tulagi because of the color of the shells' splashes, her single searchlight, and her position. "We headed west at maximum speed, zig-zagged and flashed fighting lights and passed on TBS that we were being fired on by our own forces. Own forces then ceased firing on us." The ship firing on the *Talbot* was probably the *Wilson.*[2]

The *Blue* had no indication of the presence of the enemy until she saw planes over the battle area intermittently flashing red and white lights, as though signaling. Her report indicates that firing continued every now and then, mostly in the obscured area near Savo Island, until 0215, "when the attention of this vessel was diverted."[3] Forty-five minutes earlier, the *Blue*'s radar had failed to pick up the seven Japanese ships racing in to attack the southern group of ships.

From a position nine miles west of Savo Island, when all action with the *Vincennes* group had ceased, the *Blue* made a sound contact and sighted an unidentified ship to the southeast. Lieutenant Commander Williams looked at the bearing of the contact to determine whether it was from a surface vessel or a submarine. He identified the ship as a small two-masted schooner with a slow-speed auxiliary engine, set on an easterly course, probably the same vessel the Japanese had mistaken for a destroyer much earlier. Satisfied that the vessel was an innocent passerby, the *Blue*'s commanding officer reversed his patrol and continued at twelve knots.

A minute later the *Ralph Talbot*—still illuminated by what she believed to be lights from friendly ships, Lieutenant Commander Callahan thinking that fire had ceased because the attacking ships had realized their mistake—was fired on again. This time the *Talbot* recognized her attacker as the enemy, a cruiser with one stack. Thought to be of the *Tone* class, she had crossed from port to starboard at close range, apparently slow to recognize the *Talbot.* A nerve-racking thirty seconds passed for the destroyer before the ship, now on her starboard quarter and making high speed, turned on her searchlights and opened fire. This was the speedy light cruiser *Yubari,* the only ship in the Japanese force with a distinctive single funnel.

Callahan now had the enemy in sight. As the *Talbot* obtained a range on the *Yubari,* she was illuminated by another searchlight from the *Tenryu.* The *Furutaka,* using the lights of these two light cruisers, also came in to attack. The glare of lights momentarily blinded the *Talbot*'s signalman, who was training the director, so that he could no longer see the target. The torpedo officer took the director, at a distance of 3,000 yards firing three torpedoes from her after starboard tube in the direction in which the enemy had last been seen. The right torpedo in tube no. 3 did not fire, and Tube no. 2 was out of commission owing to the earlier shell hit. Men on the bridge and main deck and in the engineering spaces, however, reported hearing underwater explosions, similar to those of depth charges, two or three minutes after the starboard battery was fired. It was not definitely known whether a hit was scored.

A shell from the *Yubari*'s first salvo hit the *Talbot*'s starboard quarter, below the bridge, and her no. 4 gun. A second shell hit the after end of the chart house, destroying both radars and cutting the automatic gun-train and -elevation apparatus. Three more hits came in quick succession, killing twelve men, after which the *Yubari,* slightly damaged, went her way. She left the *Ralph Talbot* with a big fire in her chart house, power and steering gone, and listing 20 degrees to starboard.[4] With no means of communication, the *Talbot* stood toward the western shore of Savo Island, fighting fires, throwing gear overboard, and making repairs. She limped to the anchorage on two boilers.

The *Talbot*'s ordnance department had been put out of commission, and her living quarters were no better off. A hundred men were without mattresses, blankets, and clothing, these having been either destroyed or immersed in salt water and oil. Only one of the four living compartments could still be used, so that most of the crew had to sleep topside. The ship, moreover, needed to be completely reprovisioned. Thousands of pounds of bread, crackers, meat, fresh and canned vegetables, fruit, powdered milk, cereal, ice cream, flour, butter, sugar, eggs, and catsup had been ruined.

The *Blue* had a much less eventful night. Shortly after her encounter with the two-masted schooner, she witnessed the scene with the *Talbot* northeast of Savo. From a distance she also saw the attacks on the American cruisers, and possibly the *Vincennes*'s identification lights turned on to warn the *Wilson* and the *Helm* that she was friendly. Twelve minutes later the *Blue* sighted an unidentified ship rounding Cape Esperance, taking a southwesterly course at average speed. She increased speed to twenty knots and sped after the ship, signaling her for identification but receiving no answer. This was the disabled destroyer *Jarvis,* limping along at about ten knots. The *Jarvis* obviously expected to be attacked by the *Blue.* Once recognition was established, the destroyer slowed to eight knots and continued on her journey.

The only ship in the fifteen-mile area of Savo Island not to fire a shot, and the first to be seen by Mikawa's force, the *Blue* took no offensive action, inflicted no damage on the enemy, sustained no loss or damage, and, of course, failed to sight Mikawa's force as it slipped past in the night.

The destroyer *Yunagi*'s performance must have been as disappointing to the Japanese as that of the *Blue* was to the Allies. A few minutes before the rest of the force separated, the *Yunagi* had fallen out of formation to engage the *Jarvis.* She opened fire at 0155. Lieutenant Shizuichi Okada, her commanding officer, reported that he broke off the action about 0200 after firing torpedoes on a ship at the rear of the southern force. At that point, the illumination light on the *Yunagi*'s gyrocompass broke down. "The *Yunagi* was turning when the light went off," he said. "As a result we could not make out the bearing. Although we intended to follow the front ship, we lost sight of her and reversed course."

By this time, also, the *Yunagi* was running out of fuel. Unable to run at high speed, she followed the slow *Furutaka.* Okada did not realize that the force had split into two groups and now saw only three of the original seven cruisers. At 0220 he received Mikawa's message ordering the ships to a speed of thirty knots. Gradually the *Yunagi* was overtaken by the other ships.

At 0240 the *Tenryu* sighted the *Chokai* at a distance of about 9,900 yards, and at 0320 the western group gradually converged on the eastern. Five minutes later, the *Yunagi* caught up with the force and took station astern the *Yubari.*

By 0340 all units of the Japanese force were in original battle line order: the *Chokai, Aoba, Kako, Kinugasa, Furutaka, Tenryu, Yubari,* and *Yunagi.* For the first time in two hours, Mikawa had direct tactical command over his force.

13

The End of the *Canberra*

When Mikawa left the four Allied cruisers in flames, Admiral Crutchley had received no information as to the nature of the battle or its results. He ordered the *Australia* to patrol a line seven miles west of the X-ray area, covering the transports and cargo ships and keeping within the antisubmarine screen. Close to 0226, he sent out a message to the *Chicago, Vincennes,* and *San Juan* groups asking them if they were engaged. The *Chicago* replied, "Were, but not now"; the *San Juan,* "This force not in action. Appears to be surface force between Florida Island and Savo." No reply came from the *Vincennes.* Crutchley also tried to communicate with the *Astoria* and the *Quincy* but was unable to raise them. Once more he queried the *Chicago,* and at 0245 received a reply from Captain Bode: "We are standing toward Lengo on course 100 degrees." This did little to ease Crutchley's mind.

At 0235, as the *Quincy* went down, parachute flares were dropped over Florida Island to silhouette the transports off Tulagi and Gavutu. It seemed that more action was to come. Admiral Crutchley's original orders to the seven destroyers of the striking force—the *Selfridge, Patterson, Mugford, Helm, Henley, Bagley,* and *Wilson*—had been to rendezvous five miles northwest of Savo Island. His new orders were for all destroyers not in action to concentrate on the *Australia.* This signal was sent in cypher, and many of the ships either could not understand it or did not receive it. Most of the destroyers merely followed one another, ready to open fire at any moment in case a ship turned out to be the enemy.

Confusion resulting in the inability to pick up the correct rendezvous orders at least helped to save many men from the sunken cruisers.

The *Canberra,* lying helpless about five miles southeast of Savo, continued efforts to control her fires with the use of buckets and milk cans. There was a shortage not only of containers but also of ropes with which to lift them from the sea. If we recall, ammunition was being dumped overboard, and wounded, Captain Getting among them, crowded the main deck, covered with blankets, oilskins, and hammocks to protect them from the heavy rain. As men slipped on the bloody, sloping decks, a faint flashing light appeared off the starboard bow. Friend or foe? The unknown ship came around the *Canberra*'s stern and into view. She was the *Patterson,* standing by on order of the *Chicago.* It was now just after 0300. Commander Walsh, commanding in place of the badly wounded captain, asked the *Patterson* to send a signal to Admiral Crutchley reporting his ship's position, at the same time warning the destroyer to beware: the *Canberra*'s 4-inch ammunition was likely to go up any moment.

Visibility was less than a mile, the sea choppy, with rain lashing both ships and every now and then violent streaks of lightning followed by heavy thunderclaps. As the *Patterson* closed in, loud rumbling sounds started up and came at irregular intervals as the cruiser's ammunition exploded. Walsh signaled the *Patterson* again: "You had better wait!" The destroyer retreated about two miles away to deliver Walsh's message to Crutchley.

An hour later the *Patterson*, badly damaged herself from the encounter with the two Japanese light cruisers, returned to the *Canberra* and was asked if she could send over hoses and pump water to fight fires. Three two-inch rubber hoses were hauled across, but these could not be coupled directly to the *Canberra*'s hose connections. Two were played on fires in the starboard pom-pom magazines and between decks through a hole burned into the deck planking. Men connected the hoses by hand so they would not burst apart. The *Patterson* then produced a small portable fire engine, but the ignition, wet from rain, could not be started. Despite these setbacks, Commander McMahon still considered it possible to bring the fires under control with the destroyer's hoses. Heavy rain also helped.

The *Canberra* was short of everything—torches to light the way below, medical supplies, drinking water and water to quench fires, respirators, gas masks. Legs were broken off mess tables and stools and put over the side with rafts and planks to be secured to guard rails. Two cutters were towed to the port side of the forecastle to receive wounded. One was found to be full of holes. Water came in too fast to be controlled by bailing, and the wounded, already aboard, had to be transferred to a second boat.

As the *Canberra* prepared to deliver her wounded to the *Patterson*, Admiral Crutchley received Captain Bode's signal, sent out some time earlier, telling him of the *Canberra*'s condition and his own. The *Chicago*'s signal, "Surface action near Savo, situation undetermined," did little to enlighten Crutchley. At 0315 he saw several lightning flashes east of Savo, which he took for gunfire. He was now seriously concerned for the safety of the Australian cruiser. Since he could not communicate with her directly, and had been told by Bode that two destroyers were standing by, he sent off a message to the *Patterson* asking for information on the *Canberra*. The reply came back, "Disabled on fire in position seven miles southeast of Savo Island." This added to the admiral's confusion.

Soon afterwards, the transfer of wounded to the *Patterson* began. Men stood at the portside 5-inch machine gun to keep it from accidentally firing while the destroyer was alongside. Surgeon Commander Downward, principal medical officer, and Surgeon Lieutenant Morris went with the wounded men, while Captain Getting was carried from the compass platform and put aboard. Several plasma infusions were administered in the *Patterson*, including one to Captian Getting.

One of the hoses provided by the *Patterson* continued to play on the starboard pom-pom magazine, where a large fire was still setting off ammunition. By this time the fire in after control was out and another on the catapult considerably reduced. The aircraft had burned itself out without its four bombs exploding.

Calls came for the first boat to be lowered quickly. Rafts were cut adrift and placed under the port bow, a large one being released from the port screen so that it would float clear if the ship foundered.

When the *Patterson* had been alongside the *Canberra* for about half an hour, she passed a signal received from Admiral Turner: "Unless able to join retirement, destroy your ship. Time for retirement is 0630. This is urgent."[1] There was not a chance of getting the *Canberra* steamed up by that time. Her list had increased to 17 degrees, and internal explosions continued.

At 0410, the *Patterson* reported to Crutchley that the *Canberra* was out of commission. Five minutes later, with the wounded still being transferred, Commander Walsh reluctantly gave the order to return hoses to the destroyer and prepare to abandon ship.

Turner's order took the heart out of everyone. Repairs were more or less given up as men searched the ship for remaining wounded. Abandonment was delayed because, orders or not, able-bodied officers and men would not leave until everyone had been accounted for.

Others worked on the fires near the pom-pom magazines. It seemed now that most of the fires had been subdued. If a ship were available, it was felt, the *Canberra* could be towed to safety.

The *Chicago*, having dispatched the *Patterson* to go to the aid of the *Canberra*, at 0342 slowed down to five knots. Captain Bode had been caught by surprise during the battle and was determined to make up for it. At 0410 he saw what looked like heavy gunfire toward Savo Island.[2] He changed course and proceeded in that direction.

Meanwhile, the *Patterson* sent another signal to the *Canberra*: "Please expedite. It is now 0505. How many men do you have?" Walsh thought there were about six hundred. Could the destroyer take them all? "We can try," Commander Walker signaled back. On his orders, men were lined up around the *Canberra*'s deck and able-bodied men instructed to take the wounded aboard using cutters and lifelines.

Three stretcher cases were already on the *Patterson* when she sent an urgent message: "Out all lights, all hands stand clear, let go wires!" Almost immediately, she signaled that she had to depart because there was a hostile ship on her port quarter. In the *Canberra*, the order was called to take cover and beware flying wires. The *Patterson* shoved off at high speed, still pumping water into the cruiser and embarking men over the rails. Lines securing her snapped. Planks and rafts were smashed, men tossed into the water. One wounded rating, suspended in midair between the two ships, was rescued with the help of lifelines.

The *Patterson*'s parting words as she scraped alongside the cruiser were cheering: "We'll be back!" Aboard the *Canberra,* nonetheless, sheer panic reigned. One man jumped onto the destroyer's deck before she left. Others fell flat on their faces, those nearest the port guard rails scrambling across the backs of men further inboard. They listened in the dark, waiting for firing to begin. Blinding flashes of lightning accompanied by great claps of thunder added to the panic. One bolt struck the ship somewhere aft, followed by a tremendous crash and a loud hissing sound. Heavy explosions came from the 4-inch-gun deck, one so strong and prolonged that men forward cried out, "Here she goes!" and tried to dig into the deck, expecting the ship to blow up.

Just before the enemy ship opened fire with tracers and greenish-blue star shells, there were flashing lights. Shells burst close by and fragments whined high over the *Canberra.* Someone screamed "Jap cruisers!"

Able seaman St. George had been waiting in line to board the *Patterson* when she shot away. The next second, yanked off his feet, he went flying toward the *Canberra*'s davit head, suspended by the ankle, and then dropped to the deck. He had been standing in the falls of a cutter, the lower block of which was on the *Patterson*'s deck. Luckily for him, the rope fell from his foot. He looked up, saw a shell rise over his ship, and dropped flat, praying harder than he ever had before.

From the *Canberra*'s deck, Lieutenant Commander Mesley saw a strange ship with searchlights blazing and guns firing as the *Patterson* replied with three salvos. Using her lights for the first time that night, the destroyer illuminated a shape on her port beam. It looked like an American cruiser. Yeoman of signals Gunthorp could not believe his eyes. How could the enemy be an American? "Whoever she was," he said, "she gave me the biggest fright of the whole action by opening fire with what seemed to be secondary armament." He slid on his stomach to the starboard side of B deck and blew up his life jacket, waiting for the *Canberra* to go down.

Mesley thought the ship resembled the *Chicago*, although she seemed to be painted a somewhat lighter color. Suddenly, the *Canberra* lurched. He was sure she was about to capsize. "Stand by to abandon ship!" he called, but she only rolled another couple of degrees, then steadied. "Wait, wait!" Mesley shouted. A minute or so later all firing ceased and the two battling ships disappeared in opposite directions.

The strange ship was indeed the *Chicago.* The sounds Captain Bode had taken for heavy gunfire came from the thunderstorm. He had tracked the destroyer by radar for some time, and with visibility worsening had seen neither the burning *Canberra* nor the destroyer. He did not issue an order to fire, but when his ship was lit up by the *Patterson*'s searchlights, guns nos. 1 and 5 opened fire anyway. The officer controlling the starboard battery ordered cease-fire and sounded the cease-firing gong, but by this time the *Patterson* had returned fire.

The *Patterson*'s report says that, as the "enemy" appeared "somewhat like the *Chicago,*" Commander Walker fired emergency identification signals. Captain Bode, in the *Chicago*, immediately repeated the order to cease-fire. The *Patterson*, he later said, at first made the wrong emergency identification signal. Both ships ceased fire when the proper signals were seen.

From the *Australia*, Admiral Crutchley saw the short bursts of gunfire. Fortunately for his peace of mind, he did not know that his ships were at each other's throats. Concerned for both the *Canberra* and the *Patterson*, at 0532 he ordered the commander of Destroyer Squadron 4, in the *Selfridge*, to investigate the condition of the two ships. The *Patterson*'s earlier message had confused him; he was unsure whether it referred to the condition of the *Canberra* or of the *Patterson*. He gave instructions that both ships were to be abandoned and destroyed if they could not join in the withdrawal, now planned for 0730.

Everything had gone wrong for the *Chicago* since being ordered at short notice to take over from the *Australia*. She had probably caused some damage and casualties on the light cruiser *Tenryu*, but she had failed to give orders to her own group and to alert the *Vincennes* group.

Captain Bode felt that his main concern was to intercept and engage enemy ships with the entire available force, so long as there appeared to be any probability of engagement. He "did not detach a destroyer to stand by the *Canberra*, but was about to do so when on standing in toward that vessel at about 0245 we thought the *Bagley* [was in the vicinity and] had stood over toward her. . . . I considered this proper at that time."[3] Not until much later did he realize his error in not supporting the *Canberra*. At the time he could not see her because of low visibility, although he knew where she should be.

All was quiet and dark again. The *Chicago* continued on her course, discovering nothing—no enemy ships, no sign of gunfire. Her battle was over.

The *Patterson* had drawn all the fire from the *Canberra*, but even though the cruiser had not been hit, all chances faded of saving her or removing the rest of her wounded. She was now listing about 25 degrees to starboard, and fires, assisted by a stiff breeze on the starboard side, were raging out of control once more. Even with the most powerful pumping plant, it would have taken a miracle to salvage the ship. Billowing clouds of smoke poured through the seams of the ship's boiler casings. Without the help of the *Patterson*'s hoses, she was fast becoming a burned-out shell.[4]

After the *Chicago* and the *Patterson* disappeared, the *Canberra* continued arrangements to abandon ship and collected parties on the quarterdeck and forecastle. The only thing to do was to wait in the rain, hoping for the best. As dawn was breaking, a destroyer and then a cruiser were seen off the *Canberra*'s bow. One was the *Blue*, the other the renegade *Chicago*. Captain Bode, once again acting as commander of the group, directed the *Blue* to help remove men from the cruiser. When the

The last hours of HMAS Canberra. *The USS* Patterson *is close alongside. (80-G-13488, National Archives)*

Canberra signaled that she still had four hundred men on board, the *Chicago* stood by and circled the ship. This was the first indication Bode had that the *Bagley* was not in the vicinity.

The *Blue* was on the *Canberra*'s port side forward. Seconds later the *Patterson* returned. She was asked to tie up at the starboard bow, but, calling out that there were still a number of men on the quarterdeck, she went alongside the port quarter instead and took them off.

The *Patterson,* with many dead and wounded of her own aboard, received a total of 400 officers and ratings, including about 70 wounded. The *Blue* took 353. Then the destroyers proceeded to transport area X-ray and transferred all of the *Canberra*'s survivors, including Captain Getting and eight of her own wounded, to the attack transport USS *Barnett,* which subsequently passed some men to the *Fuller*.

Lieutenant Commander Plunkett-Cole and Commander Walsh, both badly wounded by shrapnel, were taken by the *Blue.* As the destroyer steamed away, Plunkett-Cole saw the *Canberra* listing about 35 degrees to starboard, burning fiercely amidships, and showing signs of fire between decks, both forward and aft. Her turrets were still trained as they had been before the enemy shells hit her.

Commander Walsh could no longer see. As the *Blue* moved off, he heard men give three cheers for the *Canberra.* They told him that her ensign was still flying. Both halyards had been dismantled to provide ropes for buckets fighting the fires.

Reluctantly, Admiral Crutchley sent a dispatch to the Australian Naval Board saying that the *Canberra* had been badly damaged and was on fire, and the crew was abandoning ship. The *Patterson,* rescuing her crew, would scuttle her.

HMAS Canberra *just before she sunk. (137295, Australian War Memorial)*

At 0644 he received a report from the *Selfridge*, returning from the destroyer rendezvous, saying that the *Astoria* was in flames and that four destroyers were picking up survivors. A further message from Admiral Turner advised him that the *Quincy* had apparently sunk. There was no news of the *Vincennes*. It was also believed that the *Ralph Talbot* had sunk. Destroyer Squadron 4 had received her call for help, but no further word came. She was last seen seven miles north of Savo Island. Turner's message concluded, "Believe ships ran into submarine and surface torpedo traps."

The *Selfridge* was sent to finish off the *Canberra*, the sun just rising as she approached the burning cruiser. She fired an incredible 263 rounds of 5-inch shells and four torpedoes, fitted with magnetic pistols. One torpedo exploded under the *Canberra*. Two others passed beneath her without exploding. Another missed her and exploded in the wake of the *Ellet*, coming up at full speed. The *Canberra* refused to go down.

The *Ellet*, which had spent the last few hours picking up survivors from the *Quincy*, saw the *Selfridge* firing on the ship at about 0730. Unable to make contact by TBS, her commander thought that the *Selfridge* was engaged in battle with a disabled Japanese cruiser. The

Ellet closed, setting course to cross the bow of the enemy, and at 5,000 yards scored several hits. She then ceased firing, having heard from the *Selfridge* that the cruiser was the *Canberra.*

The *Ellet* had expended 106 rounds of 5-inch ammunition when at 0747, as the *Canberra* had not sunk, she was ordered to complete the job. Nine minutes later, from close range, she fired one torpedo into the cruiser's starboard side, just under the bridge. Close to 0800, the *Canberra* went down.

Five men died in the *Patterson* that morning. Three were buried from the destroyer, two taken to the *Barnett* for burial. Captain Getting died on board the *Barnett* during the passage from Tulagi to Noumea, a few days after his forty-third birthday.

14

Picking Up the Pieces

Many hundreds of men, mostly from the *Vincennes* and the *Quincy,* were in the water by 0300. From beginning to end, the action against the *Vincennes* group had taken about twenty-two minutes; the fight to survive in the dark, oil-covered, shark-infested sea went on for six or seven hours, and for some men very much longer. The *Quincy* had gone down so quickly that there was no time to launch boats, and life jackets thrown overboard were so securely lashed together that a few scarce knives had to be used to cut them free. Floater nets, rolled up and tied together in canvas covers, were almost impossible to release. Straps on life jackets had rotted through or been burned. Hundreds of 5-inch-shell tanks, which had been tossed over the side or which floated clear when the ship sank, saved lives, but many men who couldn't swim had no means of support.

Lieutenant Andrew, the *Quincy*'s second senior surviving officer, collected dozens of rafts and floater nets and, with the help of Ensign A. F. Cohen, organized a raft convoy. They made constant forays into the water, repeatedly swimming into the darkness to round up floundering men.

The *Quincy*'s signal officer, Lieutenant Clarke, swam as fast as he could to get away from the sinking ship. When he looked back, she was down as far as the hurricane deck and sinking. A man was screaming nearby and Clarke swam over to find that he could not swim. Clarke gave him his life jacket, the man clawing at him until at last, tied firmly into the jacket, he floated away. Clarke swam to a 5-inch ammunition tank, glimpsed in a flash of lightning or gunfire, and clung to it until it sank. A life jacket floated by and he put it on. Then he saw one of the *Quincy*'s crew, a man who was rapidly tiring, and stayed with him until a raft, leaking and crowded, appeared. They swam to it and clambered aboard. Clarke was the only officer present. When the destroyer *Ellet* appeared he stopped his men from calling out, as he thought it might confuse the destroyer. Someone gave a signalman a flashlight to summon the ship, and soon a rescue boat was lowered from the destroyer.

They were among the fortunate. Lieutenant James Smith and several dozen men tried to support themselves on a floater net enclosed in canvas. It was impossible to unroll the net. As a result, many of the men, so close to rescue, lost their lives.

Quartermaster Tom Morris, seriously wounded, owed his life to chief boatswain's mate George John Strobel, who helped him off the port side of the *Quincy*'s fantail, found a cork float, and with his belt tied him and Seaman Second-Class Albert Samuel Blaser to either side of the rolled-up net. They were picked up by the *Ellet.* Morris spent nearly a year in the hospital. Blaser died of injuries.

Some men spent as long as ten hours in the water, clutching in the dark at shell canisters, debris, anything that would keep them afloat. Elmer Hollis, from the *Quincy*'s no. 3 turret, went overboard with a mattress, which helped him stay alive until a destroyer picked him up. Storekeeper Lawrence Bly, also from the *Quincy,* floated on a raft with other wounded men for two long weeks because the rescue ships did not see them before leaving on 10 August for Noumea. An American scouting plane spotted the raft and dropped food and water and medical supplies. Some men died of injuries before a destroyer finally rescued them.

Only when rescue ships blinked recognition signals were men permitted to swim to them. The *Ellet* and the *Wilson* picked up hundreds of men between 0400 and 0640. All those collected by the *Ellet* were provided with dry clothing, hot coffee, and cigarettes and put below decks, where they turned in to bunks. The wounded were tended to by the destroyer's medical officers and those from the *Quincy,* who performed amputations, set broken limbs, and did their utmost to ease the pain of the fearful burns many men suffered. Around noon, the transport *American Legion* took some survivors off the *Ellet.* Over five hundred men, shoeless and with no clothing save that provided by the destroyer, were issued fresh uniforms.

The *Wilson,* having received no orders, was patrolling astern of the *Helm* when at 0530 word was received over the TBS to return to area

X-ray. En route, new orders arrived for her to pick up survivors. "There were many men in the area four and one half miles to the southeastward of Savo Island," Lieutenant Commander Price recorded. "Some were on rafts, some in life jackets and some swimming. . . . The work was slow for most of the men were near exhaustion and had to be lifted bodily out of the water. The area was combed thoroughly and it is believed that all survivors were picked up." Price had special praise for the courage of Lieutenant John Feick, Lieutenant Joseph F. Illick, Ensign Arnold C. Mealy, and Ensign Andrew T. Fischer, who time after time dove into the shark-infested water to rescue helpless men and carried heaving lines to nearby rafts so that they could be hauled alongside the ship.

Lieutenant Commander Craighill from the *Vincennes* ordered able-bodied men off the raft he had found and finally managed to fill it with seriously wounded. They had been in the water for about ten minutes when, through the blackness, they heard the sound of voices and saw the shapes of people on other rafts nearby. These carried Captain Riefkohl, the navigator, and several other officers, including the wounded executive officer, Commander Mullan.

Riefkohl, washed over the rails with his orderly and chief yeoman, had found a raft in record time. In it he met up with the mess attendant who had been on the operating table when surgeon Commander Blackwood was killed. He still held his broken jaw together with one hand, with the other doing what he could to help more seriously injured onto the raft.

Presently, many rafts were floating together and Captain Riefkohl and Lieutenant Commander Craighill, assisted by other able-bodied personnel, began administering first-aid to the wounded. Men were calling to each other in the water, offering to help and shouting for stragglers to join them. At first Riefkohl ordered flashlights to be used to attract ships, but none were seen. Then he banned the use of lights unless it was certain that a ship was friendly. Lights, he feared, would attract enemy submarines. He also passed word that men were not to attempt to swim for Savo, where there might be enemy outposts.

After swimming for about five minutes, Chaplain Robert Schwyhart joined up with the raft flotilla. Dixie cups, toilet paper, pieces of lumber, and life jackets floated around them. At one point in the oily darkness of the water the chaplain felt a head and called, "Come on up here with us! Get a hold of the boom!" There was no response. The body floated close by and at last the chaplain asked for help. They forced the man underneath the boom to the other side, then he floated away.

Some time later they joined up with four more rafts fastened together, all so full they were almost submerged by the weight of the survivors. After the sun had been up for about an hour, the masts of destroyers appeared in the distance. They came nearer and nearer and were recognized as Allied. From one of the ships came a blinking signal: "There is an enemy submarine in the near vicinity. Keep yourselves out of the water as much as possible. We are going to drop depth charges." The destroyers took up position in a triangle and let go their charges, fifteen in all. In fact, there were no submarines, Japanese or American, for miles. Soon a destroyer, the *Mugford,* approached and men climbed her cargo nets to safety.

Earlier, Warrant Officer Frederick Moody, pharmacist attached to the *Vincennes*'s aft battle station, had swum away from the sinking ship and gone about fifty yards when he heard someone splashing ahead of him. Moody and the sailor stuck together and watched as the *Vincennes* settled down, "just as if she wanted to go to sleep." They continued swimming without knowing where the nearest shore lay. In search of a raft, they heard someone floundering about and swam over to find chief watertender M. S. Iwanicka, who recognized Moody's voice. He was badly wounded, his entire back lacerated by shrapnel. Iwanicka could not swim, but he floated along with the other men. This made three of them. It was slow going, but there was no advantage to be had from hurrying. A little later they ran into one of the *Vincennes*'s bakers, a man named Weist from Pennsylvania who had a distinct Dutch accent. "I think I hurt pretty bad, Doc. I don't think I make it maybe." He had a broken leg and shrapnel injuries. The baker from Pennsylvania made four. They continued and soon came across Bill Kramer, a machinist's mate and a very strong swimmer. Five hours after they abandoned ship, the *Helm,* returning from the wrong rendezvous point, came along and took them all aboard. Then Moody and his fellows pitched in, recovering survivors and helping the wounded. One of the wounded, Warrant Officer Edward Forster, a white-haired chief machinist, was in a great deal of pain but insisted that the younger men be looked after first. Forster had been with the *Vincennes* when she was first commissioned. He died the next morning, lasting little longer than his ship.

As men were hauled aboard the *Helm,* Lieutenant Commander Carroll was surprised to see a young, fully clothed officer come over the rails looking as though he was about to attend a dress parade. Lieutenant

Commander Di Giannantonio, assistant engineering officer in the *Vincennes*'s after engine room, had had his pistol, shoes, gas mask, and cap when he walked off his ship into the sea. During six hours in the water he lost all these articles and swam off time after time to retrieve them, even his cap. "I remember how much I paid for it," he told Carroll, "and was damned if I was going to lose it now."

Life photographer Ralph Morse jumped into the sea as the *Vincennes* began to list, leaving all his battle shots and exclusive pictures of the marine landing on Guadalcanal in the ship's safe. He swam around in the black water, eventually meeting up with two fellow bridge players from the cruiser. Another officer they knew later joined them. There were three life preservers between the four of them, so they took turns holding on. This lasted about eight hours. "Luckily, it was a very noisy battle with shells going off and torpedoes hitting ships," Morse wrote. "I guess any shark in his right mind got the hell out of there."

A destroyer picked them up at last and took them to Noumea. Rumors were everywhere, as Morse recounted: "The island blocked out our radars"; "the Japs hid behind the islands"; "the spotter plane did not report seeing the Jap fleet"; "the spotter plane reported the Jap task force, but the admiral did nothing about it. You name it and there was a rumor for anything you might decide happened that night."

Chaplain Schwyhart, safe aboard the *Mugford,* joined forces to help the doctors. With only sufficient strength to climb the nets, some pickups died minutes after collapsing on the deck. Their bodies were placed in blankets, weighted down with 5-inch projectiles, and after a brief burial ceremony put over the rails. At noon, survivors from the *Mugford* were transferred to the transport *Barnett* for the journey to Noumea. Chaplain Schwyhart worked with a medical officer and chief pharmacist's mate from the *Canberra* who organized volunteers to assist with the wounded on a regular watch schedule. Apart from officers and men from the four lost cruisers, there were thirty-five Japanese prisoners, fifteen of them wounded. Chaplain Schwyhart arranged for volunteer corpsmen to care for the prisoners. The American and Australian sailors at first shunned this task, but on a tour of inspection the next day, Schwyhart found that the group of volunteers caring for the prisoners had grown from two to about fifteen. One wounded Japanese spoke a little English; the men tried in vain to get information from him.

Many more wounded died on board the *Barnett.* They were wrapped in weighted canvas bags and buried from the fantail. The *Canberra*'s Roman Catholic chaplain and Chaplain Schwyhart conducted a short, nonsectarian service, as it was impossible to determine who among the dead was Protestant and who Catholic. Those buried that morning were Captain Getting of the *Canberra,* veteran machinist Warrant Officer Edward Forster from the *Vincennes,* whom Warrant Officer Moody had met aboard the *Helm,* and a third man, unknown to anyone except Chaplain Schwyhart. He was a Japanese prisoner.

While rescue ships continued to drag men from the sea, the *Astoria* began her second battle. Her engineering officer, Lieutenant Commander Hayes, reported to Captain Greenman, who had returned in the *Bagley* with a repair party, that he had been able to enter the engine rooms and no. 4 fireroom and that, if power were provided, it might be possible to get up steam. The fires had moderated; there could be access over the gun deck on the starboard side of the forecastle. The hand-operated gasoline pump that executive officer Shoup and his men had heard earlier was secured to a life raft alongside moved aft and used to pump water. The *Astoria* was peppered with 8-inch-shell holes above the waterline on the port side, in the hangar bulkhead, below the galley, and abreast of fireroom no. 1.

The extent of the fire forward could not be determined, for men could get no farther than fireroom no. 1. Finally it was decided that fireroom no. 4 offered the only opportunity to get up steam. A brigade was formed, using buckets and powder cans in an effort to subdue the topside fires and to improve access forward. Lieutenant Commander Topper and his crew penetrated all accessible parts of the ship below decks to determine damage to the hull and see if the ship was taking on water.

Before the *Bagley* left, an attempt had been made to assemble the dead on the after deck. Now the sailmaker and his assistants prepared all the bodies that could be found for a mass funeral service. About thirty bodies were sewed up in weighted canvas. The pharmacists' mates collected identification tags and put them into a box.

The list on the ship at this time was about 3 degrees, no more than it had been for at least three hours. At 0700, two hours after the *Bagley* had reported the *Astoria*'s condition, the fast World War I destroyer minesweeper, the *Hopkins* (Lieutenant Commander Benjamin Coe), came within hail of the crippled ship and was requested to tow her to shallow water off Guadalcanal.

The *Astoria* began listing more and she was now dead in the water. The *Hopkins* maneuvered under the bigger ship's stern and collected her tow line. Going ahead slowly, the line streamed and tightened. So far, so good. For a second or so it seemed that, ever so slowly, the *Astoria* was moving, but the chain carried away when speed increased to ten knots. The minesweeper maneuvered to pass the tow a second time, making one unsatisfactory approach and backing clear. The next approach was better: the towing cable was passed around the base of the winch on the *Hopkins* and shackled to her own port, the *Hopkins*'s stern held against that of the cruiser with a manila hawser.

Hoses, gasoline handbillies, and a submersible electric pump were taken aboard the *Astoria* to help with the fires. However, the power lead that was to be spliced into the *Astoria*'s electrical system was useless because of the difference in voltage. An hour and a half later, towing commenced again. On Captain Greenman's orders the *Astoria* was turned 300 degrees to head for the distant shore of Guadalcanal. Cheers echoed from the cruiser as she gained about three knots headway, but she continued in the wrong direction, her rudder apparently off center, the tow wire too short. It was an unequal tug of war.

The *Hopkins* put on full speed, twenty knots on one engine, back one third on the other, and full rudder, to counteract the *Astoria*'s turning tendency. Like a giant battered crab, the cruiser pulled sideways, fighting against the strain. The cable held and both ships believed that she could be beached. Below decks, salvage parties made repairs, plugging holes with clothing and mattresses. The sea was calm and there was a breath of a chance that if they reached shallow water, the battle would be won. Captain Greenman received word that more help was on the way in the shape of the destroyer *Buchanan,* and at 0800 he made a report via the *Hopkins*'s radio expressing the hope that the ship could be salvaged with additional supplies of power and water.

Meanwhile, Topper kept an eye on a mark he made on the *Astoria*'s well deck. With the list to port increasing, the waterline on the port side had dropped about 12 degrees. He could now get into the forecastle. While there, he noticed bubbles of yellow gas escaping up the port side of the ship at about turret no. 2. There were several internal explosions forward and rumbling noises indicating that bulkheads had carried away. Topper directed everyone to leave the forecastle and went back aft to report to the captain and the executive officer. Captain Greenman had not given up the fight. The ship, he believed, would not list much more, so he decided to make another attempt to extinguish fires in the wardroom and below.

About 0900, the *Wilson* came to the ship's rescue. She put a working party aboard to assist the *Astoria*'s fire party and pumped water on the fires for an hour or so. The *Astoria*'s need for power for the submersible pump now became less urgent. The *Hopkins* called for more tow wire, but soon after 1100 both she and the *Wilson* were called away to screen the transports. The *Buchanan,* it was reported, was coming in to help fight the fires, and the 6,000-ton transport *Alchiba* would take over the tow. The *Wilson* and the *Hopkins* took with them several hundred survivors plucked from the sea for transfer to the *Hunter Liggett* at the transport area.

Topper kept an eye on his mark on the well deck. Several of the holes forward, above the armor belt, were shipping water, and the list was increasing rapidly. The mattresses and pillows crammed into holes had not worked, and now, despite further efforts, there was nothing left to plug up holes. With the list to port so rapid, Topper, executive officer Shoup, and chief engineer Hayes realized that plans should be made to abandon ship. They went to the forecastle and recommended to Greenman that the *Buchanan* be directed to take off personnel.

The *Astoria*'s time was running out. Before the *Alchiba* reached the cruiser, her bulkheads collapsed, fires were racing through her, and the list increased to a terrifying 30 degrees. The *Alchiba* was close in, waiting to take over the tow, when right at noon Captain Greenman ordered abandon ship. The main deck awash, men slid down lines or jumped into the water, clutching at anything that would keep them afloat. By the time Captain Greenman and executive officer Shoup left, water had risen to the barbette of turret no. 3. The *Astoria* now had a list of 45 degrees.

From the *Bagley* they watched as men made their way down the slanting sides of the *Astoria* into the water. Some men poised for a shallow dive. Others stepped into the sea and began to swim. Soon the sea was a mass of bobbing heads as hundreds of men took off toward the waiting destroyers. It looked like the start of a marathon. When gunnery officer Truesdell went over the side, he saw the 8-inch guns of turret no. 3 "kissing the water."

The long fight to save the ship was over. The *Astoria* turned over on her port beam, rolled slowly, and settled slightly by the stern. Her bow rose a few feet above water, and at 1215, without further ado, she disappeared below the surface. There had been no time to conduct a burial service. In their canvas shrouds, the *Astoria*'s dead went down with her.

The *Bagley* had reported the *Astoria*'s condition at 0500, when there was still a possibility that the cruiser could be beached. She had fought alone for two hours before the *Hopkins* came to the rescue, and then the hard-working minesweeper struggled for another two hours to tow her to the shore before being called away. The *Hopkins*'s efforts were not appreciated by the *Astoria*'s gunnery officer, Lieutenant Commander Truesdell.[1] They were, in his words, "reluctant and slight. . . . The *Hopkins* was scared." In any case, Admiral Turner believed, the deep water around Savo Island would have made it most difficult for destroyers to beach the cruiser without themselves going aground. "Destroyers make very bad towing vessels," he said. "In addition to that, it would have been the height of military unwisdom to have beached the *Astoria* on Savo Island and then to have abandoned her for later capture by the Japanese. The *Astoria* was far better off at the bottom of Ironbottom Sound, than beached on Savo Island."

The *Ralph Talbot* had fought her own lonely battle, against the three cruisers of the Japanese western force, the *Furutaka, Tenryu,* and *Yubari,* operating with the assistance of searchlights from the destroyer *Yunagi*. She was still fighting ten minutes after Mikawa's decision to retire.

The Japanese destroyer *Yunagi* also fought alone, sinking the *Chicago,* so she claimed, then encountering another "light cruiser of the *Achilles* class." Her commanding officer, Lieutenant Okada, says that he did not see the American destroyer *Jarvis*. Despite this assertion, a translation of Cruiser Division 18's war diary shows that she "inflicted damage on the ship, which had tried to escape."

Admiral Turner had ordered the commander of the *Jarvis,* Lieutenant Commander William W. Graham, to stand by for an escort and then proceed via Lengo Channel to Efate, where he would report to Commander, South Pacific. After the attack, the *Dewey* had towed the *Jarvis* toward Beach Red. There were still a few miles to go when she restored power and the *Dewey* cast off. The *Jarvis* proceeded at five knots, and about 0430 anchored in about three fathoms near the eastern end of Beach Red, five miles east of Lunga Point, at which time a working party from the *McCawley* arrived to give assistance.

On his way to the anchorage, Captain Flynn, commander of Destroyer Squadron 4, inspected the *Jarvis,* reported her condition over TBS to Turner, and recommended that she proceed alone to Sydney for repairs.[2] Turner made no recommendation at the time, but later in the afternoon, when Flynn came aboard the *McCawley,* the admiral told him that the *Jarvis* was to go to Efate via Lengo Channel, escorted by a destroyer as soon as one could be fueled. He sent a boat to bring the executive officer of the *Jarvis,* Lieutenant James H. Hay, to the *McCawley*. Hay, reporting that his captain believed the ship could safely make seven knots, strongly recommended she be sent to Sydney. Turner disapproved and issued explicit oral orders for the captain of the *Jarvis.* She was to wait for an escort. He mentioned that Lengo Channel was free of mines; the ship should proceed via sheltered waters and close to shore, so that she could be beached if Lieutenant Commander Graham considered it necessary.

In vain, the destroyer *Hovey* searched until sunrise for the *Jarvis.* Soon after daylight a plane from the *Saratoga* saw the crippled destroyer, southwest of Guadalcanal. She seemed to be in poor condition, down at the bow and trailing oil. This was the last friendly sighting of the *Jarvis.*

Torpedo bombers of Japan's Twenty-Fifth Air Flotilla found her in the afternoon. The pilots, mistaking her for a light cruiser, attacked without mercy. The *Yunagi*'s war diary reports that on 9 August "our air force was ordered to attack and destroy the damaged destroyer, which split and sank." Lieutenant Commander Graham had jettisoned all his boats and rafts after the earlier torpedo hits, and now 247 officers and men, the destroyer's entire complement, went down with her, including two men picked up by the *Hopkins* that day and later returned to the *Jarvis.*

Although the destroyer's commander probably did not receive the full visual dispatch confirming Turner's orders, or the written orders sent by boat, there was no doubt in Turner's mind that her commander had received the oral orders he gave to the *Jarvis*'s executive officer. "Her commanding officer, the late Lieutenant Commander William W. Graham, by departing from Guadalcanal on August 8, 1942, in the manner in which he did, chose to act contrary to explicit orders from me which I believe he received and understood. Had he survived the loss of the *Jarvis,* I would have recommended him for court-martial for disobedience of orders."[3]

The *Jarvis*'s dead brought the Allied loss to 1,275 officers and men killed or missing. More than 700 were wounded. The figures break down as follows:

	Killed or missing	*Wounded*
The *Vincennes*	332	258
The *Quincy*	370	167
The *Astoria*	216	186
The *Canberra*	84	109
The *Chicago*	2	21
The *Ralph Talbot*	16	23
The *Patterson*	8	11
The *Jarvis*	247	

As details reached Mikawa from the Japanese ships, it appeared that a total of one enemy light cruiser, eight heavy cruisers, and five destroyers had been sunk, and five heavy cruisers and four destroyers damaged. However, based on the *Chokai*'s view of the action from the bridge, final estimates were five enemy heavy cruisers and four destroyers sunk.

The report noted that one of the heavy cruisers had carried an admiral's flag. (This was the *Vincennes,* which had hoisted a red-striped flag similar to a Japanese admiral's flag.) The *Chokai* had been hit in "some ten places," including the operations room, turret no. 1, hull, and funnels. She lost thirty-four men in action and had forty-eight wounded. The *Aoba* reported no personnel casualties. Two of her torpedo tubes were rendered useless, "cause unknown." She suffered fires in the launching-tube chambers and elsewhere, "because of the wind." The *Kako* reported neither casualties nor damage. The *Kinugasa* had one man killed, one wounded. Her port steering control room was damaged, a storeroom flooded by a shell hit, and her towing gear damaged. Her report noted "hits in no. 1 engine room and interior fires caused damage." The *Furutaka* reported neither damage nor casualties. In the light cruiser *Tenryu,* twenty-three men were killed and twenty-one wounded when shell fragments hit the deck. The *Yubari* reported no casualties. Damage was confined to "some scratches from light fire of enemy destroyer."

During the battle, the Japanese fired a total of 1,844 shells, making 159 definite hits on the Allied cruisers and destroyers and not less than 64 likely hits, a total of about 223. The Allied ships fired a total of 471 shells, making about 10 hits: 4 on the *Chokai,* 2 on the *Kinugasa,* 3 on the *Tenryu,* and 1 on the *Yubari.*

"The element of surprise worked to our advantage and enabled us to destroy every target taken under fire," Mikawa wrote. "I was greatly impressed, however, by the courageous action of the northern group of U.S. cruisers. They fought heroically despite heavy damage sustained before they were ready for battle. Had they had even a few minutes' warning of our approach, the results of the action would have been quite different."

Part Four

THE AFTERMATH

15

Turner and Crutchley "Did Their Best"

Soon after the Battle of Savo Island, the U.S. Navy began a series of inquiries into the disaster. Admiral Ghormley conducted the first, giving a critical report to Admiral Nimitz on 17 October. Ghormley believed that the destroyer screen, consisting of the *Blue* and the *Ralph Talbot,* had been too weak to warn of the approach of Mikawa's force from the northwest. With its disposition, the screen almost completely depended on radar to detect the approach of enemy surface forces. Radar detection was not reliable because of the proximity of land.

The orders were faulty in requiring the destroyers to "shadow" an enemy force and report it frequently. Lack of sea room among the islands did not permit tactics of this nature. A high-speed enemy force would have come dangerously close to its objective before the destroyers could institute tracking or shadowing. No definite task had been assigned to the *Australia* and *Vincennes* groups, and no provision made for coordination of these two groups in the event of contact by the radar guard.

Ghormley cited eight reasons for the excessive Allied losses:

> 1. The special instructions for the screening group were too indefinite in regard to what the units of their group were to do and how they were to accomplish their tasks.
>
> 2. No special battle plan was prescribed to cover the possibility of a surface ship night attack on 8–9 August.
>
> 3. The night disposition relied principally on radar to detect the approach of enemy surface vessels.

> 4. OTC [officer in tactical command] of the screening group with his flagship was, in obedience to signal, absent when the action occurred.
> 5. The information of discovery of unidentified aircraft prior to the action failed to reach all of the cruisers involved, nor did it reach Commander Task Force 62 (Turner) or Commander Task Group 62.6 (Crutchley). The vessels which did receive this information failed to attach proper significance to the report.
> 6. The cruisers were in the usual condition of night readiness for vessels engaged in patrolling.
> 7. Surprise.
> 8. The tactical requirement of being on the defense.

In a typically pertinent comment, Admiral Nimitz noted: "The basis of the Japanese victory, which is the basis of most victories, was their bold offensive spirit and alertness. Our forces were fatigued after several days of offensive operations and were engaged in protecting our transport groups which were discharging important supplies. This . . . accentuates the necessity for the best possible measures to guard against surprise."

A more detailed inquiry was made under the direction of Rear Admiral R. S. Edwards, Admiral King's chief of staff. Officers combed the war diaries and battle reports of the various ships involved. The result, "Secret Information Bulletin No. 2: Battle Experience Solomon Islands Actions," was also critical:

> It is felt that the basic concept of the defense of our transports off Guadalcanal 8–9 August was wrong. Our cruisers should have been kept concentrated, and our destroyer scouts, in as great a number as could be, should have been projected far enough westward to ensure timely and sure warning. The fallacy of dividing defending forces is as old as war. In modern naval warfare tactical surprise is such a devastating thing that it must be guarded against above everything else. Placing sole dependency upon two destroyers so located that their radar was apparently not to be depended upon for protection against a tactical surprise was, in this case, disastrous.
>
> The two groups of cruisers off Savo were steaming around squares, five miles on the side, in column at 10 to 12.5 knots [*sic*]. Each cruiser had two destroyers, one on each bow of the leading ship at 1,500 yards. Speed is the best protection for cruisers and destroyers. A high-speed patrol west of Savo Island should have been more effective.

Why the report of the Japanese surface force allegedly sighted at 1127 on 8 August did not get to the proper authorities was a mystery, the report said. In fact, the real mystery, as we now know, lay in an entirely different quarter. Despite overwhelming evidence that Stutt's signal was received during the day, this was never acknowledged, not even in this frank report, which went on to say:

> During the afternoon of 8 August a report was received that three enemy cruisers, three DDs and two PCs or AVs had been sighted at 1025 Zone 11 time on course 120 degrees T, speed 15. The reported position was about 300 miles to the north-west of our position. Another report apparently on the same force reported two CAs, one CL, one ship of *Southampton* class, some DDs not remembered and some unidentified at about 1200 (Zone 11) about 25 miles south of the first position. This should have been ample warning provided it was given to proper authorities.

The report pointed out that there had been notable lapses in communication. "The failure of the report of the approaching enemy force to get through to Rear Admirals Turner and Crutchley was most regrettable. Several of their subordinates had the information, but—probably assuming that the seniors had it also—did nothing about it."

While Admiral Edwards' report was still being put together, Admiral King directed Admiral Arthur J. Hepburn, former commander in chief of the U.S. Fleet, to report to CinCPac and conduct an "informal inquiry" into the circumstances attending the loss of the *Quincy, Vincennes, Astoria,* and *Canberra.* In addition to examining those circumstances, Hepburn was to give his opinion as to "whether or not culpability attaches to any individual engaged in the operation. Recommendations are not desired."

Hepburn had commanded U.S. submarine chasers under Admiral Sir Lewis Bayly, RN, Commander in Chief, Western Approaches, during World War I. A battleship captain during the 1920s, after promotion to rear admiral Hepburn commanded the control force of the U.S. Fleet and then served as member of the naval technical staff for the London Naval Conference in 1922, later as naval adviser at the disarmament conference in London in 1930. From June 1936 to January 1938 he was Commander in Chief, U.S. Fleet. From May to December 1938, he headed a committee preparing recommendations for extensive base development in the United States and its possessions for submarines, destroyers, mine craft, and naval air. His comprehensive report was accepted in its entirety and must be regarded as a major contribution to the U.S. Navy's success in World War II.

Now sixty-six, tactful, diplomatic, experienced, and on familiar terms with his British allies, Hepburn appeared to be an admirable choice to conduct the informal inquiry that King had in mind. He wasted no time, reporting to King in Washington, D.C., on 23 December and the following day conferring with and interrogating Vice Admiral Ghormley, who had been replaced as South Pacific commander by Admiral Halsey. Hepburn left Washington the day after Christmas and arrived in Pearl Harbor on 2 January, where he reported to Admiral Nimitz and met his newly appointed aide, Commander Donald J. Ramsey, a destroyer captain with experience in the judge advocate general's office in Washington. Meanwhile, Vice Admiral A. S. Carpender, commander of the Southwest Pacific naval forces, advised the Royal Australian Navy and passed on Admiral King's request for cooperation.

After arriving in Honolulu, Admiral Hepburn became ill and was hospitalized at Aiea. He remained there until 25 January. During the next seventeen days, he examined the CinCPac files on the Savo Island battle and interrogated Lieutenant Commander H. B. Heneberger, the senior *Quincy* survivor, and the navigator of the *Chicago,* Commander Elijah W. Irish.

Hepburn left Pearl Harbor on 11 February and arrived in Noumea, New Caledonia, a few days later. He spent a day there having talks with Admiral Halsey before flying to Brisbane to see General MacArthur. Appendix C of the admiral's report noted that on 17 February 1943 he visited MacArthur and told him he wanted

> to interrogate Admiral Crutchley. General MacArthur already knew of my mission and was of opinion that the most appropriate procedure would be take up the matter with the Prime Minister of Australia. I demurred to this, as I feared that a false impression might be created in the minds of the civil authorities. The investigation was merely in the fact-finding stage, a strictly administrative procedure. General MacArthur agreed that as Admiral Crutchley was serving under direct command of Vice-Admiral Carpender, USN, it would be proper for me to confer with him directly.

Admiral Crutchley, a key figure, arrived in Brisbane the following day under orders from Admiral Carpender and made a written submission in response to questions on the disposition of the forces and other matters connected with the battle. The two admirals traveled together to Melbourne on 20 February.

In his submission to Admiral Hepburn, and in the amplifying answers to questions raised by the admiral, Crutchley defended the disposition of the forces on the night of 8–9 August. His primary responsibility, he said, had been the defense of the transports. He believed, on the basis of intelligence, that the principal threat came from Japanese submarines known to be either in or approaching the area. He did not have enough destroyers to both protect the transports and strengthen the *Blue* and the *Ralph Talbot* on radar picket duty. Allowing a pickup range of six miles with radar, he believed that the two destroyers had an excellent chance of detecting any surface force attempting to enter the transport area from either side of Savo Island or from the east via Lengo, Sealark, or Nogela channels. The probable entrance of an enemy force would be from either side of Savo Island, but light craft, particularly, might use the other channels from the east. Accordingly, Crutchley decided to cover the three entrances by dividing his force in three, protecting the channels on either side of Savo with his heavy cruisers and the transports off Tulagi with his light cruisers.

Crutchley considered the Allied disposition to be sound because the enemy attack was intercepted. "Although we now know that the enemy force was numerically superior to either one of our heavy cruiser groups, our forces *did* [his emphasis] achieve our object which was to prevent the enemy from reaching the transports."

Fortuitously, as Hepburn was preparing to leave Melbourne for Canberra, a column by Drew Pearson appeared in American newspapers blaming both Crutchley and Turner for the Savo Island defeat.[1] According to Pearson, Vice Admiral F. J. Horne, assistant chief of naval operations, had told the House and Senate Naval Affairs Committee that the captains of the sunken cruisers had not ordered their men to battle stations and that an unnamed Australian admiral (in fact, Crutchley was English) had been in charge of a screening force of cruisers and destroyers. Both the Australian officer and Turner, Pearson went on, knew a Japanese force was in the vicinity, but they did not expect attack; therefore the Australian admiral left the *Canberra* (the journalist mistook her for the flagship) and spent the night on Turner's flagship, twenty-five miles from the scene of battle. Meanwhile, the officers under Turner and the Australian received no orders. Vice Admiral Horne "admitted that the Australians had not sent their troops to New Guinea to the extent [*sic*] requested by General MacArthur."

The Australian legation in Washington, having asked the State Department for a transcript of the proceedings before the House and

Senate committees, was informed that the hearings had been secret, and in any event, that shorthand notes were not taken. There was no transcript available.

The naval attaché at the Australian legation took the matter up with the Navy Department and saw Captain Ellis M. Zacharias and Rear Admiral Harold D. Train, director of naval intelligence. They agreed that Pearson's statements were incorrect. Train, who had been in touch with Admiral Horne, stated definitely that Horne had not made the statements attributed to him in the article. Horne, infuriated about the report, had informed the chairman of the House committee that if such misstatements were going to be printed, he would never again testify. According to Train, during the hearings Horne had been asked a number of yes-or-no questions, for example, "Was an Australian in command of the cruiser screen?" and "Was Admiral Turner in command of the whole force?" Both answers were yes. From such questions, the Navy Department said, Pearson had manufactured the article. Apparently Pearson had a reputation for untruthfulness and would like nothing better than to start a controversy. It was suggested that he had received his information from a member of the committee, but Admiral Train thought the State Department could have leaked it.

There were enough inaccuracies in Pearson's report to justify some sort of face-saving denial, but neither the Navy Department nor the Australian legation saw any purpose in countering the allegations. That would only draw attention to the humiliating defeat at Savo Island.

The incident nevertheless prompted the Australian prime minister John Curtin to ask his navy minister for an inquiry. Had the dispositions enabled the cruisers to operate their radar most effectively? Were the ships ready for immediate action, and was the radar apparatus in working order? Sir Guy Royle, chief of the naval staff, responded that the dispositions were sound, that the Royal Australian Navy was not in any way to blame for the loss of the American cruisers, that in fact, as a result of the action of the *Canberra,* the cruisers should have received ample warning to prepare for all eventualities, "which unfortunately they failed to do." As for the radar, the *Canberra* had had a surface set of type 271 that had invariably given good results on previous occasions, but it was installed in the ship only a month before the action took place and there were not enough experienced operators.

Curtin's concern that the Royal Australian Navy might be censured by the Hepburn report was allayed when the admiral arrived in Canberra. Crutchley had impressed him as a highly intelligent and competent officer. Hepburn told Sir Guy Royle he was impressed by the thoroughness with which Crutchley and senior staff officers had worked out the dispositions of the screening force and by the reasons for those dispositions. And at a meeting of the Advisory War Council, Hepburn announced that the result of his inquiries had been much more reassuring than anticipated. He was happy to say that he would return to Washington with a much more agreeable task than he expected to perform when he first arrived in the South Pacific.

After his one-day stop in Canberra, Admiral Hepburn returned to Brisbane and spent another four days there before going on to Noumea, New Caledonia, the headquarters of the South Pacific Command. Appendix C of his report, which lists the names of all officers he spoke with, does not mention that he interviewed or interrogated anyone during his second stay in Brisbane. One can assume that he did not. Nor did he make a serious effort to determine whether the Hudsons had broken radio silence to warn the task forces of approaching Japanese cruisers. In a comment on the receipt of Stutt's messages in the evening of 8 August, he noted that

> This despatch was received on the Bells schedule by CTG 62.6 [Admiral Crutchley] and the CTF 62 [Admiral Turner] on the Fox schedule. It was also received by at least one of the carriers under CTF 61 and by other units of the task force. Whether the sighting plane made a report at time of sighting, or made the report upon return to its base, it has been impossible definitely to determine. It is the policy of the RAAF radio stations in operational areas to destroy their files after one month. The pilot of the plane in question could not be identified.

In his two days in Noumea, Admiral Hepburn interviewed Admiral Turner and Captain DeWitt Ramsay, commanding officer of the *Saratoga,* and examined South Pacific Command files. He was in Pearl Harbor between 9 and 26 March to prepare his report and interrogate Captain W. G. Greenman, captain of the *Astoria.* Two more interrogations, of Captain Riefkohl and Captain Bode at Corpus Christi, Texas, on 2–3 April, completed his assignment, and on 7 April he was back in Washington, D.C., to serve as chairman of the U.S. Navy's General Board.

In January 1946, nearly three years after Hepburn filed his report—it had been circulating under a "secret" classification—James Forrestal, secretary of the navy, wrote to the chief of naval operations for his comments on a proposed release of the report.[2] The letter was annotated with various remarks recommending the release of any portions that would not cause "international friction." One recommendation, endorsed by the Joint Chiefs of Staff, was to withhold a copy from the Australians. A copy had to go to the Australian Naval Board, the annotation said, as the board had been asked to cooperate with Admiral Hepburn. In fact, a copy had been sent to the board as early as October 1943, and Crutchley had been advised of the finding that exonerated him. Missing from the report in the Australian Archives, however, are the vital annexes to the report that might lead an independent investigator to conclusions differing sharply from Hepburn's. The Australians received the findings, but not, apparently, the evidence.

In a cable to Canberra, the Australian naval attaché in Washington said that the U.S. Navy Department had proposed that all reports on the Battle of Savo Island be declassified, with the object of making them available to the Office of Public Information and private individuals.[3] Documents marked for declassification included a report by Rear Admiral Crutchley to Rear Admiral Turner, reports by the executive officer and engineering officer of the *Canberra* and by the commanding officer of the *Hobart,* as well as reports from the American ships involved. The Australians had no objection, they replied, provided all relevant papers, including the Hepburn report, were also published. They presumed that Admiralty concurrence would also be sought. Further comment would be made after the available papers had been studied.

Back came the reply from Washington that the Navy Department did not want to release the Hepburn report for "diplomatic" reasons. It wanted to publish only those parts of the Savo Island reports consisting of operations orders, war diaries, and ships' action reports. The message described the Hepburn report as entirely factual and added, "All opinion and controversial matter has been removed, and it is in no way critical of Crutchley and the Australian ships." The Australian government voicing no objection, operations orders, war diaries, and action reports were duly declassified.[4]

Even accepting that the Battle of Savo Island remains a highly sensitive topic, it is difficult at first sight to imagine any legitimate reason for the protracted delay in releasing the report, other than that the navy might have wanted to spare the feelings of the relatives of Captain Bode of the *Chicago* who, just over two weeks after being interrogated by Admiral Hepburn in Corpus Christi, took his own life. Only the unfortunate Bode, and to a lesser extent, Captain Riefkohl of the *Vincennes,* of all those who might have been censured, came under critical attention in Hepburn's report.

"During this investigation," said the Hepburn report,

> there has not come to light, either directly or by hearsay, a single incident reflecting upon the conduct under fire of any officer or enlisted man. In adjudging culpability in circumstances such as those under consideration, there is generally a twilight zone . . . between culpable inefficiency on the one hand and a more or less excusable error of judgment on the other. It is hardly possible to construct all the conditions of an emergency as they may have reasonably influenced an officer who had to take an instant decision on the spot. There is only one instance in the circumstances immediately attendant upon the Savo Island battle in which censure is definitely indicated and in which the foregoing considerations do not apply. That was in the action, or inaction, of the commanding officer of the *Chicago* in not taking the head of column position upon departure of *Australia*. In night action, especially, follow-the-leader tactics are always a most important resource, and may be the only resource, of the commander of a detachment to impose his leadership on a group. The failure of the commanding officer of the *Chicago* to take this position is, at the least, a severe indictment of his professional judgment. At the same time, it would be difficult to sustain a charge that his decision, or lack of decision, resulted in greater damage than actually occurred. The most apparent possibility is that the *Chicago* would have been sunk instead of the *Canberra*. *Chicago*'s movement to the westward, away from the scene of action, for almost forty minutes after the action opened, and for about thirty-five minutes after the last reported contact in that direction, is also inexplicable.
>
> The leadership shown by Captain Riefkohl, commanding the *Vincennes* group, is far from impressive. His choice of patrol courses, involving a change of course every half hour, and the chance . . . of being caught on a very disadvantageous course, was not well conceived. His orders for the night and his communications to the ships of his group show more the commanding officer of a ship than a flag officer. . . . A flag officer was certainly needed in command of this detachment. It is impossible to say, however, that lacking foreknowledge of the event [*sic*], any flag officer in the area should have been shifted from his assigned task to take command.

The Hepburn report was in five parts, with a separately bound and indexed volume of annexes. Part 1 consisted of directives for command organization and an outline of operations preceding the Savo Island night action. Part 2 reviewed the battle action reports. Part 3 commented on Part 1 in the light of the latest information available to Hepburn. Part 4 was a critique of the action. And Part 5 noted Hepburn's findings of fact and opinion.

Part 3 was based largely on information regarding the composition and movement of the Japanese force, which had come to light through captured documents, prisoner-of-war reports, and other intelligence, source unstated, from the files of CinCPac. The composition of the attacking force was identified in full. "This force," wrote Admiral Hepburn, "was east of Bougainville at 1120 [*sic*] 8 August when it was sighted by an allied plane which the Japanese reported as having been 'driven off.' At the time of this contact, the Japanese ships were engaged in picking up planes." The admiral confused the sighting and the time, but his reference to the plane having been driven off repeated the phrase used in the *Chokai*'s detailed action report.[5] This intelligence seems to have been the work of cryptanalysts, and if so, indicates that they were aware some two weeks after the event that one of the Hudsons had broken radio silence.

To facilitate his work, and at the same time to interfere as little as possible with ongoing operations, Hepburn had conducted his inquiry informally. The objective was to find out exactly what caused the defeat and to determine whether any officers involved in the planning and execution of Operation Watchtower were culpable. A detailed report of this nature was clearly likely to produce evidence that had not hitherto come to light. But the report, like others, determined that the Hudsons' signals failed to reach the task forces in time for appropriate counter-action, and accepted the view that Crutchley and Turner first learned of the presence of the Japanese force at 1845 on 8 August, when the Fox schedule relayed the delayed report by Stutt. "It is established," the report said, "that news of the contact did not reach Admiral Turner, or Admiral Crutchley, until between 1800 and 1900 on the 8th."

The report ascribed the primary cause of defeat to the complete surprise achieved by the enemy. Hepburn cited the following, in order of importance, to explain why the enemy was able to achieve surprise:

1. Inadequate condition of readiness on all ships to meet sudden night attack.
2. Failure to recognize the implications of the presence of enemy planes in the vicinity prior to the attack.
3. Misplaced confidence in the capabilities of the radar installations on the *Ralph Talbot* and the *Blue.*

4. Failure in communication, which resulted in lack of timely receipt of vital enemy contact information.

5. Over-dependence on ineffective radar scouting, obviously based on inadequate appreciation by commanders involved of the limitation of the sets.

6. Failure in communications and of standard practice resulting in failure to give timely information of the fact that there had been practically no effective reconnaissance covering enemy approaches on the day of 8 August.

One reason the Allies suffered disproportionate damage was the withdrawal of the carrier groups the evening before the battle. Because of this, Admiral Turner called his conference, during which the decision was made that would result in the absence of the *Australia* from the action. The carrier withdrawal was furthermore responsible for there being no force available to inflict damage on the retreating enemy.

Admiral Hepburn's report went first to Admiral Nimitz at Pearl Harbor. In general agreement with the findings, Nimitz too believed the foremost reason for the Allies being surprised was inadequate readiness for sudden night attack. He summarized the other primary causes:

(a) Communication weaknesses;

(b) Failure of either carrier or land-based air to conduct effective search, and lack of co-ordination of searches;

(c) Failure to track after contact by RAAF plane based on Milne Bay and resultant lack of utilization of our air striking power;

(d) Erroneous estimate as to the probable intention of the enemy force, possibly based in part on the lack of appreciation that the enemy would be bold enough to attack with inferior surface forces;

(e) Over-dependence on ineffective radar scouting, obviously based on inadequate appreciation by commanders involved of the limits of the sets;

(f) Failure to take action when unidentified planes were sighted (neither Admiral Turner nor Admiral Crutchley was notified of the presence of these planes);

(g) Lack of flag officers in the cruiser forces engaged;

(h) Finally, there is the probability that our forces were not psychologically prepared for action and that they were not sufficiently "battle-minded."

Before making his own comment on the Hepburn report, Admiral King considered a memorandum prepared by Captain George Russell, his flag secretary.[6] Though the navy had taken a beating, Russell commented, it did not necessarily mean that "somebody had to be the goat. . . . The operation was undoubtedly badly planned, and poorly executed, and there was no small amount of stupidity. But to me it is more of an object lesson in how not to fight than it is a failure for which someone should hang."

Fletcher and Noyes had been relieved of their commands, Russell said. No reason was assigned, but the inference was that Noyes, at least, had been tried and found wanting. Captain Riefkohl was not censured, but he was definitely stamped as falling short of flag officer caliber, and his career as a naval officer ended. Admiral McCain had failed to search the area where the Japanese might have been after Turner, in effect, asked him to do so, but apparently Hepburn did not feel that he should be called to account for it, and in any event, in view of subsequent events (McCain had taken over the Bureau of Personnel), "such action would be awkward, to say the least." Admiral Turner was pretty much given a clean bill of health. Admiral Ghormley was relieved, presumably because of the defeat. The only individual Hepburn directly censured, Russell went on, was Captain Bode, whose conduct could scarcely have been responsible for all the losses involved. He was now dead, the inference being that he had not wanted to face the music.

Russell's memorandum suggested two courses of action to Admiral King. He could accept the report, and except for the lessons learned, treat the matter as a dead issue. Or he could reexamine in detail the conduct of every officer involved.

Admiral King opted for the former course.

Commenting on Nimitz's opinion that surprise was the immediate cause of defeat, King remarked that he was inclined to agree.[7] The question thus arose whether any officer should be held accountable. Considering that this was the first battle for most of the ships and flag officers involved—that it was the first time most of them had been in the position of "kill or be killed"—the answer to that specific question, in his judgment, was no. They simply had not learned how and when to stay on the alert. The deficiencies that manifested themselves in the action, particularly with reference to communications and readiness, together with erroneous conceptions of how to conduct an amphibious operation like Watchtower, had long been corrected. Furthermore, adequate administrative action had been taken with respect to those individuals whose performance of duty did not measure up.

He saw nothing to be gained by further action, and deemed it necessary to record his approval of the decisions and conduct of Rear Admirals Turner and Crutchley. In his judgment, those two officers were in no way at fault. Both had found themselves in awkward positions, and both had done their best with the means at their disposal.

16

The Tangled Web

For another thirty years, the Hepburn report gathered dust in U.S. Navy archives. Not until 3 May 1973 was it declassified. By that time most of the principals involved in the battle were dead. Meanwhile, Rear Admiral Samuel Eliot Morison's version of events had become standard, repeated and embroidered time after time by other writers who, without a source note, denounced the Hudson crews for their failure to break radio silence and warn the American commands.

Morison, a Harvard professor, was commissioned as a lieutenant commander in the U.S. Naval Reserve after an interview with President Roosevelt and Secretary of the Navy Frank Knox in 1942. His job was to write the history of U.S. naval operations during World War II. In fifteen volumes, he went on to cover the action in every theater, assisted at various times by a number of naval officers. For the period including the battle of Savo Island, they included Commander James N. Shaw, who later retired as a rear admiral, and Lieutenant Roger Pineau, USNR, who would retire in the rank of captain. Morison insisted that he was not an official historian in the accepted sense. The navy provided him with full assistance but did not attempt to "prejudice my conclusions or set the pattern of my writing."

Every now and then, both before and after Morison published his version of events off Savo Island, a flurry of official anxiety about the battle rustled the files on both sides of the Pacific and the Atlantic. The transpacific exchange that accompanied the Drew Pearson column in 1943 was repeated in March of the following year when the *Times-Herald,* of Washington, D.C., published a report that virtually blamed Crutchley for the disaster.[1] British and Australian officials in Washington took issue with the Navy Department and reported in "most secret" dispatches to the Admiralty, and the Australian Naval Board, that Frank Knox would take steps to refute the story. When the British press failed to pick it up, it was felt more sensible to let the matter rest.

After the war, Captain Riefkohl attempted to have his reputation cleared without success. The still classified Hepburn report and the Naval War College's *War Analysis,* which repeated Hepburn's findings about the Hudsons' role, were the last word. In November 1963, however, A. J. Sweeting, acting general editor of the official Australian war history, wrote to members of two Hudson crews.[2] Could they help the project's naval historian to write more fully about the reconnaissance carried out by the RAAF prior to the Battle of Savo Island? "Morison makes much—too much, I believe—of the time taken by both Hudson pilots to report these sightings," he wrote.

"It is glaringly evident that Samuel Morison," Eric Geddes, Stutt's radio operator, wrote to Sweeting, "for reasons best known to himself, or in an apparent endeavor to cover up the deficiences of the American war machinery of the day, searched for a scapegoat. The inaccuracies of his report, although strongly worded and incriminating, make it . . . clear that his research was half-hearted and insincere. Further evidence of his insincerity is his failure to make a personal assessment of the situation, and, realizing the absolute absurdity of it, investigate the affair as you have done. This surely would have required less intellect than the decision [whether to break radio silence] which confronted the men he slandered."[3]

Having digested the crews' responses, Sweeting wrote to Lloyd Milne on 3 January 1964: "I agree with you that any blame for forwarding the sighting report lies elsewhere than with the Hudsons. Whether at this distance from events we can establish the real cause of the delay is another matter. My main concern was to clear the Australian pilots."

This letter stirred Nancy Milne, Lloyd's wife, to action.[4] But the closer she came to the facts the more difficult her task became, with the Australian government apparently determined to prevent her from making disclosures that might rock the transpacific boat. On 1 January 1985 she wrote to the director of public information, policy coordination division, Australian Department of Defense, applying under the Freedom of Information Act for Royal Australian Navy documents relating to the sightings of Mikawa's battle fleet by the Hudsons. Her research, she pointed out, had revealed that Morison's and other's version of the battle had been established to be incorrect. It was her aim to send a correct account of the part played by the RAAF to the Australian War Memorial, which had informed her that any documentary evidence could be included in updates of the Australian war histories. She also wanted to send the material to the Navy Yard in Washington, D.C., and if permission was granted by the Australian Archives, to seek publication answering the allegations made against the airmen and the RAAF operational command. "These men of the aircrews risked their lives to gather and pass intelligence concerning the enemy and have been sadly maligned by 'history,'" she added.

On 10 January, the officer in charge of business relating to the Freedom of Information Act wrote to say that her letter had been sent to the Australian Navy Office for attention. Eleven days later she received a letter from the assistant secretary, information policy, Department of Defense, advising her that he could not grant her access under the Freedom of Information Act. She should apply directly to the Australian Archives in Melbourne. Mrs. Milne returned to the archives. Some months later, she had equipped herself with enough information to list twenty-four signals that she would like to see. She filed a request on 11 September. More than two months passed before she received a letter from the regional director of the archives. "As requested, this material has been examined by our Access Regulation section and is available for you to consult in our Brighton search room," the letter said.

> It has, however, been decided to restrict access to some information contained in items Flag Signals of 8 August 1942 in accession series MP 1074/9, Flag Signals of 8 August 1942 in accession series MP 1074/7 and Mis Signals (Flag Out) of 8 August 1942 in accession series MP 1074/8. Your are entitled under the Archives Act to receive Statements of Reasons for the decision to withhold material. We are, however, unable to obtain them from the Department of Defence, which made the decision to withhold material. An explanation of your rights to seek review of these decisions is enclosed.

Two months later, another letter from the regional director enclosed the statement of reasons. "You will note that only two signals, 1141Z/8 and 1142/Z, are withheld from public access," this letter said. "The remaining twenty-two signals, previously withheld, have been re-examined and are now available for public access."

The date and time on the two signals indicated that they were sent at 1141 and 1142 on 8 August 1942, and thus that they might have some relevance to Willman's and Stutt's sightings. The statement of reasons provided other clues. "Both documents," it said,

> identify foreign governments as recipients of information gained through signals interception activities against specific targets. This finding is based on the inclusion of authorities of the foreign governments as addressees of the documents. This provides detail of intelligence collaboration which the foreign governments concerned have asked that we protect. The public release of the information could adversely and substantially prejudice Australia's present intelligence relations with foreign governments concerned. Release could therefore reasonably be expected to harm the defence, security and international relations of the Commonwealth [Australia].

All of this despite the fact that the U.S. government, by this time, had released voluminous works relating to signals interception and the role played by combined teams in Australia in radio traffic analysis and cryptanalysis.

For another five years the signals remained undisturbed, only to be taken out for fumigation. However, when the authors requested the declassified signals in April 1990, the archives replied that the fumigation process had gone wrong. The signals had become a "health hazard" and could not be made available until after sanitizing. In fairness, it must be said that this decision was quickly reversed. Copies of all signals were produced for inspection—only to be found unrelated to events off Savo Island on 8–9 August 1942! Better still, the Department of Defense assigned three officials to examine the Frumel files and other material to determine whether this organization had played any part in relaying the Hudson signals. Nothing was discovered in the documents that threw any light on the matter. By this time, however, documents available in the Washington Navy Yard irrefutably confirmed that Stutt's signal had been received by the task forces off Guadalcanal.

One of the arguments advanced by those who blamed the RAAF Hudsons for their failure to alert the Americans was that if only they had done their job, and got the signals through in time, all would have been well. But what if they did get their messages through and disaster followed?

Captain Riefkohl had no doubt whatsoever that the *Vincennes* had intercepted Stutt's signal long before it was transmitted on the Fox and Bells schedules.[5] During the captain's interrogation on 3 April 1943,

Admiral Hepburn said: "You had those contact reports sent out that day and you figured on the possibility of these people [the Japanese] coming in contact at night, but you apparently didn't think it amounted enough to be in Condition One. Is that right? Or didn't you?"

"No, sir, I didn't because of the fact that the higher command had the information on it," he replied.

"You mean you were waiting [*sic*] orders from them?"

"Not altogether. I received the report at 1015 in the morning [*sic*] and from what it said I figured the fellows on the carrier planes would get them in the afternoon. I expected to get a report on that. . . . The point is that everybody knew the attack was coming in the morning. The crew and everybody had been up since four o'clock that morning and had been fighting all day long and the day before been up since two o'clock. I was considering the desirability of keeping the personnel in the best condition for the morning attack which apparently was definitely coming."

"You apparently made the same guess everybody else did," said Hepburn.

"My assumptions were based on the information I had—not on what the admiral had. I felt he had this information and if necessary would give us a warning."

Captain Greenman was no less emphatic that Mikawa's presence off Bougainville had been reported early enough in the day for the carriers to take action. "The report was made to me some time after an air attack we had that morning," he told Hepburn. "The report was made either in the morning or some time before the afternoon action. This report came to me as having been picked up by a coastwatcher near Bougainville and [it] stated that the ships were pursuing a south-easterly course, speed 15. I believe it was an intercepted message from a coastwatcher."

"That report was received not later than in the morning?" asked Hepburn.

"It was earlier than three o'clock in the afternoon," Greenman replied.

"You are sure it was reported as coming from a coastwatcher?"

"As I recall, it was reported as coming from a coastwatcher on Bougainville."

"You don't know whether the *Vincennes,* the *Quincy* or anyone else caught it?

"No sir," he said. "We intercepted messages of this sort for general information."

Morison commented that Greenman and Riefkohl's belief that they had picked up a signal giving Mikawa's whereabouts originated with the sighting by the submarine S-38 on 7 August. "HMAS *Australia* was the only allied ship guarding the coastwatcher radio circuit and she received no coastwatcher report, so no other ship could possibly have got one," he wrote. The S-38 sighted Mikawa in St. George's Channel, between New Ireland and New Britain, not off the coast of Bougainville. Yet almost every ship knew that sightings had been made off Bougainville. Several officers made their calculations based on this and concluded that if the force continued to Guadalcanal, it would arrive some time after midnight on 8–9 August. If Crutchley's statement about the channels that he guarded was correct, he did not monitor coastwatcher frequencies. Others did. For example, when coastwatcher Mason sent his signal on 7 August that Bettys were overhead and clearly on the way to Guadalcanal, the *Canberra*'s boatswain's mate piped over the loudspeakers, "The ship will be attacked at noon by twenty-four torpedo bombers. All hands will pipe to dinner at eleven o'clock."

In his operation plan, Admiral Ghormley specifically required that signals on coastwatcher frequencies be enciphered and retransmitted to *all* ships. Moreover, several ships had heard the report that the Japanese formation included a ship that looked like a British *Southampton*-class cruiser. If this was received during daylight it could have come only from a signal Willman radioed from his aircraft.

Admiral Turner told Hepburn that he too had received the information during the afternoon, and that he had considered sending out a force that night to meet the Japanese ships.[6] He made no mention of this, however, in his comment to Nimitz on the Hepburn report. There he implied that his first news of the contact came at about 1820. Hepburn did not accept Turner's word for it.[7] He noted: "Admiral Turner's recollection was that [a report of] three cruisers, three destroyers, and three gunboats, or seaplane tenders [*sic*], was received by him in the early afternoon, but no confirmation of this."

When he was writing his account of the action, Morison also consulted Turner.[8] In his papers, under the heading "The Plane Sighting," the following passage appears: "TOR August 8 1036 (2236 Love). 'Air sighting 0001Z/8 (1101 Love) position 05°42S′ 156°05E′2 CA, 2L, 1 small cruiser similar to *Southampton* class. Ships opened fire on plane at 1020Z/8 (1220 L). Sighted small merchant ship in 07°02S′ 156°25E′ Course 290 degrees Speed 10 (east of Bougainville)." Then in handwriting: "This despatch annotated in Admiral Turner's hand: 'Note made

Jan 10. We received a report direct from plane during pm, as I remember. Can't find any record of it.'" In brackets, Morison added, "He had some arrangement for guarding scouting planes' circuit, so he told me May 16, 1943." In what appears to be his own handwriting, Morison also noted: "Riefkohl got sighting of Japs at 1530. Said had two seaplane tenders with 'em. Turner had same thing."

In other words, Morison had reason to believe that Turner had received Stutt's contact report long before it was transmitted on the Fox and Bells schedules. Despite this, he preferred the version given in the Hepburn report and wrote of Stutt, without indicating any source, that he had completely misled the American commands as to Japanese intentions. Even more curiously, he made no mention of Mikawa's intercept of Stutt's signal, an omission that has puzzled Japanese historians ever since, especially as Mikawa and Ohmae went over the chapter before its publication and made "sundry suggestions," which if accepted were to be incorporated into Morison's account.

The battle cannot be analyzed now, as it always has been in the past, on the assumption that the Allied forces failed to receive early warning that an enemy force was within striking range. Turner knew and decided that no further precautions were necessary even if a surface attack, which he thought was improbable, occurred. Crutchley knew, although under interrogation by Hepburn he did not admit it. Acting flag officer Riefkohl knew, and alone among senior commanders stressed the need, albeit only to his own ship's company, for special alertness. There is no evidence that Fletcher knew, although it was known aboard the *Saratoga*.

Crutchley's priority was the protection of the transports. During the day of August 8, CinCPac had reported that several units of Japan's submarine Squadron 3 and one from submarine Squadron 7 were en route to the Tulagi area, reinforcing the view Crutchley had held since leaving Fiji that a subsurface torpedo attack was always the main danger.

It is open to question whether the arrangements—having the transports at anchor, the screening forces making at best 12.5 knots, only two pickets on patrol north of Savo Island, and the crews of all ships permitted some relaxation from general quarters/battle stations—were adequate for their primary purpose. They are not consistent with Crutchley's insistence that he had taken serious account of the possibility of surface action. His decision to remove the *Australia* from the screen instead of using one of the two minesweepers at his disposal for transport to his meeting with Turner and General Vandegrift in the *McCawley* left the *Australia* group vulnerable to a surprise attack. To be fair, the nature of Turner's message left him with little choice. Nonetheless, Crutchley's signal to Captain Bode in the *Chicago* that he might or might not return that night was not that of a flag officer seriously entertaining the thought that his group might be involved in a surface action. Nor was his remark to Vandegrift, when the two officers were leaving the *McCawley* after the conference on 8–9 August, that the general's mission that night was more important than his own, that of a flag officer with any sense of urgency about returning to his command. (General Vandegrift was to board a destroyer minelayer that would take him to Tulagi for a conference with Rupertus to decide how many hours of unloading would be necessary to provide him with the minimum acceptable amount of supplies.) More than four hours of darkness remained when Crutchley reboarded the *Australia* and decided to remain with the transports instead of returning to the group.

Crutchley was unaware of the radar problems encountered by the *Blue* when approaching Savo Island on the night of 7 August, but his assumption that the radar required a surface range of only six miles to ensure that nothing could get by undetected failed to account for the fact that the two pickets, at the extremity of their patrols, might be separated by as much as eighteen miles. In the event, they were fourteen miles apart when Mikawa's force approached and slipped by unseen.

In *The Amphibians Came to Conquer,* Vice Admiral G. C. Dyer argued against critics of Crutchley's nighttime disposition, although Dyer, too, was unaware that Stutt had broken radio silence, and without mentioning his name made perhaps the unkindest comment of all about the airman: "He shall remain unidentified and alone with his conscience, as far as this writer is concerned." Crutchley, Dyer's argument ran, had two entrances to block. The one in the north, between Savo Island and Tulagi, was twelve miles wide (Dyer wrongly claimed), the southern one, between Savo Island and Guadalcanal, seven and a half miles wide. If the six heavy cruisers had been concentrated to the south, an ensuing battle would have put the transports within range of enemy guns and torpedoes. If the heavy cruisers had concentrated to the north in one column at a practical cruising speed of eighteen knots, they would have left an entrance open for the enemy to slip through. "It was as simple as that," Dyer wrote.

But was it?

Handling heavy ships in groups of more than four, Crutchley found, was unwieldy at night, but a high-speed concentrated patrol south of

Savo Island would have given the Allied force the opportunity to cross the T. This maneuver was executed with outstanding success two months later in the tracks of the *Blue* by Rear Admiral Norman Scott, with four cruisers and five destroyers in line ahead steaming at thirty knots, and again by Admiral J. B. Oldendorf with crushing success in the Battle of Leyte Gulf in 1944. Ushered into the twentieth century by Admiral Heihachiro Togo with brilliance and daring in the Battle of Tsushima in 1905, the maneuver had resulted in the sinking of eight Russian battleships and the capture of four others. Of the Russian cruisers, four were sunk, one was scuttled, three were interned in Manila, and one, the *Almaz,* ran undetected along the Japanese coast and arrived in Vladivostok, to be greeted by an enthusiastic crowd peering into the distance for the rest of the fleet.

If the concentrated cruiser force in line ahead had crossed the T on Mikawa's squadron, the problem that Crutchley envisaged in leading an Allied force of more than four heavy ships would have been minimized, even without voice communication. The ships that sank that night would, in all probability, have been Japanese, not American and Australian.

Warning time was not a factor in the admiral's dispositions. Crutchley was less frank than Turner when he was interrogated by Hepburn. In his "Report of Proceedings," written soon after the action, he had referred to an afternoon sighting of Mikawa's force. He failed to make any reference to this when Hepburn interrogated him. Hepburn's questions included the following: "With respect to operations on D and D plus 1 day, what information did you have of enemy surface forces in the area? My information indicates one contact report on 8 August. This was from an allied plane who at 1127 [*sic*] sighted a force of eight ships on course 140 degrees near Choiseul Island, evidently the force with which you were later engaged. Is that correct? When did you receive this report?" Crutchley listed the Fox and Bells signals at 0717Z/8 and 0742Z/8, contradicting a statement in his "Report of Proceedings" that he had received a report during the afternoon, a fact subsequently confirmed to the apparent satisfaction of the Australian Naval History Office.

In 1950, in response to a request from the Admiralty, the Australian naval liaison office in London wrote to the director of naval intelligence in Australia asking that an appropriate signal pack, marked "RACAS [rear admiral commanding Australian Squadron] CYPHER LOG, 1st to 31st August 1942," be perused to determine what Japanese sightings had been reported in the Solomons area on 8 August 1942.[9] The director passed this request to the Australian Naval History Office, which replied on 23 March. The pack, it had discovered, contained only one reference to enemy sightings. Much more significantly, one signal in the pack stated that all air reconnaissance reports on 8 August had been passed to Task Force 44, which was Commander, Task Group 62.6—Crutchley. The signal also gave the search pattern for Milne's Hudsons on 9 August, which, as usual, followed the pattern set on 5 August.

The Naval History Office referred to Crutchley's "Report of Proceedings" and his "Night Action off Savo Island, 9/8/42," appendix no. 6, stating that during the day there had been the report of an enemy force east of Bougainville steering southeast and that it was possible at twenty-five knots for the force to have reached Guadalcanal at the time the enemy force was actually there. Referring to an attached list of sightings, it continued: "It appears obvious that sighting No. 4 on the list [Stutt's], being the largest sighting and also the most southerly one, was given precedence in attention by the task force commanders over the later sighting, No. 7 on the list [Willman's], and this research definitely indicates that Rear-Admiral Crutchley, as Commander 62.6, was in receipt of full enemy intelligence." It added that Admiral Turner, Commander, Task Force 62, had decided that this small Japanese force would not attack the vastly superior Allied force.

The office noted that Captain Gatacre (then commander), staff officer of operations and intelligence aboard the *Australia* during the Savo Island battle, might care to comment on the report before the final answer was forwarded to London. The archives do not reveal what Gatacre's comments, if any, might have been. The Australian Archives say that the RACAS cypher log has been destroyed and that the list appended by the Naval History Office to the letter for the naval intelligence director has disappeared. In his autobiography, *A Naval Career: Report of Proceedings,* however, Gatacre wrote the following:

> Over a period of some months, Hepburn and Ramsey [the admiral's aide] talked with nearly everyone who could contribute to the investigation, so it must be concluded that the Hepburn report contained nearly everything factual about the battle, as known to the allied side. After the war, the Japanese side of the story became known. I believe the following to be a fair summary of events: Japanese Rear-Admiral Mikawa collected from Kavieng and Rabaul an attack force consisting of five heavy cruisers, two light cruisers, and one destroyer, intending

> to reach the combat area at midnight 8/9 August. The force was sighted at 10:25 A.M. on 8th by a RAAF Hudson patrol aircraft; the sighting was not reported at the time; the Japanese force was not shadowed; after the aircraft had landed at its base some hours later, the patrol report mentioned having sighted a Japanese naval force of three cruisers, three destroyers and two seaplane tenders or gunboats (at least the aircrew could count up to eight!). That sighting did not reach Admirals Turner and Crutchley until 6:30 P.M. Having been sighted, and expecting an air attack, Mikawa decided to delay his arrival in the combat area till 1:30 A.M.

Gatacre said that he found out about the Hudsons' signals on the Fox schedule. "It was learnt later," he wrote,

> that whilst the plane's orders were to report immediately any enemy naval forces sighted, and to track them, it had not done so. The plane had completed its search and had returned to base: the sighting of the Japanese naval force had been part of its general report! The communications arrangement had extended to about seven hours the interval between the sighting, and Admirals Fletcher, Turner and Crutchley having knowledge of it. Crutchley, Farncomb and I discussed the sighting and its significance. It was obvious that the force could reach the combat area during the night, but its composition was not that of a raiding force; furthermore, to reach the combat area, the force would have to pass through the area of Admiral McCain's shore and seaplane tender–based air patrols, and there had been no sighting reported by them. (It was later ascertained that, because of bad weather, the air patrols were not flown that day. The Task Force commanders in the combat area were not informed!) Nevertheless, Crutchley, Farncomb and I had ample war experience to cause us to doubt the ship recognition capabilities of non-naval aviators, and to have no great confidence that they would even see a naval force from the air.

There were no flies on the bulkhead to record what Crutchley, Farncomb, and Gatacre had to say when they discussed the Hudsons' reports. At other times, they made no secret of their distrust of air force, especially RAAF, reconnaissance. Yet that Gatacre should have denied that the gist of Stutt's signal was known during the day, while Crutchley acknowledged it in his "Report of Proceedings," remains curious. As Crutchley's staff officer of operations and intelligence, Gatacre must have been aware of the signal.

Some of the doubts he shared with Farncomb about the air force seem to have been the result of the Japanese air attacks on 7 and 8

August. In his report to Crutchley on the operation written at sea on 12 August, Farncomb commented:

> Before the operation started we had heard that shore-based aircraft from the Australian Command were going to interdict on enemy aerodromes prior to our arrival in the Solomons. Our first day's experience did not inspire us with much confidence in the efficiency of the "interdiction," for not only did a large force of heavy bombers and fighters from Rabaul, 600 miles away, manage to get at us, but a team of dive bombers, quite unexpectedly, did so as well. The second day's attack by torpedo bombers and heavy bombers subsequently confirmed our opinions of the value of this interdiction, and we were glad indeed that we had U.S. naval aircraft co-operating with us.[10]

That aircraft from the southwest Pacific Area did not jump into action in response to the Hudson's signal is explained by the arrangement between the two commands: Southwest Pacific aircraft would operate against hostile naval targets only if Commander, South Pacific Area, made specific, direct requests for such attacks to Commander, Southwest Pacific Area. No request was made. Admiral Ghormley believed that MacArthur lacked the aircraft to cope with Japanese shipping while attempting to inderdict airfields, with the curious result that although B-17s had Mikawa in full view off Rabaul on 7 August, they concentrated their attack on the Vunakanau airfield, dropping ninety-two 500-lb bombs on the runway. Whatever damage they did was insufficient to prevent the Bettys and Zekes from taking off the following day; a few of these bombs splashing around Mikawa, on the other hand, might at least have encouraged second thoughts about the hazardous raid that Captain Kami was selling so ardently.

Both the *Wasp* and the *Saratoga* were aware of Stutt's signal. According to Clark Lee, the *Wasp* considered sending a force to attack Mikawa and, for reasons that cannot be established, decided not to. Turner also decided against sending a surface force. So far as McCain is concerned, the distance of his forces may have been one of the factors responsible for his inaction.

The accounts by Hepburn, Morison, and all the others of the Hudsons' failure to break radio silence have their origin in "A Partial Summary of Communications," prepared by Commander Ramsey.[11] "The best information indicates that the aircraft [Stutt's] which made the sighting did not make a radio report, but made a verbal report upon arriving at Milne Bay during the late afternoon on 8 August," he wrote.

"It appears that once the sighting was given to Townsville, it was passed on without delay." Almost every statement in this report is wrong. Stutt did break radio silence. His verbal report was made early in the afternoon—he landed at Milne Bay at 1255. The dispatch classified "emergency" went out from Milne Bay one hour and fifty-five minutes after he landed. In Townsville, it was unaccountably delayed for hours before going out on the Fox and Bells schedules.

Ramsey, in turn, depended on a report prepared for him by Lieutenant Commander D. L. Grant, USN, force communications officer in the Southwest Pacific Area, who said that he had been unable to determine whether the Hudson had made a report at the time of the sighting or had returned to base, reporting on arrival.[12] "It was the policy of RAAF radio stations in operational areas," Grant went on,

> to destroy their files after a month and for radio stations in nonoperational areas to destroy their files after six months. Since the sighting was made seven months prior to the opening of the interrogation, we have been unable to locate the original sighting report. All authorities who might . . . have retained a copy of this sighting report have been queried but none has it on his files. I have spoken to ACH [area command headquarters] Townsville on the phone in hopes someone might remember the sighting, but have had no answer yet.

In fact, the RAAF information concerning the Hudsons' signals was held in the central war room in general headquarters at the Australian Mutual Provident building in Brisbane.[13] It would have been readily available. Since Admiral Hepburn was on the spot, it would have been a simple matter to procure the documents.

In the course of his investigation, Commander Ramsey did not check the frequency on which the Hudsons transmitted, or the means adopted to monitor their reports. "The Operation Instruction," he wrote,

> does not appear to state the frequency that South-West Pacific aircraft were to use in communication with South Pacific bases. It therefore appears doubtful that any of the Task Force commanders in the South Pacific area would necessarily be guarding frequencies used by South-West Pacific aircraft in making contact reports. . . . It is possible that a despatch giving frequencies used by South-West Pacific aircraft in making their reports was sent to the South Pacific Force, but no record of such could be located. It thus appears that no provision was made for guarding of South-West Pacific aircraft frequencies by the South

> Pacific forces. It is concluded that it was the intention of Commander South-West Pacific Area that despatches from aircraft under his command were to be transmitted first to him and then relayed as necessary.

The fact is that the details of all Hudson reconnaissance flights were relayed in advance to CinCPac and to the South Pacific task forces, together with the frequency to be used, which, to ensure that it was monitored with constant and urgent attention, was a coastwatcher channel. Moreover, that MacArthur should have wanted to check urgent radio sighting reports before "relaying them as necessary" to the task forces off Guadalcanal, even given the state of U.S. Navy-Army hostility, and MacArthur's personality, is nonsense.

In his discussion with Admiral Hepburn, the *Chicago*'s Captain Bode and Commander Irish confirmed that reports of Mikawa's force had been received during daylight hours.[14] Again, the Hepburn report chose not to accept this evidence.

Turner and Crutchley, knowing of the sighting and deciding against changing the disposition of the screening force to meet a possible surface threat, based their decisions on what they thought Mikawa *would* do, not on what he could do. Turner, in reporting to Hepburn, blamed the rain storm for the northern force's disaster: "I have been told by several officers in the northern division that they heard firing to the south but saw very little of it due to the rain, and thought probably that a submarine was being attacked. Some officers saw some star shells and some tracers but not very much. The existence of this rain squall between the two divisions is considered to have had a marked influence on the action."

On the lack of warning from the radar pickets, Turner said he had assumed that the *Blue* and the *Ralph Talbot* would detect the approach of the vessels at a distance of up to twelve to fourteen miles.

> Knowledge possessed by me and the staff concerning radar was practically non-existent. Admiral Crutchley had an officer whom he considered well qualified in radar. I consulted with him and some other officers with some experience. All seemed to think that this scheme was satisfactory. I considered then, and I still so consider, that it was essential to divide the cruisers into two divisions, about ten miles apart, for covering both sides of Savo. Concentration in case of attack seemed almost sure. If I had to do it over again I would put additional destroyers out on the screen, would still divide the cruisers into two divisions, but would draw them a little further to the eastward of Savo Island in order

> to miss the rain which prevails there during the night. This is purely hindsight, as I felt on 30 July and on 8 August that the arrangement was OK.

Turner maintained that it had never been his intention to withdraw the *Australia* from the screening force. He believed Mikawa could not arrive before about midnight, and that it was essential that he talk to Crutchley and Vandegrift about his proposal to withdraw the following day.

Vandegrift and Crutchley left the *McCawley* about 1155. Vandegrift headed for Tulagi and Crutchley for the *Australia.* "Unfortunately, the boat had a difficult time and took about an hour reaching the *Australia,*" Turner said. "Admiral Crutchley decided to join the *Hobart* [*sic*] in the close screen instead of returning to his usual station. I was not informed of this decision."

Thus as Mikawa approached Savo Island the *Vincennes,* in command of the northern group of ships, had no idea that the *Australia* was not in her usual place in the screen, or what the group's plans were. The *Chicago* did not know that Crutchley had decided not to return, and Turner did not know Crutchley's whereabouts.

Captain Greenman in the *Astoria* was equally ill informed.[15] "Did you know that the *Australia* had been hauled out?" Hepburn asked him.

"I had no knowledge until several days later," Greenman replied. "I presumed she was there and was somewhat incensed because the admiral hadn't given any information as to where his ships were. It was so necessary to the orientation of our screening vessels, I was quite concerned."

As for the unidentified aircraft that appeared over the task force, the *Australia* was informed during Crutchley's absence, and he was told half an hour after his return to the ship. The information was not passed on to Turner in the *McCawley.*

The stress of the full two days' action, the weariness of officers and men, the excessive use of TBS between ships, and perhaps above all, the ships' lack of experience working together, had all begun to show before the first shots in the battle were fired. Yet rarely in the history of naval warfare has any force, warned that it might be attacked, taken so few precautions. On the other hand, as Admiral Nimitz acknowledged, Mikawa had demonstrated brilliantly just how important the element of surprise could be. "The Japanese are masters of amphibious warfare," Nimitz said.

They have demonstrated their ability to land large bodies of men and material on open beaches with no facilities other than those they brought with them. In the battle of Savo Island they have proved their ability and capacity in night action. They have demonstrated again that an inferior naval force led with boldness and resolution can undertake night attack against a superior naval force with good prospects of success. It is to be hoped that we will profit by their example in the future and turn against them the lessons they have so ably taught us.

17

They Couldn't Read the Signals

As soon as the war ended, the army and navy ministries in Tokyo and the army-navy Imperial General Staff ordered their organizations and forces to destroy all secret documents to keep them out of Allied hands. For several days the chimneys in the army and navy offices in Tokyo belched smoke. Almost all important documents were either destroyed or disappeared. Then the U.S. occupation forces arrived and scooped up any surviving documents they could find and sent them back to America. However, some remained, either on the bookshelves of government organizations and libraries or in private hands. Among them was a single copy of the *Chokai*'s detailed action report.

One of the documents taken back to the United States was the detailed action report of the *Furutaka,* which was used extensively in the Naval Wars College's "War Analysis." In this work no mention was made, however, of the *Chokai*'s report. After the establishment of the War History Office under the Japanese Defense Agency in October 1955, the Japanese began to collect surviving documents on the war and to negotiate with the U.S. authorities for the return of captured documents. Among them were the war diaries and detailed action reports of Eighth Fleet ships engaged in the Battle of Savo Island. Two and a half years later, Japan succeeded in negotiating with the U.S. authorities for the return of the documents. Most were returned, but not the detailed action report of the *Furutaka.* As for the *Chokai*'s detailed action report, that was still missing, along with several dozen copies of the report known to have been mimeographed after the battle. The war diaries and action reports of each ship were submitted to the investigation division of the Japanese Navy Ministry, so that identifying a document if it existed would prove no problem.

For several years the War History Office had no success in tracing a copy of the *Chokai*'s report. However, just before his death in November 1963, Engineer Lieutenant Ryohei Kataaoka, a division commander in the *Chokai* from September 1941 to November 1942, sent his files, including a copy of the *Chokai*'s detailed action report, to the War History Office, which authenticated it. The existence of the action report validated beyond reasonable doubt the statements made by Captains Riefkohl and Greenman to Admiral Hepburn that they, too, had received Stutt's signal.

But for Nancy Milne's efforts to clear the names of the Hudson crews, the missing clue might have remained forever interred in the War History Office archives. The unanswered question is whether a copy of the report found its way to the United States during the occupation. If Commodore Bates, in preparing his "War Analysis," and Morison had had access to the document, they surely would have arrived at different conclusions. In the absence of firm evidence to the contrary, it must be accepted that the *Chokai*'s report was not among the documents that found their way into American hands.

This does not explain the contradictions in the Hepburn report and its accompanying documents, nor the fabrication about Stutt having tea before his debriefing. On the one hand, there is the evidence from Turner that he got at least one of the Hudsons' signals in the afternoon—early in the afternoon, according to Hepburn. On the other, there are the conflicting reports from Commander Grant in Brisbane and from Commander Ramsey, who had conducted the inquiry into communications. Despite having heard from Turner himself that he had received a signal during the afternoon, Hepburn seems to have been convinced otherwise by Ramsey. The admiral put his name to the report that decided that Turner, Riefkohl, and others were wrong: the Hudsons had not broken radio silence, and their messages were delayed for hours, too late for the carriers or McCain to do anything about Mikawa. Morison embroidered this with the story about Stutt and his tea, and writers ever since have repeated it, adding for good measure their own biting comments.

The question arises whether political, naval, or even personal reasons lay behind this turn of events. The Savo Island defeat touched off international sensitivities. An English admiral commanding a joint U.S.-Australian force was likely to be the subject of some criticism in the

United States, win or lose. These sensitivities were reflected in the way that Whitehall and Canberra reacted to the occasional American criticisms of the Australian ships and of Crutchley. There is no evidence, however, to suggest that any political pressure was exerted. Nancy Milne had many obstacles to overcome in her research, but the Australian government needed no persuasion from anyone else in restricting access to secret files, especially where they related to the forbidden fruit of signals intelligence. All three navies, British, Australian, and American, would undoubtedly have found it easier to live with the account that placed so much emphasis on the Hudsons' allegedly delayed reports than to put blame elsewhere. The error of relying overmuch on the radar screen provided by the *Blue* and the *Ralph Talbot,* for example, would surely have received more attention if lack of early warning had not been seen as a primary cause of the disaster. Interservice jealousies and personal differences colored the thinking of officers like Farncomb and Gatacre. The facts were misrepresented, sometimes, we suspect, deliberately. But basically there appears to have been overriding, inbuilt resistance on the part of all who originally inquired into the Savo Island battle to the idea that the task forces had actually been informed in ample time to meet any threat that Mikawa might pose. The Australian board of inquiry into the loss of the *Canberra* was no exception. In the thousands of words of evidence presented to the board in late August 1942, there is nowhere a suggestion that the *Canberra* was warned only after dark on 8 August. A report prepared by Lieutenant Commander Plunkett-Cole aboard the rescue ship soon after the battle failed to give specific times for the receipt of the warning signals. Yet, under examination by the board, he left little room for doubt that they had been received during the daylight.

"During daylight on 8th August 1942, apart from the air attack which you have already described, were any other reports of enemy aircraft or surface craft received?" he was asked.

"We were warned of a further impending air attack which did not materialize—we were warned to expect it about 1600," he replied. "Other than that there were three enemy reports, only one of which I personally saw. I have mentioned that in my report. There was a force of cruisers, destroyers, and either transports or seaplane tenders in an area about 400 miles away."

Both Lieutenant Commander Mesley and Lieutenant Commander Wight indicated that there had been reports of enemy surface craft during the day.[1] Yet the board decided that a report "was received after dark of an enemy force about 400 miles away at 1030 that day." It made no reference to signals received in daylight. The board, it seems, simply could not bring itself to believe that warning signals received so long in advance failed to evoke any response in the task forces. Its finding may well have had an impact on Admiral Hepburn's thinking—and on everything that has been published since.

The author of the Hepburn report was not Admiral Hepburn but Commander Ramsey, who, having retired as a rear admiral, wrote to Morison on 5 January 1949 suggesting that it would be helpful if the two got together before Morison tackled Savo Island.

> The report I wrote has never been released and probably will not be. Of course, the vitally interesting part of the report is what I did not put into it. This was because of the restrictive nature of our directive covering the inquiry. I presume that I should some day write a story on it myself, because, although I included with the report most of the data which formed the basis of the report, I doubt whether anyone besides myself could use it effectively. Particularly of importance are the conversations I had with some of the officers concerned.[2]

Ramsey went on to say that he was in Boston fairly frequently and would contact Morison next time he was there.

Unbeknownst to Ramsey, Morison was well advanced with his work covering Savo Island. Attached to a letter dated 3 June 1948 from Roger Pineau to Morison researcher Commander James C. Shaw is a note that reads:

> Commander Roeder (of the annex, who was in Australia at the time) seemed to think that the routing of the sighting report from the Australian Hudson (Savo Chapter, pp. 8 and 9) was not exactly correct. Told him I thought it had come straight from the Hepburn report (had it?). He did not remember the exact details himself tho' present when the message was sent out. If our account is from the Hepburn report, it should be accurate enough: but if our source is doubtful, perhaps I should research the trail of that message again. It seems important to me because the mention of an eight-hour delay looks like someone was remiss: and if so we should be more specific about it. Please let me know.[3]

In Morison's voluminous office files there is nothing to indicate the origin of his story about Stutt and the cup of tea. To assume that it is his fabrication is to do much less than justice to a distinguished historian. Since the story is without foundation—no authoritative document contains the information—someone reasonably expected to be in possession of the facts must have told him. When requested by his informants, Morison kept his sources secret. In the absence of source material on the matter in his files, it seems likely that the information came by word of mouth as a result of inquiries following Pineau's suggestion that someone had been remiss. If so, who was the informant?

Morison's phrase, that Stutt "had his tea," is confusing. "Tea," in the Australian vernacular, is an evening meal. Since Stutt returned to Milne Bay early in the afternoon, far too early for the evening meal, he might have had a cup of tea, but not tea. An American unfamiliar with the Australian idiom would probably not have understood these nuances. There were Americans at Milne Bay who could have been privy to the facts. A feasible explanation, however, is that Morison was told the story by an Australian, probably an Australian with no affection for the RAAF, and that he found it fitted Commander Ramsey's scenario.

Although the task forces received Stutt's signal, apparently no one knew where it had come from. Opinion seemed to be divided after the battle whether a coastwatcher or an army plane was the source. No one mentioned the Hudsons. In the absence of evidence that the Hudsons had, in fact, broken radio silence, the long delay before the Fox and Bells reports arrived appears to have been accepted as confirmation that the pilots, in Pineau's words, were remiss.

That the Hudsons' frequency differed from the coastwatchers' in the Solomons may have added to the confusion. Again, because of the inadequacy of shipboard communications, signals may not have been picked up by receivers guarding the main channels, and the same signals may well have been received at different times—in the clear and in cypher. Admiral Turner remembered that one signal had arrived during the afternoon, but he could find no record of it, probably because it was picked up by one of the sixteen field sets in the *McCawley*.[4] Captain Greenman may have received the signal through the same sort of arrangement, for he could clearly remember its receipt, while his signals officer could not.

At 1500 on 8 August, the *McCawley* received another signal from an unknown source. This appears to have been an intelligence officer's assessment: "One desdiv and units of another desron en route to Florida Island." Like the other signals, it rang no alarm bells either in the task forces or in the Southwest Pacific Area Command. An analysis made at area command headquarters in Townsville, which the *McCawley* received at 2230 on 8 August, said: "Lack of opposition to our raids at Salamaua and Lae indicates movement of enemy aircraft from these areas. Opposition strongly encountered at Rabaul. Movements of naval vessels and APs indicates possible occupation of Bougainville and Buka in strength, and possible use of Kieta airdrome."

In a note for Admiral Hepburn prepared on 21 February 1943, Crutchley listed the frequencies monitored by the *Australia* from 7–9 August: Fox, Bells, Fletcher's warning net, fighter direction, and Turner's antisubmarine and search patrol while the planes were operating. The *Hobart* guarded South Pacific reconnaissance by day, the *Australia* by night. Southwest Pacific reconnaissance was not guarded, he said, but these reports were rebroadcast by Bells.

Thus it would appear that there was no provision for monitoring coastwatcher frequencies. This would be consistent with Crutchley's explanation at the time that he had first received the report on the Fox and Bells schedules. How, then, did the *Australia* receive the coastwatcher's warnings from Bougainville and Buka? Why, in his original report, did Crutchley say that he had received the report during the day? Did the *Hobart* get the signal and pass it on to the rear admiral commanding the Australian Squadron? Why did Morison write that only the *Australia* guarded the coastwatcher net if she did not guard that net at all?

Many other questions remain unanswered. Why did Admiral Mikawa and Captain Ohmae fail to inform Admiral Morison that the *Chokai* had intercepted Stutt's signal on the morning of 8 August? Since both Mikawa and Ohmae read Morison's account of the action before it was published, and were free to suggest changes, why did they not include this vital information? Why did Captain Ohmae, in his article in the Naval Institute *Proceedings* in December 1957, fail to make mention of it? Roger Pineau assisted Morison in preparing the account of the battle and edited the *Proceedings* article. He has no explanation for the general silence about the Hudson's signal.[5] He says that the *Proceedings* article, written eight years after Morison's volume 5, simply overlooked the Hudsons' sightings. A search of Captain Ohmae's papers in Japan for the original manuscript of the article was unsuccessful.

Either the Japanese failed to reveal to Morison that the signal had been intercepted, or Morison was reluctant, like the Australian board of inquiry, to accept that warning because of the weight of evidence available. Did Morison believe that Admiral Turner had invented the story when he told him that he had received the message in the afternoon? On 9 August 1942, despite the excessive secrecy surrounding the receipt of messages on some ships, even at junior levels, knowledge of the enemy's presence nearby had spread. Thus, chief radio electrician W. R. Daniel, USN, writing to the commanding officer of the *Quincy* detail on 19 August 1942, reported: "Intelligence was ample, timely and accurate; yet the Japanese ships were not sighted until 0150 9 August at their battle stations and firing at us from the darkness. No force had intercepted them prior to their arrival, despite the fact that we had notice of their composition, speed, position and course as early as 1600 on 8 August."

Several ships carried the obsession with secrecy to disastrous lengths. Intelligence on which the lives and security of the force depended had, in many cases, a restricted circulation. "The Nelsonism system epitomized by the phrase 'a band of brothers' is as important today as ever," wrote Lieutenant Andrew, a survivor from the *Quincy*. "Realization of this fact is not general. Too often the spirit, best illustrated by the young coding board officers who slyly hint of knowing all, but tell nothing, is prevalent. At times it even appears as though some officers hope to increase their own importance by thus withholding information even from their seniors. This deplorable tendency extends even to restricting the information given commanding officers." Another officer from the *Quincy* noted that "dispatches . . . which were decoded by myself reported a Japanese force on 7 August, course 140 degrees, headed toward the Guadalcanal area, yet no definite action was taken to meet this force."

Lieutenant Commander Heneberger, the *Quincy*'s senior surviving officer, told Admiral Hepburn that he personally had not expected a surface attack, and that his commanding officer had not issued any special instructions regarding possible encounters with Japanese surface forces on the night of 8–9 August. In talking to communication personnel at a later date, however, Heneberger found that a dispatch had been received indicating an enemy force was headed in the direction of Guadalcanal. "What distribution was made of it, I do not know," he said, "except that it was never received by myself, or transmitted to the main battery control officer. In the *Quincy,* after much discussion on the subject, all heads of department were permitted to go to the communication center and read the file of secret dispatches daily while at sea, or engaged on a mission in order to keep abreast of what was going on in our theater of operations."

A fourth *Quincy* officer commented:

> War is still a matter of communications. Personnel charged with the responsibility of controlling guns in a high-speed war such as the present must be kept posted with all pertinent information regarding enemy movements. On the evening of August the eighth, subsequent information revealed, several reports of enemy movements were sent out by reconnaissance forces in the area and each of these reports indicated the possibility, even the probability, of an enemy attack on our forces. None of this information was made available to the officers controlling the guns. . . . The location and activity of the carrier support groups were unknown, and it was assumed that these carrier support groups were capable and were actually protecting the operation from any and all surface attacks.

An initially persuasive but misleading finding in the Hepburn report was that the search sector through which Mikawa approached was less than half covered on 8 August because of weather, and that this important information did not reach Admiral Turner until the day after the four cruisers had been sunk. The area in question was sector 2, stretching from the New Hebrides northwest toward Bougainville and east of Malaita, embracing Santa Isabel Island and the southern cape of Choiseul Island and adjoining waters to the west. The left half was searched only 80 percent, out to 650 miles, and the right half not at all. Even if the aircraft had completed its flight to the full 750-mile limit, however, and searched every inch of the sea, it would not have seen Mikawa. Not until 1720 did it reach a position opposite the halfway point on Choiseul Island, beyond the 750-mile limit of the B-17s' flight. Two Avengers from the *Enterprise* were in this general area at 1610 and missed Mikawa by thirty miles. Although the B-17s traveled for a distance of 650 miles, instead of the assigned 750, their flight had reached its extremity by 0715, more than three hours before Stutt sighted the force off the west coast of Bougainville. Mikawa was well over a hundred miles away. No afternoon search was ordered, despite warning signals arriving each day from Pearl Harbor about the extent and nature of the Japanese surface buildup.

As for Turner's request to McCain to cover sector 280 degrees to 310 degrees from Malaita, it called for a morning, not an afternoon, search. Admiral Hepburn did not know what action was taken on Turner's dispatch, although it would have been easy enough to obtain the information: McCain's aircraft did make the flight, as requested, and missed sighting Mikawa by about sixty miles.

In his request to McCain, Turner failed to indicate how far he expected the aircraft to search, although his reference to the Southwest Pacific Area could have been taken to mean that he wanted it to go beyond the set boundaries. No doubt he expected the flight to be made from Malaita by long-range PBYs, and not by B-17s with extra belly tanks from the New Hebrides. But the PBYs at Malaita became operational only on 8 August, and in any event, McCain did not use the slow-moving planes in areas where they might be expected to meet Japanese fighters. He decided to use the B-17s instead. They crossed into MacArthur's territory, as did all other flights in this sector, but did not go far enough. The question then arises, what, if anything, Turner or Fletcher would have done if either an Avenger or the B-17s had sighted Mikawa. Turner had already decided that Mikawa was headed for Rekata Bay on Santa Isabel; the selection of a course that would have made it necessary to go through the channel between Santa Isabel and Choiseul might not have caused Turner to change his mind. He had looked again at Crutchley's nighttime dispositions and decided they were adequate. Crutchley had erred once; he could err again. As for Fletcher, confirmation of Mikawa's presence is likely to have indicated threat, not challenge.

If failure to follow up the Hudson's signal emerges as the most serious error of all, many other factors contributed to the Allied defeat. Overreliance on radar, especially in areas where land mass interfered with reception; the ever-present threat of submarines; the disregard of warnings of plane sightings; and the delay in changing from condition 2 of readiness to general quarters all added to the distaster that overtook the Allied ships.

Operation Watchtower was hastily planned and inadequately prepared, but this was by necessity, not design: the airfield at Guadalcanal had to be taken before it became operational, and the Japanese, on the move, had to be stopped. All too rarely in war does time permit the concentration of force that a commander would like. Most of the cruisers were poorly trained for night action. Admiral Layton's ill-advised comment that the Japanese lacked night-fighting skills, coupled with the *Australia* group's lack of confidence in air force intelligence, did not encourage a rational assessment of what Mikawa might do. Captain Bode and Captain Riefkohl found themselves with flag responsibilities for which they were neither prepared nor equipped. While Admiral

Fletcher took no part in the battle, he nevertheless remained a significant player. If he had not indicated his determination to withdraw, the meeting between Turner, Crutchley, and Vandegrift in the *McCawley* is unlikely to have taken place on the night of 8 August. The *Australia* would have been in her proper place at the head of the southern column, with Crutchley in command.

In his comment to CinCPac on the Hepburn report, Turner echoed Admiral Nimitz:

> I have concluded that our forces, both sea and land, at that time simply were not battle-minded. None had been in surface action of any kind. Few had even been in action against aircraft or submarines. Training schedules had very largely been relaxed since the beginning of the war. There had been few co-ordinated battle exercises and very little target practice. The Navy was still obsessed with a strong feeling of technical and mental superiority over the enemy. In spite of ample evidence as to enemy capabilities, most of our officers and men despised the enemy and felt themselves sure victors in all encounters under any circumstances. Accentuating this was a mental uncertainty as to the methods and capabilities of fellow members of this heterogeneous force. An illustration of the state of mind we all were in is given by our previous disregard of the urgent necessity for stripping ships of inflammable materials. The net result of all this was a fatal lethargy of mind which included a confidence without readiness, and a routine acceptance of outworn peacetime standards of conduct. We were not mentally ready for hard battle.[6]

In the same report, however, Turner gave the impression that he had not received the Hudson's signal during the day, and that four dispatches from the Southwest Pacific Command, which reached him about 2230 on 8 August during his talks with Crutchley and Vandegrift, combined with the false information in the Fox report at 1830, had led him, after lengthy conversations with Crutchley, to conclude that the chances of a night attack were small.[7]

The *Chokai* apparently received the Hudson signal between 1026 and 1103, and at least some units in the task force got the signal around the same time. Riefkohl believed he had received it as early as 1015, which would have been impossible, of course. Greenman got it before noon. Turner told Hepburn that he had it in the afternoon, or early afternoon, and confirmed this in his discussion with Morison. If the *McCawley* had picked up the signal at the same time as the *Chokai,*

Turner would have known of Mikawa's presence off the coast of Bougainville more than eleven hours before the Southwest Pacific Area Command signal arrived during his conference with Vandegrift and Crutchley. If, in fact, the signal arrived midafternoon, he would still have had another three or four hours of daylight in which to establish to his own satisfaction the location, composition, and probable intention of the enemy force, and whether it constituted a threat. Prudence demanded at least a late-afternoon search, if not by carrier aircraft, McCain's land-based force, or PBYs from Malaita, then by seaplanes from the cruisers. The *Quincy* carried no less than five seaplanes. They had been used for spotting friendly fire, marine spotting, and antisubmarine patrols. During the action on the night of 8–9 August, they quickly caught fire and served only to illuminate the *Quincy* for Mikawa's gunners. On searches and as the essential preliminary to night action, Mikawa had used his cruiser-borne seaplanes to full advantage; the notion that Allied cruiser planes might have been used in the same way does not appear to have entered Turner or Crutchley's mind, although their range was more than adequate for the task. Two years later, during the invasion of Saipan, Turner faced a threat in many ways similar to that at Guadalcanal. With the approach of Japanese surface craft three days after the landing, he withdrew the transports temporarily, returning them as soon as the danger had passed. Off Savo Island he sensed no real danger.

Admiral Fletcher's role was even more unusual. To Admiral Hepburn, he defended his decision to withdraw, notwithstanding Mikawa's attack. At noon on 8 August, he said, Task Force 18 had reported that it had fuel for only thirty-one hours at twenty-five knots. Those figures would have been reduced by 15 percent if operating conditions on 9 August were the same as those the previous two days. It was not practicable to fuel destroyers from cruisers when they had only sufficient fuel for fifty hours at twenty-five knots. During the continuous flight operations, of 7–8 August, speeds of twenty-five knots and over were necessary. Because the task forces were equally short of fuel, it would not have been possible to retire one task force at a time. When the task forces did refuel on 10, 11, and 12 August, they required 176,212 barrels of fuel. At this stage, some destroyers had only 500 barrels of fuel remaining. If the carriers remained another day, that is, through 9 August, they were to operate in the same waters as on 8 August—southeast of Guadalcanal and in the vicinity of San Cristobal. This decision was believed sound in view of the presence, on 8 August, of forty planes equipped with torpedoes. With the task forces in the position in which they would have been had they remained in the area, and sufficiently fueled to operate indefinitely at high speed, Mikawa probably would not have been located by a search the next morning. However, the attack forces would have had to launch from a minimum distance of two hundred miles, with the carriers much further north than they would be expected to operate.

In a letter to Hanson Baldwin of the *New York Times* on 8 July 1947, Fletcher said that he had been reluctant to comment on the actions in which he had been engaged during the war, because his memory after five years was not as trustworthy as the reports and records made at the time.[8] Fortunately, however, his memory seemed fairly clear on certain matters Baldwin had raised. At the time of the conference off Fiji, he had expected to remain off Guadalcanal until the landing was completed, if it was not unduly delayed. He recommended the withdrawal because of a shortage of fuel.

> We were surprised to find the destroyers running short almost at once and the carriers and cruisers used much more fuel than we expected. This was probably due to the fact that we were in the doldrums and forced to run at thirty knots practically all of the daylight hours because of our almost constant landing and launching of planes. We had to fuel one destroyer the night of the seventh, I remember. We figured if we stayed one more day (which we might possibly have done if we had fueled destroyers at night) we would be caught in a very bad position if enemy carriers appeared on the ninth. I think we all expected that they would show up shortly after the landing operations.

The "we all" did not encompass naval communications intelligence, which, day after day, had warned precisely what Japanese ships were in the region. These did not include an aircraft carrier.

As for fuel, according to Lieutenant Commander Simpler, commander of Fighting Squadron 5 in the *Saratoga,* the carrier was a "veritable oil barge herself."[9] Simpler, who detested Fletcher, may not have been the most reliable witness, but in fact the fuel situation was much less critical than Fletcher said.[10] The cruisers were all half full or better. Among the carriers, only the *Enterprise* was running low, and she had enough fuel for another three days. Some of the destroyers were running low, but not to the point where an early withdrawal was indicated.

While the Zekes had shocked the Wildcats and the Bettys had posed a serious torpedo threat, the loss of sixteen fighters—not the twenty-one Fletcher claimed—had not seriously reduced the force. The means to continue fighting remained; only the will was lacking. Long before Ghormley's signal to withdraw, the *Saratoga* was heading south, leaving the transports, their screen, and the marines on Guadalcanal and Tulagi to fend for themselves. Ghormley, in faraway New Caledonia, had no reason to doubt Fletcher's implied claim that he was short of fuel, or even that there were large numbers of Japanese planes in the area. Thus, the battle was over, and Mikawa was busy putting distance between himself and Savo Island, before Task Force 61 received the flash report that some sort of action had taken place.

As we have seen, in the fallout from the battle, those who suffered most were Captain Bode, Captain Riefkohl, and the crews of the Australian Hudsons. Although Bode probably should have taken the lead in the *Australia* group when Crutchley went to the *McCawley,* Crutchley's signal that he might or might not return was less than helpful. Commanders should not be so imprecise. Moreover, as Bode was well aware, moving ships into formation in darkness is both difficult and dangerous. Whether the *Chicago* would have played a more useful role in the battle if she had not headed away is also open to question. She probably would have gone down instead of, or with, the *Canberra.* Bode's gravest error was his failure to warn the *Vincennes* group, the rest of the task force, and even his own screen, that an enemy attack had begun.

Riefkohl was left completely in the dark about the *Australia* group's plans. He did not know that the *Australia* had closed on the *McCawley,* or that he was in overall command of the two groups. Alone among all commanding officers, he warned of the possibility of attack in his night orders, but, remarkably, he failed to warn the other members of the *Vincennes* group of his concern. "I felt quite certain that our aircraft would attack the Japs that afternoon, and, if for any reason they were not attacked, we would be alerted by our force commander," he wrote to Vice Admiral Arthur S. Carpender, then the U.S. Navy's director of public relations, on 30 August 1946, pleading for the publication of a true account of what happened during the battle. "As we received no alert, I naturally assumed that the enemy had been attacked. Due to the possibility that some of the ships might have escaped undamaged, and, being Japs, might continue in their mission, I issued the warning to my ship."

As for the Australian air crews, the survivors have been involved in a continuing effort to establish the facts relating to their part of the operation on 8 August. Of his crew, only Lloyd Milne and radio operator "Dutch" Holland survived the war. Milne, Bill Stutt, and Wilbur Courtis live in Melbourne. Milne returned to his work in the Department of Aviation after resigning his commission in the RAAF after the war. Courtis became a teacher at Melbourne's Scotch College. Stutt recently retired as chairman of the Moonee Valley Racing Club in Melbourne. Holland and Eric Geddes live in retirement in New South Wales, John Bell in Western Australia. There were times when each man was bitter. Now, fifty years after the fact, they are pleased that history may put the record straight. Willman and his navigator, John Davies, are both dead. All efforts to identify other members of the crew have been unsuccessful.

The Battle of Savo Island involved highly sensitive issues affecting Allied solidarity and morale at a critical stage of the war. Britain, Australia, and the United States could not afford at the time to engage in a public debate over the conduct of the battle. Columnists like Drew Pearson were all too ready to take issue.

Admiral King responded sensibly to Captain George Russell's advice that he treat the Hepburn report as a dead issue. Quite apart from the issue of Allied solidarity, flag officers with potential were in short supply. A full-scale inquiry that produced all the facts might have destroyed the careers not only of Crutchley and Fletcher but also of Turner, who in subsequent operations proved to be a brilliant amphibious commander, and perhaps even McCain, who with Vice Admiral Marc A. Mitscher led the carrier war when the kamikaze campaign was at its height. It would also have strained relations between Britain and the United States, and the United States and Australia, to no one's advantage other than Japan's. There was everything to be said for profiting from lessons and getting on with the war.

Today, however, the most important lesson of all has been overlooked in the flawed reporting and diagnoses of Admiral Hepburn and a succession of historians. Savo Island should be remembered as a battle that was lost not simply because of the weariness of those involved, or a failure of communications, or the fable of a Hudson pilot and his tea, but rather because of a grave underestimation of Japanese capacity and training and the most unfortunate rejection of intelligence. The senior officers were exhausted, and communication was a nightmare. This does not alter the fact that Turner and Crutchley received detailed and timely information about Japanese concentration and movement. The S-38, the B-17s, and the Hudsons erred in details, granted, but they did provide the essential complement to the hard intelligence from radio traffic analysts in Melbourne and Pearl Harbor. Disaster lay in the failure to read the signals right, and in the failure to appreciate the Japanese capacity for surprise. To consider what might have happened if one or the other, or both, of the arms of the Japanese offensive, either toward Port Moresby or in Guadalcanal, was successful is to venture into unfruitful hypothesis. However, the manpower figures are illuminating.[11] Despite their enormous losses, on 15 August 1945, when the fighting ended, the Japanese still had 103,500 troops in the Bismarcks-Solomons area and another 35,000 in New Guinea. They failed in their plan to isolate Australia, but because of the Allies' Savo Island blunders, they came perilously close to succeeding.

Overstretched as they were, they would have been even closer if Admiral Mikawa, having effectively disposed of four of the six Allied heavy cruisers and badly damaged a fifth, had returned to finish off the transports. His original order leaves no doubt that the transports were the primary target. To concentrate on them before he dealt with the heavily armed cruisers, however, would have opened the way to defeat. But now the harvest was waiting to be reaped.

Mikawa made his decision on the bridge of the *Chokai,* heading north. Captain Hayakawa was in no doubt that the Eighth Fleet should have finished the job. "Our subsequent operations will become very difficult if we leave the enemy force as it is," he told Mikawa and his flag officers. "The enemy will complete the airfield and finish unloading the transports. The enemy's fighting ships are now totally destroyed. Let's go back to the transports." Mikawa agreed, but the bold Kami had become cautious. "The Americans have battleships and aircraft carriers south of Guadalcanal," he said. "It is inevitable that we'll be attacked from the air. We need to put 300 miles between us and the carriers before sunrise."

Lieutenant Commander Saburo Kiuchi, who was on the bridge and overheard this conversation, recalls that both Mikawa and Onishi appeared to agree with Kami. Ohmae and Kami gave little advice that Mikawa did not accept. Ohmae's view was that it was essential to clear the area and get beyond range of carrier planes before daylight. Mikawa personally wanted to return but acquiesced to his staff's argument that it would take three hours to make another run-in, including the time for reassembling and reforming.[12]

Mikawa's aide, Lieutenant Takahashi, remembers that no one spoke once the decision was made. The bridge grew quiet as the Japanese fleet headed north at full speed.

A more adventurous commander would have elected to continue the action. Yamamoto, in a sharp reversal of his approach on 7 August, criticized Mikawa sharply for his failure to destroy the transports, though in doing so he would have risked losing all his cruisers. Of course, if Mikawa had known that Ghormley's signal approving Fletcher's request to withdraw was about to be delivered, or that the U.S. carriers would play no further part, he would not have hesitated. More surprising than Mikawa's decision to break off the action was his withdrawal as far as Rabaul. Waiting in St. George's Channel was the submarine USS S-44, under the command of Lieutenant Commander J. R. Moore. On 10 August, she fired four torpedoes into the *Kako* and sent her to the bottom in five minutes. "I cannot see why the *Chokai* and Cruiser Division 6 had to withdraw so far and with little damage," Vice Admiral Matome Ugaki noted in his diary. "Maybe there was an urgent need to refuel, but I do not think it was so urgent."

Perhaps prudence called for a discreet withdrawal, but not beyond the point of quick return. By failing to reinforce success while the Allies were still reeling from their losses, Mikawa let the last big opportunity of the war slip through his fingers. The Battle of Savo Island was a great Japanese naval victory; it was also the beginning of the end for Japan.

Notes

Works cited frequently in the notes are abbreviated as follows:

AAB	Australian Archives, Brighton
AAC	Australian Archives, Canberra
HR	Hepburn report
MOF	Morison office files
NY	U.S. Navy Historical Center, Navy Yard, Washington, D.C.
PRO	Public Record Office, London
WA	Bates and Innis, *Strategical and Tactical Analysis: The Battle of Savo Island* (commonly known as *War Analysis*)

Introduction

1. Ito, 19.

2. Ibid., 19–20.

3. Ito, 19–20; Horner, *High Command,* 181; Long, 75. See also Agawa, *Gunkan* Nagato *no shogai,* 294–96.

4. SRH 272, NY.

5. Interview with Nave, Mount Eliza, Victoria, Australia, June 1988.

6. Horner, *High Command,* 217; Advisory War Council minute no. 1013, CRS A 2682, vol. 5, AAC; minutes of prime minister's war conference, Melbourne, 10 August 1942, MP 1217, AAB; MacArthur's off the record press conference on the anniversary of his arrival in Australia (manuscript in possession of authors).

7. Buell, 222.

8. Isley and Crowl, 129.

9. Newcomb, 68–69.

10. The *Chokai*'s detailed action report, library of the war history department, National Defense College, Tokyo.

Chapter 1

For the account of the Hudsons' role on 8 August we have drawn heavily on documentary evidence, including the crews' logs, official cypher messages, the correspondence between Nancy Milne and crew members, and the correspondence between the crews and the acting general editor of the official Australian war history. We supplemented this with personal interviews with Milne, Stutt, and Courtis, and with phone conversations with and letters to Geddes. The information that the *Chokai* intercepted Stutt's message, the vital clue, came from the library of the National Defense College in Tokyo. Confirmation that Stutt's message was received during daylight on 8 August came from the inquiry into the loss of HMAS *Canberra* and from various annexes to HR, MOF, and the historical records in AAB.

1. Interviews with Stutt and Courtis, Mount Eliza, July 1988.

2. MP 1588, RACAS cypher log 1942, AAB.

3. See *WA,* 32 and 101, NY.

4. MP 1074/4, Navy Department unclassified inward signals, AAB. See also annex A to Operations Plan 1-42, South Pacific Force MP 1290/1, item 29, p. 6, AAB.

5. Interview with Milne, Mount Eliza, July 1988.

6. Interview with Courtis, Mount Eliza, July 1988.

7. Geddes letter to acting Australian general history editor, Official War History, Canberra, 14 January 1964, and subsequent interviews with authors.

8. The *Chokai*'s detailed action report, the library of war history department, National Defense College, Tokyo.

9. MP 1074, unclassified inward signals 1939–64, AAB.

10. Interview with Stutt, Mount Eliza, July 1988.

11. Nancy Milne papers and letter written by Wilbur Courtis, September 1942.

12. Dyer, 367.

13. SRH 012, "The Role of Radio Intelligence in the American Japanese Naval War," vol. 3, NY.

14. MP 1049/5, secret and confidential File 206/3/501, Navy Historical Records, Solomons Campaign, para. 116, p. 11, AAB.

15. MP 1587, File 105H, paras. 96–100, p. 20, AAB.

16. MP 1049/5, File 2026/3/501, paras. 14–19, pp. 2–3, AAB.

17. Statement by Peek to authors, telephone conversation, August 1988.

18. MP 1587, historical records File 105F, AAB.

19. Unpublished paper by Captain Emile Bonnot, USN (Ret.), 23 February 1988, sent to Martin Clemens (copy in possession of authors).

20. HR, Annex "Individual Personnel," NY.

21. Ibid.

22. MOF, Box 26, folder Notes on Guadalcanal 6, Turner, Guadalcanal, and Central Solomons, 1943, NY.

23. Ibid. MOF, Box 26, folder Savo Island, NY.

24. Ibid.

Chapter 2

For the description of Tulagi and Guadalcanal we are indebted to Martin Clemens, who granted us interviews and permission to make use of his unpublished diary. The details about the work of the cryptanalysts come from interviews with Nave and the Milne papers; SRH 016-034, narrative combat intelligence, Central Pacific Ocean Area, NY; SRH 355, Naval Security Group History to World War II, by Captain J. S. Holtwick, USN (Ret.); OP-2-G, Fleet Radio Unit, Melbourne (Frumel), NY; SRH 102, "The Magic Background of Pearl Harbor," vol. 1, NY; and "The Role of Radio Intelligence in the American-Japanese Naval War," vol. 3, NY. See also Horner, *High Command,* chapter 10, and D. Ball and Horner in *Australian Outlook* (December 1972).

Chapter 3

1. Memorandum, notes on Hanson Baldwin's interview with Turner, MOF, Box 26, folder Savo Island, NY. See also Turner memorandum for Admiral Hepburn.

2. MOF, Box 26, folder Savo Island, NY.

3. The *Dominion,* 4 July 1942.

4. SRH 012, NY.

5. Letter to Hanson Baldwin, 8 July 1947, MOF, folder Savo Island, NY.

6. Layton, 459.

7. Copy of letter, dated 25 September 1943, supplied to authors by A. W. Grazebrook.

8. Turner on HR, Box "Individual Personnel" and 2 of 3, NY.

9. Our account is from many different sources. These differ as to the severity of the disagreement between the two principals. We have sought to achieve a balance.

10. Letter to Hanson Baldwin, 8 July 1947, MOF, Box 26, folder Savo Island, NY.

11. As a result of traffic analysis reports, Japanese strength was consistently being upgraded during this period. The intelligence annex to Operation Plan A3-42 MP 1290/1, item 29, dated 30 July, states: "Information obtained by Commander-in-Chief Pacific Fleet reports Japanese plans for the consolidation and improvement of bases in the Solomons-Bismarck area with further reinforcements to arrive soon. It appears that four additional cruisers have been moved to Rabaul, and that five divisions of submarines may be operating in New Britain and Australian waters. It indicates estimated strength in the Bismarck–New Guinea–Solomons area as 11 cruisers, 13 destroyers, 15 submarines."

12. MP 1587, File 105N, AAB.

13. Kenney letter to General Arnold, 17 September 1944, OPD 201, National Archives, Washington, D.C.

14. ADM 234/376, p. 53, PRO.

15. Inabo Masao, ed., *Kimitusu nichi-ro-sen-shi* (Intelligence history of the Japano-Russian war), lectures at the Army War College, Tokyo (Tokyo: Hara Bookstore, 1966).

Chapter 4

1. SRH 012, NY.

2. Gill, 132. *WA,* 84, says it was received by Crutchley and passed to Turner.

3. *Saratoga* action report, 7–8 August 1942, NY.

4. Figures compiled from action reports of the *Saratoga, Wasp,* and *Enterprise*, NY.

5. SRH 012, NY.

6. HR, Annex T, "Communications and Dispatches," NY.

7. Interview 26 January 1945 by CNO, Office of Naval Archives and Library, *WA,* 59, NY.

8. *WA,* 60, NY.

9. Rear Admiral R. B. Gardner letter to Rear Admiral A. E. Smith, president, Naval War College, 20 October 1948, MOF, Box 27, folder Savo Island, NY.

10. MOF, Box 27, folder Savo Island, NY.

11. See Frank, 613.

Chapter 5

All officers and men of the heavy cruiser *Chokai* were killed in Leyte Gulf on 25 October 1944. There are, therefore, few survivors of the

Chokai who witnessed the earlier Battle of Savo Island. One exception is Fumio Niwa, the war correspondent whose book *Kaisen* (Sea battle) is a highly personalized history of the Battle of Savo Island as seen from the Japanese side. Niwa kindly gave us permission to quote from his book.

Admiral Mikawa's aide at the time of the battle, Lieutenant Shigeo Takahashi, and Lieutenant Commander Suburo Kiuchi were on the bridge of the *Chokai* during the battle. They were helpful in interviews, as were Lieutenant Seizaburo Hoshino, communications officer of Cruiser Division 18, and Lieutenant Nobuo Komatsu, in charge of antiaircraft batteries in the *Furutaka.* Both Hoshino and Komatsu remember that the Eighth Fleet made feinting movements to hide its intentions after the sighting by Stutt and Willman on the morning of 8 August. Two of our other principal sources are an unpublished manuscript by Lieutenant Commander Shigeo Naka, the *Chokai*'s gunnery officer, and Admiral Matome Ugaki's *Sensoroku* (Records of the seaweeds of war).

1. War History Office, National War College, *Nanto homen kaigun sakusen,* 464–65.

Chapter 6

We used Japanese, American, and Australian sources in this lead up to the battle, including ships' action reports, statements from survivors, and interrogations of hundreds of men and officers at the Australian board of inquiry held in August and September 1942. We used the Japanese war history *Nanto homen kaigun sakusen* and war correspondent Niwa's *Kaisen* for descriptions of preparations aboard the *Chokai. WA* also provided details of the Japanese approach to the southern force of Allied ships.

1. *Blue*'s action report, MP 1587, File 105E, AAB. See also NRS 211, NY.

2. MP 1587, File 105A, AAB.

3. R. D. F., "Aspects of Loss of HMAS *Canberra,* Most Secret," September 26 1942, MP 1049/5, File 2037/7/190, AAB.

4. Ibid. The first draft of a letter, dated 8 September 1942, to be sent to the second board of inquiry indicates the ignorance about radar.

5. Captain Bode memorandum for Admiral Hepburn, April 3 1943, HR, vol. 2 of 3, p. 306, NY.

Chapter 7

Interrogations of officers and men from the *Canberra* at the Australian board of inquiry provided material for this chapter, as did the detailed action report of the USS *Patterson.* We also used *WA.* Japanese details come mainly from reports of the *Chokai, Tenryu,* and *Yubari,* as well as correspondent Niwa, who was aboard the *Chokai.*

1. Informal inquiry into the circumstances attending the loss of the *Vincennes, Quincy, Astoria,* and *Canberra,* NRS 121, NY; further interrogation of Captains Riefkohl and Bode, 3 April 1943, HR, Annex M, NY.

2. Interrogation no. 61 of Rear Admiral Matsuyama, U.S. Strategic Bombing Survey (Pacific), naval analysis division, vol. 2, OPNAV-P-03-100; *WA,* 117.

3. MP 1587, File 105A, AAB.

4. MP 1049/5, File 2026-3-501, AAB.

Chapter 8

For the part she played in the battle, the *Chicago* was heavily criticized in HR and by Admiral Crutchley. Captain Bode wrote on several occasions to Hepburn to explain his actions, once from the U.S. naval station at Balboa in the Canal Zone. In his letter of 8 April 1943, he referred to the Secret Information Bulletin No. 2, which had been received at district headquarters the previous day. In an attempt to make his case, he told of firing several rounds on ships that "were only indicated briefly by several flashes sharp on the starboard bow. . . . " The margins of his letter are full of Hepburn's question marks and comments, such as "Did they?" "No," and "Confused."

Reports of the *Yunagi*'s actions are conflicting. We have used reports from her commanding officer, Lieutenant Okada, her war diary, and *WA,* 117.

1. Lieutenant Okada in an oral statement on 11 July 1957 said that he "did not see the enemy destroyer on the opposite course. . . ." WDC/160984, Cruiser Division 18's war diary, contradicts this statement: "Outside the bay she [the *Yunagi*] also inflicted damage on one ship of the *Achilles*-class which had tried to escape. . . ."

2. Captain Bode letter to Hepburn, 8 April 1943, HR, vol. 2 of 3, p. 303, NY.

3. MP 1185/8, File 1932/2/226, AAB.

4. *WA,* 120; interrogation no. 61 of Rear Admiral Matsuyama, U.S. Strategic Bombing Survey (Pacific), *WA,* 117.

5. MP 1587, File 105B, AAB.

Chapter 9

All of the cruisers in the northern group were sunk and all records lost, so that times given of the action vary from ship to ship. HR pointed out that as it was so difficult to determine the position of the group from reports submitted, it was decided that the position reported by the *Helm* "more nearly fitted the general picture" (MP 1185/8, File 1932/2/226). The *Vincennes*'s report, however, was detailed and useful to us, as were later talks between Captain R. C. Parker and Captain Riefkohl. *WA* provided more thorough research than HR, and Lieutenant Dorris's *Log of the Vincennes* gave accounts by survivors of the command ship of the group.

1. MOF, Box 26, Savo Island folder, Captain Riefkohl statements to Captain Parker, 24 October 1946, NY.
2. Dorris, 293.
3. Further interrogation of Captains Riefkohl and Bode, Corpus Christi, Texas, 3 April 1943, HR, Annex M, NY.
4. Ibid.
5. Ibid.
6. Ibid.
7. MP 1049/5, File 2026-3-501, AAB.
8. Talk between Captain Riefkohl and Captain R. C. Parker (from Parker's notes), MOF, Box 26, NY. During this talk the following was said:

> The DD skippers were new and held fast to order of Crutchley not to turn on searchlights, although a DD with initiative would have illuminated under the situation. . . . Suppose one of them had illuminated the Japs and been shot out of the water for it, it might have let our CAs get in the opening salvos and thus have changed the entire result. (Note look up the Battle of Matapan in the Mediterranean. My recollection is that one or more British destroyers *did* turn on searchlights to illuminate the Italians, who were then smothered under fire from the British BBs and cruisers before they could hurt the illuminating DDs.)

See also Riefkohl statements to Captain Parker, 24 October 1946.

Chapter 10

As all but one senior officer in the *Quincy* were killed and most records lost, there are fewer reports from this ship. Reports by Lieutenant Commander Heneberger, Lieutenant Andrew, and other survivors are included in this chapter. That provided by Quartermaster Tom Morris, who served in the *Quincy* from 1940, proved particularly interesting, as did Commander Grady Mesimer's *History of the USS Quincy, CA-39.* MOF, Box 27, was also useful, as was Hepburn's interrogation of Heneberger.

1. "History of USS Quincy (CA 39)," Office of Naval Records and History, ships' history section, Navy Department, NY, and Mesimer, 130.

2. Memorandum for Admiral A. J. Hepburn, additional information in regard to the ex-USS *Quincy,* 10 February 1943, Antiaircraft Training Center, Waianae, Oahu, HR, vol. 3 of 3, Box 1728, WWII Action Reports, NY.

3. Lieutenant Andrew, the *Quincy*'s second senior line officer to survive, wrote in his report: "Night vision is an extremely important factor. Modifications of existing ships and changes in design of new ships should be made to allow the captain of a ship to proceed from his emergency cabin to his battle station without requiring him to pass through any lighted compartments. He must be able to see clearly the second he arrives on his station. If he is unable to do so, it may easily result in improper handling of the ship."

4. MOP, Box 27, folder Savo Island, NY.

Chapter 11

Reports from senior officers and men of the *Astoria* are many and varied, and often critical. Details in this chapter come from these action reports, the history of the cruiser, Japanese sources used in previous ships' reports, Morison's and Turner's papers, and *WA.* Captain Greenman's detailed reports and those of the ship's gunnery officer, Lieutenant Commander Truesdell, are particularly interesting.

1. Notes on Savo Island from MOF, Box 26, Pacific 9 notebook, p. 13, NY. Morison noted: "Commander W. H. Truesdell who was Gunnery Officer aboard *Astoria* at Battle Savo Island gave me his view of it. 1. No sense sending *Quincy* and *Vincennes* to join *Astoria.* There were several other CLs or CAs available in Pacific. 2. Had accompanied *Saratoga* to Pearl to fuel. *Quincy* and *Vincennes* had had no battle practice since war began."

2. Interrogation of Captain Greenman, Annex "Individual Personnel," HR, NY.

3. MOF, Box 26, Pacific 9 notebook, p. 13, NY.

Chapter 12

Admiral Crutchley's "Special Instructions to the Screening Group" were especially confusing to the destroyers. The *Patterson* and the *Ralph*

Talbot had both alerted the Allied cruisers before action began and as the Japanese attacked the southern force of ships. The *Ralph Talbot,* last of the Allied ships to have contact with the Japanese, used her lights after most of the Japanese force had retired, until they were put out of commission, but during the actual battle all destroyers stuck firmly to Crutchley's orders to illuminate only when ordered. We used the destroyers' action reports, *WA,* NRS II-210 (NY), and reports from Lieutenant Okada of the *Yunagi.*

1. The USS *Wilson*'s report of action, Annex P, HR, NY.
2. MP 1185/8, File 1932/2/226, AAB.
3. NRS II-298, *WA,* 256, NY. This source notes:

> The contact on this schooner made by the *Blue* at 0215 is most significant in revealing the wakefulness of the *Blue.* For this contact was only sighted after it had come within sonar range—a maximum of about 2,000 yards in these waters. The question as to how the Japanese could have passed the *Blue* undetected seems to be answered, in part at least, by the circumstancial evidence that the *Blue* was not vigilant, at least on certain bearings. The statement of the commanding officer that the contact made by sonar echo ranging at 0215 "diverted" the attention of his ship from distant and obscure battle noises (which by this time had ceased) to the immediate presence of an unidentified ship scarcely 2,000 yards away appears most revealing in this respect.

4. The *Yubari*'s report mentions "some scratches from the light fire of an enemy destroyer." This damage was probably caused by the *Patterson*'s and *Chicago*'s fire earlier in the action. The *Yubari*'s report does not give the time she was hit. The *Talbot* did hit the Japanese destroyer at this time, but probably did not put out her searchlight: "He was simply misled by the Japanese searchlight technique which had caused a number of the Allied ships to believe they had damaged other enemy searchlights during this night action" (NRS II-298, *WA,* 300, NY).

Chapter 13

Our account of the loss of the *Canberra* is based on interrogations of men and officers by the Australian board of inquiry, personal interviews, the action report of the *Patterson* and other rescue ships, including the *Chicago,* HR, *WA,* and Admirals Crutchley and Turner's reports.

1. Commander Walsh, NRS 211-0092, 29 August 1942, NY.
2. Captain Bode memorandum for Admiral Hepburn, 3 April 1943, HR, vol. 2, p. 311, NY.

3. Captain Bode letter to Admiral Hepburn, from Balboa, Canal Zone, 8 April 1943, ibid., p. 304. Bode wrote: "It was subsequently reported that the entire crew of the *Canberra* had been removed. At that time and afterwards I was in supporting distance of the *Canberra* while remaining as clear as necessary to avoid being silhouetted until the general situation indicated the practicability of closer approach. . . ."

4. Admiral Crutchley described "a rather amazing account of the *Chicago-Patterson* duel." He said that the *Canberra*'s engineering officer thought his ship might have been saved but for this episode. "I was able to see Admiral Sir Guy Royle about this and he called in Commander Walsh, Executive Officer, *Canberra,* June 1943. Walsh said that the above inference was unjustified. *Patterson* was doing *Canberra* very little good—hoses were the wrong size etc. and she was already doomed when *Patterson* cast off. Nevertheless some future historian will probably make that inference and blame *Patterson* for the loss of Canberra."

Chapter 14

Lieutenant Donald Dorris's *Log of the Vincennes* provided reports from many of the survivors of that cruiser. Commander Grady Mesimer's *History of the USS* Quincy gives accounts of more than ninety survivors, and Quartermaster Tom Morris provided personal and vivid accounts of the *Quincy*'s fight for survival. Our account of the *Astoria*'s second battle comes from surviving officers and men and from those of the destroyer minesweeper *Hopkins* and the destroyer *Wilson,* among others. We used Admiral Turner's papers for accounts of the *Jarvis.* Allied casualties are compiled from various sources, including Gill, 152, 153; *WA,* 377; and Morison, 63. Japanese damage and casualty figures are from MOF, Box 27, NY (from excerpts from WDC documents 160623 and 161407); *Nanto homen kaigun sakusen* (Navy operations in southeast area), 464–65; Ohmae, p. 1277; and *WA,* 376.

1. MOF, Box 26, Notes on Savo Island, Pacific 9 notebook, p. 13 NY.

2. Comments submitted by Admiral Turner for volume 5 of Morison's *History of U.S. Naval Operations in World War II,* August 1950, MOF, Box 27, 19–22, NY. Turner criticized some passages by Morison concerning the *Jarvis* and those by Commander James C. Shaw (who assisted Morison), in the U.S. Naval Institute *Proceedings,* February 1950. This comment by Admiral Turner also refers to a dispatch received about noon on 9 August, originating from a coastwatcher and announcing the approach of many Japanese planes. "Until I read the article by Commander Shaw in the February 1950 . . . *Proceedings,* I always wondered why we had received

this apparently false report from the coastwatcher. Without question in my mind now, that report related to the Japanese aircraft that attacked and sank the *Jarvis* to the westward of Guadalcanal."

3. Comments on Admiral Morison's volume 5, 20 August 1950, MOF, Box 27, 2, NY. In a letter to Rear Admiral Charles Welborn, Jr., deputy CNO (administration), Navy Department, Washington, Turner wrote: "However the officer is dead. In spite of what I consider reflections upon me personally in Vol V and in a recent public article by Commander James C. Shaw, concerning uncertainty in the delivery to the *Jarvis* of my orders relating to her departure from Guadalcanal, I believe that it would be undesirable to permit publication of matters that might cause sorrow to any living relatives of Lt. Cmdr. Graham. For that reason, I bring this matter specifically to the attention of the Department."

Chapter 15

This chapter is based primarily on three reports on the Savo Island battle. The first was written by Admiral Ghormley to Admiral Nimitz a little more than a week after the battle. The second, "Secret Information Bulletin No. 2: Battle Experiences, Solomon Islands Actions," was made under the direction of Admiral King's chief of staff. The third, prepared by Admiral Hepburn and described as the result of an "informal inquiry," has since been accepted as a definitive work.

1. MP 1158/8, secret and confidential files 1932/2/226, AAB.

2. Turner papers, Box 19, NY.

3. MP 1185/8, File 1932/2/226, AAB.

4. CRS A2679/1 Item 7/1943, AAC.

5. See extract from the *Chokai*'s detailed action report, p. 15 of this book.

6. HR, Annex X, NY.

7. MP 1185/8 Department of Navy, secret and confidential files 1923–1950, File 1932/2/226, AAB. This file is also available at NY. The authors' copy came from AAB.

Chapter 16

1. MP 1185/8, File 1932/2/220, AAB.

2. Letter, 25 November 1963, Milne papers.

3. Ibid., 14 June 1964.

4. Complete file of all letters mentioned, Milne papers.

5. Further interrogation of Captains Riefkohl and Bode on 3 April 1943 at Corpus Christi, Texas, HR, Annex M, NY.

6. MOF, Box 26, folder Savo Island, NY.

7. HR, 41, para. 83, NY. "It is established that news of the contact did not reach either Admiral Turner or Admiral Crutchley until between 1800 and 1900 on the 8th" (MP 1185/8, secret and confidential files 1923–1950, File 1932/2/226, AAB). See also HR, Annex Individual Personnel.

8. MOF, Box 26, Pacific 6 notebook, 1943, p. 13, Turner, Guadalcanal, and Central Solomons, NY.

9. "The Battle of Savo Island, 8–9 August 1942," MP 1587, File 105N, AAB.

10. Farncomb letter to Commander, Task Force 44, HMAS *Australia* at sea, 12 August 1942, MP 1587/1/10 105E, AAB.

11. HR, Annex T, NY.

12. Ibid., memorandum to Ramsey.

13. Milne papers.

14. HR, Annex "Individual Personnel," NY.

15. Ibid.

Chapter 17

1. MP 1049/5, secret and confidential files, File 2026/3/501, AAB.

2. MOF, Box 24, folder Acknowledgments and Criticism, NY.

3. Ibid.

4. MOF, Box 26, Pacific 6 notebook, 1943, Turner, Guadalcanal, and Central Solomons, NY.

5. Captain Pineau note to authors, 5 May 1990.

6. Turner was wrong. The *Australia* had seen surface action (and been under air attack) off Dakar in 1940. The *Canberra* had engaged in surface action against the *Kitty Brovig* and other ships in 1941. The *Hobart* had seen surface action in the Red Sea. Both the *Hobart* and the *Australia* had been under air attack in Admiral Crace's force in the Coral Sea battle. Crutchley had commanded HMS *Warspite* in the North Sea (when the lessons of air attack applied). The *Astoria* had been in both the Coral Sea and Midway battles. The *Chicago* had been in the Coral Sea battle. The *Wasp* had made aircraft delivery runs to Malta under threat of submarine, surface, and air attack. It is difficult to argue that after the Coral Sea and Midway battles, U.S. carrier forces were not battle-minded. As for Turner's statement that training schedules had been "relaxed," they were held infrequently, mostly for lack of time.

7. Memorandum for CinCPac, 13 May 1943, HR, NY.

8. Ibid.

9. MOF, Captain Pineau letter to Morison, Box 27, folder Savo Island, NY.

10. *WA,* 94, NY. See also Morison, vol. 5, 28.

11. Major-General Charles A. Willoughby, "Mobilization and Disarmament of Japanese Forces," *Military Review* (July 1946):27–30.

12. MOF, Box 8, folder Ohmae Toshikazo, Answers to Captain Pineau's Questions, NY.

Bibliography

Works in the English Language

Agawa, Hiroyuki. *The Reluctant Admiral: Yamamoto and the Imperial Navy.* Translated by John Bester. Kodansha, Tokyo, 1979.

Ball, D. "Allied Intelligence Co-operation Involving Australia during World War II." *Australian Outlook* 32, no. 3 (December 1978): 229–309.

Barbey, Daniel E. *MacArthur's Amphibious Navy: Seventh Fleet Amphibious Force Operations, 1943–45.* Annapolis: Naval Institute Press, 1969.

Bates, Richard W., and Walter D. Innis. *Strategical and Tactical Analysis: The Battle of Savo Island, August 9, 1942.* Newport, R.I.: Naval War College, Department of Analysis, 1950.

Buell, Thomas B. *Master of Sea Power: A Biography of Fleet Admiral Ernest J. King.* Boston: Little, Brown, 1980.

Costello, John. *The Pacific War.* New York: Morrow, 1980.

Custer, Joe James. *Through the Perilous Night: The Astoria's Last Battle.* New York: Macmillan, 1944.

Dorris, Donald Hugh. *A Log of the Vincennes.* Compiled, supplemented, and edited by Jonathan Truman Dorris. Louisville: Standard Printing, 1947.

Dyer, G. C. *The Amphibians Came to Conquer: The Story of Admiral Richmond Kelly Turner.* Washington, D. C.: Department of the Navy, Naval History Division, 1971.

Feldt, Eric A. *The Coast Watchers.* New York: Nelson Doubleday, 1979.

Frank, Richard B. *Guadalcanal: The Battle and the Legend.* New York: Random House, 1990.

Gatacre, G. C. O. *A Naval Career: Reports of Proceedings.* Sydney: National Press and Publications, 1982.

Gill, G. H. *Australia in the War of 1939–45: Royal Australian Navy, 1942–45.* Canberra, 1968.

Griess, Thomas E., series ed. *The Second World War, Asia and the Pacific*. The West Point Military History Series. Wayne, New Jersey: Avery, 1984.

Griffith, Samuel Blair. *The Battle for Guadalcanal.* Philadelphia: Ayes, 1953.

Hailey, Foster. *Pacific Battle Line.* New York: Macmillan, 1944.

Hayashi, Saburo, and Alvin D. Coox. *Kogun: The Japanese Army in the Pacific War*. Quantico, Virginia: The Marine Corps Association, 1959.

Holmes, W. J. *Undersea Victory*. New York: Doubleday, 1966.

Horner, D. M. *High Command, Australia and Allied Strategy, 1939–1945.* Australian War Memorial, Canberra. Sydney: George Allen and Unwin, 1982.

———. "Special Intelligence in the South-West Pacific Area in World War II." *Australian Outlook* 32, no. 3 (December 1978): 310–27.

Kahn, D. *The Code Breakers: The Story of Secret Writing*. London: Weidenfeld and Nicholson, 1967.

Layton, Edwin T., with Roger Pineau and John Costello. *And I Was There.* New York: Morrow, 1985.

Lee, Clark. *They Call It Pacific.* New York: Viking Press, 1943.

Lewin, R. *The American Magic: Codes, Cyphers and the Defeat of Japan.* New York: Penguin, 1982.

Long, Gavin. *The Six Years War.* Canberra: Australian War Memorial and the Australian Government Publishing Service, 1973.

Lord, Walter. *Lonely Vigil.* New York: Viking, 1977.

Manchester, William. *American Caesar.* Melbourne: Hutchinson, 1978.

Mesimer, Grady F. *History of the USS* Quincy, *CA 39.* Privately published, 1990.

Mooney, J. L., ed. *Dictionary of American Fighting Ships.* Washington, D.C.: Naval Historical Center, Department of the Navy, 1981.

Morison, Samuel Eliot. *The Struggle for Guadalcanal, August 1942–February 1943.* Vol. 5 of *History of United States Naval Operations in World War II.* Boston: Little, Brown, 1951.

Newcomb, R. F. *Savo: The Incredible Naval Debacle off Guadalcanal.* Sydney: Ure Smith, 1963.

Ohmae, Toshikazu. *"The Battle of Savo Island."* U.S. Naval Institute *Proceedings* 83, no. 12 (December 1957): 1263–78.

Potter, E. B. *Nimitz.* Annapolis: Naval Institute Press, 1976.

Tregaskis, Richard. *Guadalcanal Diary.* Sydney: Angus and Robertson, 1943.

Vandegrift, A. A. *Once a Marine.* New York: W. W. Norton, 1964.

Watts, A. J., and B. G. Gordon. *The Imperial Japanese Navy.* London: Macdonald, 1971.

Works in the Japanese Language

Agawa, Hiroyuki. *Gunkan* Nagato *no shogai* (The life of the warship *Nagato*). Vol. 1. Tokyo: Shincho Sha, 1975.

Hando, Kazutoshi. *Nippon kaigun o ugokashita hitobito* (Men who moved the Japanese navy). Tokyo: Rikitomi Shobo, 1983.

Igarashi, Suguru. *Kuroki Nihonkai ni kiyu: Kaigun Mihogaseki sonan-jiken* (They disappeared in the dark Sea of Japan: Naval incident off Mihogaseki). Tokyo: Kodan Sha, 1978.

Ito, Masanori. *Rengokantai no eiko* (Glories of combined fleet). Tokyo: Bungei Shunju Shin Sha, 1962.

Niwa, Fumio. *Kaisen* (Sea battle). Tokyo: Chuo Koron Sha, 1942.

Onishi, Shinzo. *Kaigun seikatsu hodan* (Free speech on naval life). Tokyo: Hara Shobo, 1979.

Sakai, Saburo. *Ozora no samurai* (Samurai in the sky). Tokyo: Kojin Sha, 1967.

Sanematsu, Yuzuru. *Joho senso* (Intelligence war). Tokyo: Tosho Shuppan Sha, 1972.

Takahashi, Yuji. *Tetti Kaikyo* (Iron-Bottom Sound). Tokyo: Mainichi Shinbun Sha, 1967.

Takemura, Satoru. *Gunkan* Aoba *wa shizumazu* (Warship *Aoba* didn't sink)! Tokyo: Konnichi no Wadai Sha, 1985.

Ugaki, Matome. *Sensoroku* (Vice Admiral Ugaki's war diary). Tokyo: Haro Shobo, 1968.

War History Office, National Defense College. *Nanto homen kaigun sakusen* (Naval operations in the southeast area). Vol. 1. Tokyo: Asagumo Shinbun Sha, 1971.

Australian Archives, Brighton

The Australian Archives in Brighton, Victoria, contain many useful documents. These include MP 1587, File 1058, "Preliminary Report, Solomons Islands Operation"; Annex A to Operation Watchtower plan 1-42, South Pacific Force, which establishes the connection between the frequency to be used by the Hudsons; MP 1587-105A, "Report of Proceedings" by Crutchley, which indicates the daytime receipt of a Hudson message; MP 1185/8, File 1932/1/226, "Preliminary Report of the Loss of the Canberra"; MP 1049/5, File 2026/3/501, the *Canberra* file, an immense document containing detailed interrogations of *Canberra* survivors, the finding of the board of inquiry; MP 1185/8, Box 12, navy office File 1932/2/226, the Hepburn report, with only one annex but extra material, including signals memoranda between the RAN NLOs in Washington, London, and Canberra, and some ministerial correspondence; MP 1587, File 105F, "Secret Information Bulletin No. 2," 24/6/43, published by CinCUS headquarters; MP 1254/1, miscellaneous papers relating to coastwatching; MP 1185/8, File 1945/2/9, correspondence relating to Chungking reports of a planned Japanese invasion of Australia; and MP 1049/5, File 1855/2/431, "Defense of Australia: General Review by Chiefs of Staff."

Australian War Memorial, Canberra

The Australian War Memorial has extensive files from the Allied Translator and Interpreter section, Southwest Pacific Area. It also holds the documents used by G. Hermon Gill when he was writing the official history and the operations record book of Thirty-second Squadron, RAAF. That book records Stutt's 8 August flight time, which differs slightly from the time entered in the log book.

National Institute for Defense Studies, Tokyo

Principal Japanese documents are to be found in the war history department of the National Institute for Defense Studies in Tokyo. These include the following:

The Eighth Fleet's war diary and detailed action report

Cruiser Division 6's war diary and detailed action report

Cruiser Division 18's war diary and detailed action report

The *Chokai*'s detailed action report on the First Sea Battle of the Solomons

The *Kako*'s detailed action report of the Sea Battle of the Solomons (7–10 August 1942)

The Eighth Fleet headquarters' report on the night battle of Tulagi Sound

An oral statement by Shizuichi Okada about the First Sea Battle of the Solomons

An oral statement by Tsuto Araki about the First Sea Battle of the Solomons

A recollection by Shinzo Onishi about the Eighth Fleet's Operation Guidance

Public Record Office, London

The Admiralty did not declassify its Savo Island files until 1987, generating false hope that some closely guarded secrets might be disclosed. They were not. "Naval Operations of the Campaign for Guadalcanal, August 1942–February 1943," tactical torpedo and staff duties (historical section), Naval Staff, Admiralty SW1 ADM 234/341 and 234/376, is a useful chronology of events leading to and including the battle. It contains Admiral Layton's reference to Japanese lack of experience in night fighting as well as some errors in detail.

The Milne Papers

The Milne papers, in possession of the authors, consist of correspondence in 1963 and 1964 between the acting official Australian war historian and members of the crews of the Hudson aircraft; correspondence between Nancy Milne and both the Australian War Memorial and the Australian Defense

Department; correspondence between Nancy Milne and the authors; correspondence between Nancy Milne and the Hudson crew members, including the letter from Commander Seno confirming that the *Chokai* had intercepted Stutt's message; various intelligence documents relating to the Hudsons' operations and others; Nancy Milne's handwritten notes covering the years of her principal research, 1983–87; photocopies of the records of navigators involved; cypher messages from the RAAF and the Royal Australian Navy relating to the Hudsons' operations and the Savo Island battle, including flight plans and radio frequencies to be used; copies of extracts from various books dealing with the battle; and sundry maps showing the Hudsons' flight plans.

U.S. Navy Historical Center, Navy Yard, Washington, D.C.

The U.S. Navy Yard has a vast collection of declassified official documents, correspondence, memoranda, etc., relating to the Battle of Savo Island and the campaign in the South Pacific. The basic documents on the battle itself are available on microfilm. These are NRS II-210, a combat narrative; NRS II-298, the Naval War College's exhaustive *Strategical and Tactical Analysis: The Battle of Savo Island, August 9, 1942;* NRS II-320, CinCPacFlt monthly operations; NRS II-514, the Cominch battle experience series; NFX 211, reports of ships participating, including casualty reports of the five cruisers; NRS 402, Japanese source material cited in volume 5 of Morison's *History of United States Naval Operations;* NRS 1976-75, the informal inquiry by Admiral Arthur J. Hepburn into the Savo Island battle; NRS 1979–58, the loss of the *Quincy, Astoria,* and *Vincennes;* and NRS 1979-II, "The Role of Radio Intelligence in the American-Japanese Naval War." Of particular importance are Morison's office files, the personal papers of Admiral Richmond Kelly Turner, and the annexes to the Hepburn report.

Acknowledgments

Years of patient research by Nancy Milne, wife of the officer in charge of the Hudsons, led not long before her death in 1987 to the discoveries that cleared the RAAF. After Mrs. Milne's death, her family handed her research to us. The evidence she had assembled prompted us to make deeper inquiries into the battle, but without her preliminary research this book would not have been written.

Special thanks are due to Martin Clemens, who gave us access to his unpublished diary, and to A. W. Grazebrook for invaluable technical assistance and for reading and providing essential comments on the manuscript. Lieutenant Commander M. J. Gregory, officer of the watch when the *Canberra* was hit by Mikawa's force on 9 August 1942, also read the manuscript and was immensely helpful in adding to our account of the action and for other useful contributions. Many others aided us in various ways through correspondence and interviews or by pointing the way to relevant documents.

Others in the United States, Australia, and Japan who contributed include Admiral Sir Victor Smith, Vice Admiral Sir Richard Peek, Commodore Bruce Loxton, Captain David Hamer, Captain Eric Nave, Commander Grady F. Mesimer, Jr., Laurence L. Morris, Robert Sherrod, Geoffrey Evans, Bob Miller, Ralph Morse, Wilbur Courtis, Lloyd Milne, Bill Stutt, Eric Geddes, Gail Schmidt, J. Griffiths, Lachie McDonald, Annabel Warner, A. W. Skinner, Jeffrey Wenger, and John Bell.

Commanders Saburo Kiuchi and Shizuichi Okada, IJN (Ret.); Lieutenant Commanders Tatsuo Takubo, Nobuyoshi Komatsu, Shigeo Takahashi, and Tatsuhiko Ishiguma, IJN (Ret.); Lieutenant Commanders Masataka Chihaya and Yasushi Kuwashima; Captains Masahiro Yoshimatsu and Shin Itonaga, JMSDF (Ret.); Commander Noritaka Kitazawa, JMSDF; and Kenji Koyama of the war history department of the National Institute for Defense Studies in Tokyo were all of great assistance.

The Australian War Memorial granted permission for the use of maps from the official history. Andrew Mason drew the map showing the Hudsons' search zone on 8 August. Kay Wotherspoon typed and retyped the manuscript.

We are grateful to Little, Brown, for permission to reprint an excerpt from S. E. Morison's *History of U.S. Naval Operations in World War II,* volume 5, and to Mr. Fumio Niwa for permission to quote from his work, *Kaisen* (Sea battle).

Index

About the Authors

Denis and Peggy Warner have collaborated on two previous military books, *The Tide at Sunrise: A History of the Russo-Japanese War, 1904–1905* (Charterhouse, 1974) and *The Sacred Warriors: Japan's Suicide Legions* (Van Nostrand Reinhold Company, 1982). The former book was a main selection of the Military Book Club, the latter a selection of Book-of-the-Month Club. Both authors have spent many years in Asia and the Pacific. Denis Warner was a correspondent for *Reporter* magazine during the Vietnam conflict and a frequent contributor to the *Atlantic Monthly*. He served as *Look*'s Asia correspondent during the closing years of that magazine and during the Second World War was a war correspondent with the U.S. forces in the Central and South Pacific.

Commander Sadao Seno, who did research for the book in Tokyo, has written for Japanese and U.S. publications, including *Proceedings*.

The **Naval Institute Press** is the book-publishing arm of the U.S. Naval Institute, a private, nonprofit society for sea service professionals and others who share an interest in naval and maritime affairs. Established in 1873 at the U.S. Naval Academy in Annapolis, Maryland, where its offices remain, today the Naval Institute has more than 100,000 members worldwide.

Members of the Naval Institute receive the influential monthly magazine *Proceedings* and discounts on fine nautical prints and on ship and aircraft photos. They also have access to the transcripts of the Institute's Oral History Program and get discounted admission to any of the Institute-sponsored seminars offered around the country.

The Naval Institute also publishes *Naval History* magazine. This colorful quarterly is filled with entertaining and thought-provoking articles, first-person reminiscences, and dramatic art and photography. Members receive a discount on *Naval History* subscriptions.

The Naval Institute's book-publishing program, begun in 1898 with basic guides to naval practices, has broadened its scope in recent years to include books of more general interest. Now the Naval Institute Press publishes more than sixty titles each year, ranging from how-to books on boating and navigation to battle histories, biographies, ship and aircraft guides, and novels. Institute members receive discounts on the Press's nearly 400 books in print.

For a free catalog describing Naval Institute Press books currently available, and for further information about subscribing to *Naval History* magazine or about joining the U.S. Naval Institute, please write to:

Membership & Communications Department
U.S. Naval Institute
118 Maryland Avenue
Annapolis, Maryland 21402-5035

or call toll-free, (800) 233-USNI.

THE NAVAL INSTITUTE PRESS

DISASTER IN THE PACIFIC
New Light on the Battle of Savo Island

Designed by Karen L. White

Set in Granjon
by TCSystems, Inc.
Shippensburg, Pennsylvania

Printed on 55-lb. Glatfelter antique cream
and bound in Holliston Roxite B vellum and Rainbow antique
by The Maple-Vail Book Manufacturing Group
York, Pennsylvania